D0214544

The Triumph of the
Flexible Society

The Triumph of the Flexible Society

The Connectivity Revolution and Resistance to Change

MANUEL HINDS

Westport, Connecticut
London

Library of Congress Cataloging-in-Publication Data

Hinds, Manuel.
   The triumph of the flexible society : the connectivity revolution and resistance to change / Manuel Hinds.
       p. cm.
   Includes bibliographical references and index.
   ISBN 0–275–98128–2 (alk. paper)
       1. Information society. 2. Information technology—Social aspects. 3. Information technology—Economic aspects. 4. Globalization. 5. Computer networks—Remote access. 6. Democratization. 7. Free enterprise. I. Title.
HM851.H55   2003
303.48'33—dc21   2003052900

British Library Cataloguing in Publication Data is available.

Library of Congress Catalog Card Number: 2003052900
ISBN: 0–275–98128–2

First published in 2003

Praeger Publishers, 88 Post Road West, Westport, CT 06881
An imprint of Greenwood Publishing Group, Inc.
www.praeger.com

Printed in the United States of America

The paper used in this book complies with the Permanent Paper Standard issued by the National Information Standards Organization (Z39.48–1984).

10 9 8 7 6 5 4 3 2 1

Para Carmen Beatriz, Eleonora y Eva María

The eternal battle between order and disorder,

harmony and chaos,

must represent a deeply felt human perception

of the universe, for it is common to so many

creation myths and so many cultures . . .

Order is equated with good and disorder with evil.

Order and chaos are seen as two opposites,

poles upon which we pivot our

interpretations of the world.

Ian Stewart[1]

Contents

Contents

Acknowledgments

I am much indebted to Hilary D. Claggett, Senior Editor, Praeger Publishers, for her enthusiasm, her unfailing support, and the many ideas she gave me to improve this manuscript. I am also indebted to my friends Elkyn and Halla Chaparro, Fernando Saldanha, and Millard Long, who, through the years, encouraged me to keep on working on my project. Claudio Loser and Ronald Scheman read the final manuscript and wrote kind words about it. My daughters, Carmen Beatriz, Eleonora, and Eva Maria, as well as my son-in-law, Martin van Dam, and my fiancée, Patricia Figueroa, gave me their enthusiasm and ideas in addition to their loving support.

Introduction

The dawn of the twenty-first century has proved unsettling. It was not what we expected. Only a few years ago, the world was full with apparently justified optimism. The new century would be free of the ideological fights that plagued the twentieth. A consensus had emerged in all countries that markets and democracy was the basis for healthy societies; the prospect of a war between superpowers seemed to have faded into the past; a "new economy" born out of the combination of computers and telecommunications was emerging with such strength that millions of people thought that it would mark the end of the cyclical downturns that afflicted the world economy for centuries; and globalization, a term never clearly defined, was uniting the world into a happy conglomerate of people who understood each other. Such optimism was not based on dreams but on realities. The world experienced a sustained economic expansion, driven in large part by the country where the new economy was first flourishing, the United States. Countries all over the world liberalized their economies and joined the ranks of democracy.

Worrying facts are deflating all these optimistic expectations. As the new century settled in, each and every one of the reasons for optimism has failed to deliver what it promised. The possibility of myriads of small conflicts springing up all over the world in a diffuse way has replaced the focused, controllable prospect of a confrontation of superpowers. The price of stocks has declined fast, with those of high-technology companies falling faster than the rest; the downturn phase of the business cycle has not only failed to disappear but, in a rare event, all major economies slowed down at the same time in the early 2000s. In a phenomenon that, surprisingly, is not very well-known, mounting statistical evidence shows that the distribution of income is deteriorating all over the world, becoming more skewed even in the most advanced nations. In the United States, for example, the annual income of the top fifth of the population was equal to 9.4 times that of the poorest fifth in 1977; by 1999, this number had increased to 15.7 times.[2] This is happening in other developed countries as well. The share of total income that the poorest 30 percent of the population gets in 12 of these countries for which data exists has declined by 18.8 percent on average in the last 10 to 15 years.[3]

The same problem is present in the international dimension: the gap between developed and developing countries, rather than getting smaller, is becoming larger. Politically, globalization, rather than being the herald of an integrated world, has become a bad word among large groups in both developed and developing countries. The reforms that developing and formerly Communist countries carried out to capture for themselves the success of the advanced capitalist, democratic societies have not produced the expected results.

Along with these problems, disillusionment with markets and democracy is spreading throughout the Third World. This is evident not just in the growing volume of cynical expressions uttered about democracy in poor countries but also in electoral decisions. Something unexpected, the illiberal democracy is on the rise in many corners of the world. People are electing tyrants and reconfirming them in their positions even after they curtail their freedoms. As told by Fareed Zakaria, the author of a recent article in *Foreign Affairs*,

The American Diplomat Richard Holbrooke pondered a problem on the eve of the September 1996 elections in Bosnia, which were meant to restore civic life to that ravaged country. "Suppose the election was declared free and fair," he said, and those elected are "racists, fascists, separatists, who are publicly opposed to [peace and reintegration]. That is the dilemma." Indeed it is, not just in the former Yugoslavia, but increasingly around the world. Democratically elected regimes, often ones that have been reelected or reaffirmed through referenda, are routinely ignoring constitutional limits on their power and depriving their citizens of basic rights and freedoms. From Peru to the Palestinian Authority, from Sierra Leone to Slovakia, from Pakistan to the Philippines, we see the rise of a disturbing phenomenon in international life—illiberal democracy.[4]

Zakaria estimates that 50 percent of the democratizing countries in the world are turning into illiberal democracies.

Most shockingly, on Tuesday, September 11, 2001, two hijacked passenger airplanes hit and brought down the twin towers of the World Trade Center in New York. A third one destroyed a portion of the Pentagon. A fourth one crashed near Pittsburgh, presumably on its way to hit Camp

David. This coordinated terrorist attack and the sordid war against liberal ideas that started with it killed the optimism that had filled the arrival of the twenty-first century. The magnitude of the terror campaign exposed in an appalling way the vulnerability of civilized societies to small but determined terrorist teams. More than anything, its viciousness brought into focus the persistence in our times of the cold, inhuman destructiveness that dwells hidden in the darkest corners of human nature, a destructiveness that sacrifices both the lives of innocent victims and those of the criminals themselves. It was a shocking reencounter with the world of primitive hatred, where empathy with the suffering of fellow human beings does not exist; where hurting others is a source of so intense a satisfaction that people are willing to give their own lives to experience it.

This raises the ominous prospect of something worse than illiberal democracies: the rebirth of destructive societies, those terrible entities that we thought we had left behind with the fall of Communism at the end of the twentieth century and the defeat, 50 years earlier, of Nazi Germany and militaristic Japan in World War II. The attack of September 11, 2001 showed that the glorification of death for the sake of obtaining some sort of heaven, here or in another life, is back.

This terrorist action was an extreme manifestation of the disillusion with liberal ideas that is taking hold of developing societies, mixed with a religious fanaticism and destructiveness that had not flared in the world for centuries.

The repulsion of liberal ideas is not a privilege of religiously fanatic groups or developing societies, however. After almost a century of absence, political radicalism is reemerging even in the most developed countries. They have come out into the light mainly with the violent protests against globalization that they have staged in several international events, disrupting them seriously and creating havoc in the places where they meet. A new intellectual radicalism is also surfacing in academia, a phenomenon that was familiar in Europe and the Third World but not in the United States. While divided about the shape of the world that they would like to see emerging—the only thing that seems to unify them currently is their opposition to globalization—these groups share the view that liberal ideas are the weapons of racial, sexual, or cultural white bigots bent on exploiting the rest of the world, economically and politically. Unbelievably, Marxist literature calling for violent revolts is reemerging, published not by editorial houses operating on the fringes of society but by prestigious academic publishers. Groups on the extreme right opposing globalization are also flourishing and some of them have engaged in terrorism. Although thus far it looks that it was only an individual incident, destructiveness of the sort displayed by the terrorist attack of September 11, 2001 flared once in the bombing of a Federal building in Oklahoma in the 1990s, carried out by a fanatic who though that modern society had taken away his freedom.

What is unsettling is that all these developments seem to be unrelated except for the fact that all of them betray the erosion of what we thought was the natural order of things. Although liberalism and democracy are not necessarily together in theory, we had grown accustomed to see them as one and the same thing in practice. We dreamed of a world where all countries were democracies, thinking that people would always opt for freedom and the rights of the individual. We thought that technological innovations would bring about progress exclusively and would always help in the elimination of the problems of humankind. We thought that increasing communication and trade would always tend to eliminate differences and misunderstandings, leading to a more peaceful world.

We should have known better. The explosion of hatred that started on September 11 took years to gather strength and we did not even adumbrate it because we were immersed in our optimism.

What is the ultimate source of this explosion of destructiveness?

The question has provoked a storm of ideas, ranging from outright accusations that Islamic religion is inherently aggressive to soul searching trying to find sins that the West could have committed in its dealings with the Islamic countries. Focusing on the current explosion of terrorism, however, produces narrow answers that fail to expose the sources of the cold-blooded destructiveness we are watching in this moment, and may even obscure their true nature.

One example of such narrow explanations is those portrayed by Samuel Huntington in his book *The Clash of Civilizations and the Remaking of World Order*. In this book, Huntington portrays an enlightened Western civilization under siege by foreign civilizations that are mostly opposed to the liberal foundations of the former. He recognizes that there are some groups within the West that also challenge those liberal values. Such groups, however, are infiltrated.

Western culture is challenged by groups within Western societies. One such challenge comes from immigrants from other civilizations who reject assimilation and continue to adhere to and to propagate the values, customs and cultures of their home societies. This phenomenon is most notable among Muslims in Europe, who are, however, a small minority. It is also manifest, in lesser degree, among Hispanics in the United States, who are a large minority. If assimilation fails in this case, the United States will become a cleft country, with all the potentials for internal strife and disunion that entails. In Europe, Western civilization could also be undermined by the weakening of its central component, Christianity.[5]

Huntington forgets that Western civilization includes not just George Washington and Abraham Lincoln but also Robespierre, Marat, and Dantón; the Spanish, French, and Italian Inquisitions; Savonarola; St. Bartholomew's night; the Paris Commune of 1871; the Opium Wars; Hitler and the Ku Klux Klan. He does not include Russia within the West, which sets Communism as an alien doctrine in his conceptual framework. Doing this, however, would ignore the fact that Communism was not a Russian or Oriental invention. Karl Marx, the main founder of the movement, was a German and he wrote *Capital*, the recapitulation of all his theories, sitting on a bench in the British Museum. Friedrich Engels, the co-founder, was an English industrialist of German descent. And Marx did not look into obscure Oriental texts for inspiration—in fact, he despised Oriental people. He inserted his philosophy within the quintessentially western philosophical tradition of Friedrich Hegel.

Thus, the Russians adopted a western philosophy to create one of the two most infernal regimes in history—the other being the western Nazi regime. Westerners also invented terrorism. In little more than a decade at the turn of the twentieth century, western terrorists assassinated hundreds of important people, including Tsar Alexander II of Russia, Empress Elizabeth of Austria, President Carnot of France, King Humbert of Italy, Premier Canovas of Spain, and President McKinley of the United States. In addition, they planted bombs that killed crowds at random in most of the capital cities of Europe. Chemical biological warfare is also an old western invention. The prohibition of using asphyxiating gas in battle dates from the 1899 international conference in The Hague that discussed arms control and arbitration—the substitution of arbitrators for armies as the means to solve international conflicts. There was only one vote against this decision: that of the United States. Its representative, the famous Admiral Alfred Thayer Mahan, at the time a Captain, said that he did not want to restrain American inventiveness.[6]

Finally, the use of God as an excuse for venting out destructiveness is not exclusive to the Muslims. Terrorism erupted in each of the main religions in the last quarter of the twentieth century: Christianity (the bombing of abortion clinics, the Oklahoma bombing); Zionism (the assassination of Yitzhak Rabin, the attack on the tomb of the patriarchs); Islam (the two World Trade Center bombings, the Hamas suicide missions); and Buddhism (the Tokyo subway attack).[7]

Thus, the problem is not one of a clash of civilizations. It is infinitely more complex than this. In fact, what Huntington does, tracing a line splitting the world in racial or cultural terms and blaming the races on the wrong side of the line for social problems is what the Nazis did. Tracing such lines is what the white supremacist groups, Osama Bin Laden, and many similar fanatics have done in our times. Searching in this direction is inappropriate not because it is dangerous—we should never delete quests because they may lead us to scary or inconvenient results—but because it does not fit the facts. Since all religions have in some moment of history justified violence in the name of God and all of them are producing violent groups in our days, the point is, why are all these radically violent interpretations of religion taking hold precisely at this time, after having been dormant for many centuries?

Moreover, what we are seeing is not unprecedented. At the end of World War I and the troubled times that immediately followed it, the tyrannical regimes that had prevailed in Europe for centuries were replaced by parliamentary democracies committed to free markets. As it happened in the 1990s, people thought that liberal democracies and free markets had become the norm in the world. Yet, within little more than a decade, liberalism seemed to have failed to make inroads in the solution of severe problems of income distribution, financial crises, and social dissolution. In fact, like today, many people thought that these problems were the result of the freedom of markets and the ravenous greed they elicited. Politically, the table turned and most industrializing societies fell into illiberal democracies and, shortly thereafter, into terribly destructive regimes of left and right denominations. These societies included the Soviet Union, where democracy lasted only a few months, fascist Italy and Japan, where it lasted for a few years; and Nazi Germany, where it lasted for almost 15 years. Along with them, many other European states that began the post-war period as democracies adopted different forms of fascism, including Spain, Greece, Hungary, Romania, Yugoslavia, and Bulgaria. The same process took place in the developing countries that had followed Europe into the adoption of democratic institutions and liberal economic regimes, most noticeably in those of Latin America, which were captured by military tyrannies. This turnaround was preceded by a growing disillusionment with liberalism that resembles the one we are starting to see.

What we do have in common with the turn of the last century? Why is liberalism under attack just a few years after it seemed to have triumphed definitively, for the second time in one hundred years?

I propose an answer to these questions, one that provides a framework to understand not just the terrorist attacks but also all the other problems I mentioned in the initial paragraphs of this introduction: the economic tribulations that were visible well before the terrorist attacks, the perceived failure of liberal policies in eliciting fast progress in developing and formerly Communist countries, the negative turn in the distribution of income in both developed and developing countries, the growing instability of world markets, the increasingly violent reaction against globalization and the emergence of nonterrorist but illiberal regimes. All these disturbing events are part of the same phenomenon: the disruptions caused by a new process of technological innovations that will change our lives as deeply as the Industrial Revolution did during the last two hundred years. This new revolution was set in motion by connectivity, the power to manage complex tasks from afar in real time, an ability that the combination of computers, telecommunications, and by fast means of transportation has made possible. This revolution is the core of the new economy.

It has become commonplace to say that these developments will change the way we live. Different from globalization, which has been widely demonized, people pay lip service to the benefits of connectivity. This optimistic view is natural because most people focus their attention on the new world that will emerge—the global village and the new economy, which many people thought were with us already. Few people, however, realize that the new economy is still far in the future and that, however beneficial it would be, the transition to it implies the disruption, even the destruction, of what we have today in terms of skills, investments, ways of life, and even basic institutions for our social order. When thinking that the new economy would be a miraculous engine of uninterrupted growth—to the point that it would signal the end of the economic cycles— and would be accepted by everyone as the conveyor of a better life, we forgot the experience that we had from the Industrial Revolution. Yes, in the long run, the new industrial technologies made possible a better world in all dimensions of life. In addition to unbelievable wealth, the Industrial Revolution brought about democracy and human rights, which in turn made possible a society that, whatever its flaws, is more advanced in terms of freedom and social cohesion than any other society in history. In the process, however, the Industrial Revolution created enormous social and political conflicts, which in many societies led to bloody revolutions and the installation of terribly destructive regimes. In fact, the new democratic industrial state had to fight its way against Nazism and Communism, the most destructive regimes that the world has seen. These regimes were products of the same Industrial Revolution that created democracy and human rights—they emerged as alternative ways to manage the industrial society that was rising from the ashes of the feudal and mercantilist societies of preindustrial times.

Destructiveness may emerge from technological innovations for a simple reason. Profound technological advances, while opening the road for a better future in the long run, are terribly disruptive in the short term. They render obsolete the capital accumulated in physical assets, in human knowledge and skills, and, even more fundamentally, in the shape of the institutions linking together the fabric of society. People who thought they had their future assured suddenly find that their skills have been turned obsolete by the new technologies or by the new styles of life derived from them. Activities that had been for decades the mainstay of an economy suddenly become unprofitable, either because their product disappeared or because, to be profitable, they have to be relocated to another part of the world. This brings about all kinds of economic and social disruptions, including unemployment, negative turns in the distribution of income, bankruptcies, frequent financial crises, and depression. Life becomes unstable, the future unbearably uncertain. Through these effects, rapid technological progress threatens the very foundations of social life: that subtle web of links that introduce order in our relationships with our fellow human beings, giving shape to what we call society. Disruptions like these elicit a strong resistance to change in every society, which in many instances takes radical forms and leads to chaos, terrorism, violent revolutions, and the installation of fundamentalist regimes that reassert the social order of the past on the new society that is emerging.

This is what was starting to happen 100 years ago, under the influence of the last stage of the Industrial Revolution, that which introduced electricity, the telephone, the internal combustion engine, the car, and the airplane. As the new technologies advanced, rendering obsolete then current skills and instruments of production, societies experienced drastic shifts in the distribution of income, terrible financial crises, and social dissolution. Existing institutions crumbled. As the new century dawned, the conflict that had arisen in the nineteenth century on how to manage the new industrial society became more intense and eventually led to bloody revolutions, two world wars and the most horrendous bloodbaths that the world has known—the Communist massacres of the 1930s in Russia and the 1950s and 1960s in China and the Nazi Holocaust. The signs of this conflict were apparent in the terrorism of the early 1900s, in the collapse of the preindustrial tyrannical regimes at the end of World War I, in the brief dally with liberalism at the end of it, and in the emergence of fundamentalist regimes that reimposed a tyrannical social order of the past on the new industrial society. One thing led to the other.

This is what is starting to happen in our times as well. Certainly, we have not seen any sign of destructiveness in any of the developed countries. However, we have seen the collapse of the most rigid of all societies, those that, like the autocratic regimes that fell after World War I because they were inconsistent with the new world of industry, could not withstand the impact of a world based on connectivity: the Communist regimes. Moreover, we are seeing the reemergence of fundamentalist opposition to change and its success in dominating entire societies. Throughout the last quarter of the twentieth century, we saw the collapse of several rigid regimes in the Middle East. They, however, were not replaced by liberal democracies. On the contrary, as it happened in Russia and Germany in the early twentieth century, they were replaced by even more rigid and destructive regimes in Iran, Iraq, and Afghanistan. The reaction of these regimes against liberalism is not primarily economic. The fundamentalists feel that they are defending their social order, their religion, and their moral principles against the erosion that the liberalization of customs brought about by a more connected world inflicted on them.

They are afraid that, without the rigid principles that have supported their social order for centuries, their societies will collapse into chaos. That is why they have reasserted their archaic, tyrannical principles of social order in a more radical form than the regimes they replaced. They are the most extreme harbingers of the resistance to change that is likely to extend to other places as the world becomes more connected. They are the exact equivalent of the resistance to change that became imbedded in Communism and Nazism 100 years ago.

Current resistance to change, however, is not circumscribed to Muslim fundamentalists. It is also flaring in the romantic defense of archaic societies put forward by intellectuals who denounce liberal political and economic ideas as part of the cultural penetration of the West in other parts of the world—defending, in fact, mechanisms of exploitation that have kept these societies away from progress throughout their histories. Resistance to change is also moving those who claim that government intervention in the economy to protect settled interests would be the best response to the challenges of the transformation. This was the way the preindustrial economies were organized, the way in which the Nazi and Communist regimes returned.

The fantasy of the 1990s is over. The confrontation between the impersonal forces of change and the natural resistance to it will permeate our century as much as it permeated the previous one.

The new conflict that is starting could prove to be more difficult than the last one because the geographical span of the controversy is much wider than a century ago. While the Industrial Revolution brought about an internationalization of the economies—a first globalization—the ideological conflicts were settled mostly within countries, and, with some catastrophic exceptions, like the Austro-Hungarian Empire, those countries were racially and culturally homogeneous. Now, the interdependence of countries has reached a level without precedent in history. Precisely as a result of connectivity, what happens in one country affects the domestic life of the rest of them. Also, the population of the developed countries, those that led the way during the Industrial Revolution, is no longer homogeneous racially and culturally. Creating a political consensus about the way society should face the challenges of the transformation—the unemployment, the financial crises, the negative trends in the distribution of income—may be much more difficult today than 100 years ago. The problems that must be resolved to create the social cohesion that is essential for a society to overcome its challenges are daunting.

It is within this context that the feeling that something is fundamentally wrong with free markets and capitalism is creeping back all over the world. Since the logic of connectivity is barely starting to affect our social order, we can expect that the tensions of the transformation will only increase in the future, and that the resistance to it will correspondingly become stronger. The conflict on how to manage the connected world will become more intense. We do not know what will happen, which side will win the confrontation.

In this respect, we should remember that the shape of the society that would emerge from industry was in doubt throughout the painful process of adaptation to the Industrial Revolution. Fortunately, the defeat of Nazi Germany and the collapse of the Soviet Union ended the process with the triumph of the liberal democracies. It could have gone the other way. Today, the technologies that have made connectivity possible can be used for the good or for the bad. Rather than being the vehicles for freedom, they can be the mechanisms of control. As it was a century ago, the conflict on how to manage the new world of connectivity may be settled on the side of freedom or destructiveness.

These considerations pose two fundamental questions. What makes the difference between the societies that react positively to technological changes, creating a superior social order from them and those that react negatively to them, generating in the process bloody revolutions and destructive regimes? What are the policies that governments and societies can adopt to ease the transition toward the more humane and efficient society that connectivity is offering, avoiding a repetition, at a higher level of technological power of destruction, of the tragic events of the twentieth century?

These questions summarize the subject of this book. The issues they pose go well beyond the conventional economic approach—the design of economically efficient policies—to cover the complex interaction of political and economic events that give shape to a society. The aim of the book is not that of predicting what will happen—which would be a futile exercise, particularly because we are living through highly nonlinear times. Rather, the book aims at identifying the links between our current actions and the emergence of either creative or destructive regimes in the next turn of history. This is different from looking for the policies that would maximize growth and efficiency. While efficiency is essential for humane progress, it is not true that efficient systems will always lead to humane societies.

I split the discussion of the subject in two parts. I start the first part with the analysis of two issues. First, I discuss why we can be sure that connectivity is causing a technological transformation as deep as the Industrial Revolution. Second, I analyze the sources of each of the responses elicited by a technological revolution—development, stagnation, and destructiveness—interweaving the experiences of the Industrial Revolution with the challenges posed by the new transformation that is just starting in our times. In the second part, I turn to extract the conclusions of this analysis for the policies that we should pursue if we want to creatively absorb the tensions that connectivity is creating in our world.

NOTES

1. Ian Stewart, *Does God Play Dice? The Mathematics of Chaos* (Oxford: Basil Blackwell, 1989), p. 5.

2. U.S. Congressional Budget Office, *The Economic and Budget Outlook, An Update* (Washington, D.C.: U.S. Congressional Budget Office, 2000) Table 1.

3. Jean-Marc Burniaux, Thai-Thhanh Dang, Douglas Fore, Michael Forster, Marco Mira d'Ercole, and Howard Oxley, *Income Distribution and Poverty in Selected OECD Countries* (Paris: OECD, 1998), Economics Department Working Papers No. 189, Table 3.1, p. 37.

4. Fareed Zakaria, "The Rise of the Illiberal Democracy," *Foreign Affairs* 70, no. 6 (1997). The article is also available in Patrick O'Meara et al., eds., *Globalization and the Challenges of the New Century* (Bloomington: Indiana University Press, 2000), p. 181.

5. Samuel P. Huntington, *The Clash of Civilizations and the Remaking of World Order* (New York: Simon & Schuster, 1996), pp. 304–5.

6. See Barbara Tuchman, *The Proud Tower, A Portrait of the World Before the War, 1890–1914* (New York: Bantam Books, 1967), pp. 271–307.

7. See Mark Juergensmeyer, *Terror in the Mind of God, The Global Rise of Religious Violence* (Berkeley: University of California Press, 2000).

PART I

Resistance to Change, Stagnation, and Destructiveness

CHAPTER 1

The New Economy

How do we know that the marriage of computers and telecommunications is the dawn of a new technological revolution? What makes it different from other important innovations of the recent past—like, for example, the discovery of nuclear power or the invention of space rockets? What are the implications of this difference for the life of the common citizen? I deal with these questions in this chapter. I first present the reasons why we can be sure that we are watching the beginnings of a process that will change our societies as deeply as the Industrial Revolution did. Then I focus on the impact that this process is having on the way enterprises operate, and, through them, on the functioning of the economy as a whole and the life of the average individual.

We can visualize the difference between a normal innovation and one that triggers a technological revolution by picturing progress as a straight line leading from lesser to higher development. A normal innovation accelerates the speed at which society moves along that line. A technological revolution shifts the direction of the line, redefining the direction of progress.

This shift in direction is what the Industrial Revolution did when it started in England, 200 years ago, with the development of the steam engine, the invention of the railroad, and the massive introduction of machinery in the textile industry. These inventions, and the immense economic progress they unleashed in Britain, opened the eyes of the entire world to the enormous gains that could be obtained by harnessing the forces of nature for productive purposes. This new awareness triggered a string of innovations that has not ended as yet, going from steam to elec-

tricity, to internal combustion, and then to nuclear power; from the railroad, to the steamships, to the airplane, and then the space rockets; from
the telegraph to the telephone, the radio, and television; from iron, to steel,
to the sophisticated new materials that now cover space vehicles.

The cumulative effect of all these inventions transformed the life of
every person in the industrializing countries. The industrial society is not
just bigger and richer than the feudal society it replaced. It is completely
different in almost all the dimensions of human relations. Industrialization was revolutionary not because the inventions that propelled it were
astonishing but because it transformed society in fundamental ways. A
discovery that does not change the way we live so deeply is not revolutionary, even if it is as impressive as a nuclear electric plant or a space
rocket.

The technological innovations of the Industrial Revolution elicited two
main changes in the shape of social order. The first was the substitution
of horizontal networks of private parties for the vertical command of the
state as the main mechanism to ensure the functioning of the economy.
This changed the way in which consistency was achieved in the decisions
that people make continuously about selling, buying, investing, and saving, as well as about all other economic activities. Such consistency has
two dimensions: one is geographical—assuring that particular regions are
supplied at any given moment—and the other is temporary—assuring
that decisions taken today will be consistent with the needs of the future.
Before the revolution started consistency in both space and time was ensured by rigid regulations, issued by the local landlord or the national
sovereign, as the case could be. The Industrial Revolution, however, introduced so much complexity in the economy and disturbed the existing
economic relations in such a drastic way that the ability of governments
to control the economy collapsed in the early years of the process. One by
one, the barriers created by governments to control trade, capital flows,
and competition fell under the sway of the powerful industries that
needed inputs from distant places and massive markets to unload their
production—overflowing in this way the limited boundaries of the pre-
industrial states and their capacity to command their economies. Gradually, and with some measure of intervening chaos, a network of contracts
between private parties replaced the authority of the sovereign as the
main mechanism to ensure economic consistency. The role of the state
focused on the enforcement of these contracts.

The second grand response to the challenges of the Industrial Revolution was the creation of the modern democratic system, which was also a
substitution of horizontal mechanisms of social control for the traditional
vertical structures that had assured the social order in the past. Thus, the
Industrial Revolution forced a transformation of societies from their previously vertical shape to one in which, while important elements of ver-

ticality remained in place, horizontal networks exercised the ultimate powers of social control.

To determine if connectivity is in the same category as industrialization as a shaper of social relations, we have to analyze what the main changes are that it would elicit in society and compare their magnitude with those brought about by the Industrial Revolution. This is what I do in this chapter. At the end of it, I find that, from the point of view of the trend to transfer power to horizontal networks, connectivity is just a continuation of what started with industrialization. Yet, the way in which it is pushing for the same end result is so different from the ways of industry that we can say that connectivity is inaugurating a new technological era.

The end of World War II in 1945 marked the end of the Industrial Revolution. This end did not come as a result of a stop in the string of innovations aimed at harnessing the forces of nature. On the contrary, after that date, technological progress continued at a faster pace than before. However, its revolutionary impact on society subsided for two main reasons. First, as new inventions were coming along, technological progress became the steady state. Once this happened, societies settled in the industrial age and innovation became a normal part of life. If anything, the new generations became used to the idea that new and more powerful machines would be invented. Second and more importantly, the mainstream innovations of the postwar era were not conceptually different from those that had come along for the previous 150 years and, therefore, did not rock the institutional setting of societies. Nuclear plants are thousands of times more powerful than those based on steam. Yet, both of them do the same thing. A fast jet is a marvelous invention, but it is the same basic machine as that first flown by the Wright brothers at the beginning of the twentieth century, and even as the first locomotive that ran in England 100 years before. At a higher level of generality, it is a machine, a mechanism built to multiply the power of the muscle by the application of some physical principles. The same can be said about a space rocket or a nuclear plant. They all are applications of the same principle: mastering the physical sciences to apply them to extend the power of people over nature.

All this changed in the early 1980s. At that time, the manifestations of a new technological revolution started to be visible. We know that it is a new revolution because it went in a direction different from that of the Industrial Revolution. Rather than multiplying the power of the muscle, it aimed at multiplying the power of the mind—individually and through the immediate association with other minds across the world. This shifted the direction of progress into a new dimension. More accurately, it opened infinite dimensions of progress that did not exist in the industrial age. It converted the straight line that represents progress into one of those fans that ladies used to wave to refresh themselves before air conditioning was invented.

The new revolution is frequently called the Informatics Revolution because it is based on the explosive flow of information made possible by the marriage of computers and telecommunications. This, however, is the input of the revolution. The revolution is the explosion of connections between people that this flow of information makes possible. It multiplies to infinity the contacts that people can establish with other people for all purposes, economic, political, and social—including the acceleration of innovations aiming at multiplying the power of the muscle. Therefore, a more appropriate name for the process is the Connectivity Revolution.

Different from the Industrial Revolution, the Connectivity Revolution is invisible. There is nothing like the railroads, or the huge steel mills, or the immense ports that gave a very visible presence to industrial development. The temples of the new revolution are not noisy factories but quiet campuses where people work in front of computers. Its fuel is not material. Rather, it is thoughts spread through the ether, or through hidden fiber optic cables. Its ultimate output is not visible either. It goes imbedded in the products of other activities: in the shape of their design; in the improved coordination of their production and marketing; in the reduced costs of their production; in the accelerated rate of innovation in all areas of science.[1] We can say that the revolution is not in the computer, the wires, or the use of the electromagnetic spectrum, but in the capacity that people are acquiring to manage extremely complex tasks through networks of brains scattered around the world.

With time, the possibility of processing and transmitting data and thoughts at the speed of light will transform our social and political environments in radical ways too, both directly as a result of the creation of new linkages between individuals and groups in society, and indirectly through the social and political effects of the economic changes the new revolution is eliciting.

The first manifestation of this revolution was the joint ability of computers and telecommunications to transfer money across the world in real time, crippling the governments' ability to enforce controls on capital transfers across borders. A global market for financial transactions on line was gradually created. This, in turn, pushed for trade liberalization as the flowing capital generated infinite numbers of business opportunities. For the general public, it started as a curiosity, a means for gadget freaks to play and enjoy themselves. Children went massively into it.

As this was happening, another, more secret dimension of the technological revolution was changing history. The increased connectivity and the explosion of creativity that computers were eliciting in the West resulted in a qualitative differentiation between the military might of the United States and that of the Soviet Union. Understanding that this would lead to an irretrievable decline of their country, the Soviet leaders decided to abandon central planning and gamble for a decentralization of economic decisions within the still Communist framework of the Soviet Union. This led to the ultimate chaos and the collapse of the system and the country. Being the most rigid of them all, the Soviet Union was the first country to fall victim to the disruptive trends of the new revolution. Other societies are already feeling the same pressures that crushed the Soviet Union.

Grasping the true nature of the Connectivity Revolution requires the realization that taking full advantage of it requires three different sets of actions. The first is to acquire the art of coordinating complex activities horizontally. The second is to use the technological possibilities created by modern computers, telecommunications, and transportation to expand the geographical span of such coordination. The third is to take full advantage of the networks thus created to generate value added based on knowledge and logistics. It is only when the three are combined that success in business is assured.

The ability to coordinate complex activities horizontally does not depend on the availability of computers and telecommunications. It can be exercised without any physical equipment. Conversely, the availability of computers and telecommunications does not guarantee that such ability would be developed. This ability is an advance in the art of organization.

In fact, a Japanese company, Toyota Motors, pioneered this approach to management decades before computers and telecommunications extended the possibility of carrying out coordination from afar. The company adopted the new horizontal approach after World War II, when it had to rebuild its facilities with a very limited capital budget. In those times, the heyday of Henry Ford's mass production techniques, automobile production was controlled by huge American enterprises, which produced large volumes of standard cars in extremely expensive factories. Each model was profitable only if it could be produced in very large quantities. Toyota could not afford these facilities, and had to produce a wide diversity of vehicles for the domestic market. Thus, it had to operate with less hardware and produce in smaller runs than the most efficient plants in the world.

What Toyota developed to face this challenge was called Lean Production. The essence of Lean Production is to substitute human capital for physical capital, making full use of the ultimate comparative advantage of humans over machinery: the ability to coordinate autonomously and to innovate. One of the practical rules of the approach is to transfer the maximum number of tasks and responsibilities to those workers actually adding value to the product on the production line, reducing intermediate supervisory levels, and encouraging workers to take responsibility in finding new ways to improve the efficiency of the plant. In this way, Toyota reduced the need for vertical enforcers of organization—the supervisors—by empowering the workers to associate with each other in a horizontal way. The gains obtained by Toyota with this new system, however, were not limited to the reduction in the number of supervisors. Most of them came from the increased creativity and efficiency that the new system elicited. The horizontal networks of workers proved more efficient than the vertical structures they replaced.

A telling example of the innovations introduced by Lean Production is the way it delegates the power to stop a line of production. The cost of stopping the entire line of production in a large factory is very high in terms of lost output. In the traditional car factory only the plant manager could make such a decision. Toyota empowered all workers in the line to stop it if they found a mistake, be it a defective batch of components, or a problem of coordination. The line was restarted only when the solution to the problem was found. When Toyota first introduced this concept, car producers around the world thought that it was a sign of the company's ignorance of what makes a plant profitable. Indeed, stoppages became very frequent soon after the system was introduced. Once production was resumed, however, Toyota had resolved, for good, the problem that had motivated the interruption of the production process. Soon the Toyota plants were running with fewer stoppages than those of their traditional competitors, and turning out products with higher quality and much lower costs. Today, plants managed under this principle work almost without interruption, so that their utilization is close to 100 percent, while a manager in a plant run on the traditional principles of mass production was seen as very good if the stoppages were on the order of 10 percent of the production time. Not only that but by the 1980s, the time needed to assemble a car was 14 hours in a Toyota plant and 36 hours in a typical American factory and the assembly defects per car were 45 in the Japanese factory and 130 in the American one. The coordination was so efficient that the Japanese facility carried the inventories needed for two hours of production while the American one accumulated the needs for two weeks. All these, and many other indicators of productivity, were better in the Toyota plants because of Lean Production.[2]

By the early 1990s, other enterprises had become immensely successful by independently developing horizontal approaches to organization and extending them to all the aspects of a company, particularly in the emerging personal computer industry in the United States. The practice is extending so fast that there are people predicting the end of the concept of a job as a structured slot with well-defined responsibilities within a clear command structure. As far back as 1994, a *Fortune* article was noting how this was happening in many path-breaking companies.

Study a fast-moving organization like Intel and you'll see a person hired and likely assigned to a project. It changes over time, and the person's responsibilities and tasks change with it. Then the person is assigned to another project (well before the first project is finished) and then maybe to still another. These additional projects, which also evolve, require working under several team leaders, keeping different schedules, being in various places, and performing a number of different tasks. Hierarchy implodes, not because someone theorizes that it should but because under these conditions it cannot be maintained. Several workers on such teams . . . used the same phrase [when interviewed]: "We report to each other."[3]

The end product is a corporation where decisions are not the result of vertical flows of information and commands, but of horizontal communications and coordination between individuals. Companies with decision-making power closer to the customers have a clear advantage in both speed of response and creativity, the crucial features of successful enterprises in the new world. Many enterprises have not attained success in this new kind of organization, producing chaos in their staff rather than a better capacity of response. For this reason, many people have come to think that this is a fad, bound to disappear. It is not. Those enterprises that succeed in this difficult art, combining it with the immense possibilities that modern computers, telecommunications, and transportation are opening, will certainly win the markets.

The second and third elements of the Connectivity Revolution—the exercise of horizontal coordination at a distance and the use of this capability to engineer an increase in the value added per worker all over the world—are associated with globalization, a process that many people identify as the engine of the transformations now taking place in the world's economy. In fact, globalization is just one of the consequences of the real source of change, connectivity. Understanding this point is essential.

In fact, globalization is a phenomenon that clearly exemplifies the difference between the industrial and the connectivity ages. Many people think of it as just a rapid expansion of cross-border trade and investment. These people would be surprised when learning that the current ratio of international trade to world production is approximately equal to that prevailing 100 years ago. Industrialization prompted an enormous expansion of international trade and capital movements during the nineteenth century that went as far as the current expansion has gone in terms of trade and further in terms of capital flows. We have forgotten this old globalization only because protectionist policies dominated the twentieth century, causing a drastic fall in the international flows of goods, services, and capital—a trend that started to be reversed only in the last half of the century. In 1998, trade represented 26 percent of gross domestic product (GDP) in the 16 major economies—less than five percentage points over the average of 1913, which was 21.3 percent. The overall increase of less than five percentage points, spread over 85 years, would hardly justify the great importance that people attribute to globalization.[4] The same can be said about the flows of investment across borders. The ratios of world-wide capital flows to world GDP in the early 1990s were about half of those prevailing in the late 1880s. The biggest international investor of the late nineteenth century, Britain, invested abroad a much larger share of its own GDP than any of the large investors of our days.[5]

Our current globalization, however, is much more than a repetition of what happened in the nineteenth century: an expansion of trade. We can grasp its truly innovative aspect by looking at what it is doing, not to commerce, but to production processes, and noticing how such effects are linked to the Connectivity Revolution.

Connectivity is changing the production processes because it is removing many of the restrictions that enterprises had during the Industrial Revolution to choose the location of their production facilities. Until recently, the development of communications and transportation severely constrained these decisions, mainly in the direction of concentrating their operations in the smallest possible number of locations. These were determined by access to either markets or raw materials. Once a location was chosen, all operations had to be established there, including many which could have been located optimally elsewhere if the need to concentrate for coordination purposes did not exist. In this way, for example, a complex product could include both high-tech components—which could be produced only in areas with ample supply of sophisticated engineers and highly skilled workers—and simple intermediate products that could be easily produced in a developing country. Everything had to be produced within the same geographical area to ensure a close coordination of the production process.

Now, computing, communications, and transportation have developed to the point where enterprises can split their operations, and locate each of their component activities in the best possible place in the world in terms of overall costs and efficiency. Thus, a company can have its design facilities in California, its financial department in New York or London, and production facilities for each component of their product in different places in the world. These components can then be assembled in different facilities for selling in different markets. Rather than being housed under one single roof, production lines can span the entire world, coordinated by computers and connected by fast transportation facilities.

This is the truly innovative aspect of the globalization process. The revolution is in the geographical splitting of lines of production—something that could happen only as a result of the Connectivity Revolution. Thus, globalization *is primarily a phenomenon of production rather than one of trade*—even if with time, we can expect that trade volumes would increase further as globalization proceeds. We cannot understand the current globalization without making reference to its driving force, the ability to coordinate complex tasks from afar. It is just a manifestation of the new power to coordinate complex tasks at a distance—the second source of the Connectivity Revolution.

To grasp the third aspect of the revolution—the use of horizontal coordination at a distance to engineer an increase in the value added per worker all over the world—it is useful to take a look at the origins of globalization. It started in the United States during the 1980s, well before the fall of the Soviet Union, as a reaction to invasion of industrial products imported from Europe, Japan, and the Asian Tigers (Korea, Hong Kong, Singapore, and lately Thailand and Indonesia). The new entrants focused their efforts on products that the United States had dominated for decades, including cars, home electronics, home video equipment, and other appliances. The car industry, for so long the symbol and bulwark of American industry, was threatened by imports from Japan. The production of electric and electronic home goods and appliances was being curtailed by the much cheaper imports from Japan and East Asia. Household names like RCA Victor and Sylvania disappeared from the market, substituted by brands like Sony, Panasonic, and Toshiba. The same was happening in steel, chemicals, and many other sectors. Some steel communities in Pennsylvania became ghost towns. The invasion was so fast and so deep that many people predicted that the country would deindustrialize, losing its economic and political power. Claims for protection rose from all sectors.

President Reagan's government took some action to restrict trade in some sectors, with disastrous results. This was particularly evident in automobiles. The government imposed temporary quotas on the number that could be imported into the United States. The result was that foreign carmakers, which up to that moment had been successful on taking over the low-end of the market, went for the high-value-added niche to maximize profits out of a given number of cars sold, and dislodged the American companies from that profitable niche as well.

Most American companies, however, were left in the dark, and this was the best thing that could have happened to them. Take the case of Motorola as an example of a process that took place in all sectors in the economy. The company had started in the early decades of the twentieth century as the provider of radios for Ford cars and had diversified into other radio and TV products to become a powerful corporation. In the 1980s, the influx of competition from abroad eroded the competitiveness of the company. The costs of production of the new entrants were so low that trying to compete in those products was out of the question. It became clear that the wages of the American engineers and workers were too high for the price of the goods they were producing.

Motorola responded with a two-track strategy. First, it abandoned the products that had become too cheap for the sophistication of its engineers and workers, and it focused the enterprise on developing goods in which that sophistication would be their main competitive advantage. The company launched a new line of products; it concentrated on products that were out of the reach of its competitors, at least for a long while, such as portable communications equipment and microprocessors. This strategy did not resolve the problem entirely, however, because even the most sophisticated products include unsophisticated parts—the plastic cases of cellular phones, for example—that are important components of the final cost of the products. Producing these parts in the United States increased costs unnecessarily. This prompted the second part of the overall strategy: the company went global in the organization of production. Using the new opportunities presented by connectivity to coordinate complex tasks from afar, Motorola parceled out the production of the unsophisticated parts of its new products to other countries, where wages and other costs were lower than in the United States, and concentrated the production of the sophisticated parts and the coordination of the whole in the United States, where engineering creativity was higher than in the rest of the world. That raised the productivity of the company in two ways: by increasing the value added of their production through innovative design of new products and by minimizing the cost of production at a global level. Companies in all sectors of the American economy adopted the same strategy during the 1980s and 1990s, splitting their production chains around the world, according to the competitive advantages of different places. This started globalization.

Thus, globalization was only half of what started to happen in the United States during the 1980s. The most important part was the technological leap that raised the productivity of local American production. Once companies moved to produce goods and services with higher value added, the wages paid in the United States were no longer excessive because the companies were taking full advantage of the workers' superior abilities. The development of the microprocessor and the software required to making it work helped in the process. They in turn elicited the development of small computers, which could be used in infinite products, such as cars, airplanes, machine tools, hospital equipment, security systems, television sets, appliances, telecommunications, and personal computers. The microcomputers could be imbedded in all these products and more, and could also be used to make their production more efficient. The application of microprocessors to telecommunications turned computers and telephones compatible with each other, and this launched the Connectivity Revolution.

The process took place not just in companies that, like Motorola, went directly into connectivity products. Many other traditional industrial sectors, those that were most threatened by the invasion of foreign competition, adopted similar strategies, creating a strong market for the development of more efficient and faster connectivity equipment.

It is important to notice here that this growing market included not just companies that were globalizing; many companies in the United States found in connectivity a means to increase their efficiency in the domestic market as well. Many globalized domestically, in the sense that they split their production facilities within the United States, taking advantage of the differences in the sophistication of labor and costs of production inside the country. In fact, the main transformation has taken place in the domestic American economy; the international integration of the chains of production began as a complement of this domestic process of innovation, and remains largely so.

This process, at the national and international levels, is one of the key effects of connectivity. Productivity can increase in the most sophisticated economies *because* they are exporting the least productive of their activities to other countries, which allows them to concentrate on the more productive new activities. On the other hand, the transferred activities are more productive than the ones they replace in the developing countries, so that their transfer results in an increase in the overall productivity of these other countries. That is, connectivity has the potential to increase the productivity of all countries in the world, simultaneously, by just transferring activities from one place to another.

In summary, the fundamental transformation is connectivity, and globalization is a consequence. This is an important point to remember when analyzing the policies that countries may adopt to facilitate the adjustment to the turmoil of the transformation. Connectivity is extending to the entire world a value-added ladder, in which companies and countries can place themselves in accordance with their abilities, and then begin to escalate by increasing their skills. This ladder existed before, but because of the technological limitations of the Industrial Age was not available for everybody; it was fragmented across countries. Most of the ladder was in the developed countries because they controlled the key to escalate it—management capacities. Now that these capacities can be exercised around the world, all countries have access to the main ladder.

The innovations that gave birth to the Connectivity Revolution naturally lead to the creation of an economy where knowledge and coordination become the main sources of wealth.

This is becoming evident in three dimensions of economic activity. First, the price of goods and services that contain more knowledge are going up relative to those that contain less of it, even if the cost of producing them physically is about the same. The prime example of this is the difference in the price of a blank diskette and that of one containing data or software. The cost of physically producing the two is approximately the same, but the difference in the price they command in the market is enormous. Second, the same phenomenon is visible in the composition of the cost of a single product from scratch to the final consumer. Most of the value of the products is added in the nonmanufacturing portions of the process: design and commercialization. Industrial technology has become so advanced that producing anything is a relatively simple task. The value added is in the adequacy of the design to meet the needs of a specific market segment and in the logistics needed to reach that segment with the product. Third, services with a high content of knowledge are replacing industry as the most important economic activity, which is attracting more talent. In the United States, the cradle of the Connectivity Revolution, the share of factory workers in the total labor force declined from a peak of 35 percent in the mid-twentieth century to around 15 percent in the late 1990s. In contrast, "knowledge workers," those whose jobs require advanced schooling, now represent a third of the American workforce and represent the fastest growing segment in the labor markets.[6]

I review in the following paragraphs some of the consequences that the emergence of this new economy of knowledge is having in the shape of our economic activities: the shift from mass-oriented production and consumption to individualized production and marketing, the shifting balance between the power of small and big firms, the increase in productivity, and the acceleration of competition.

While the Connectivity Revolution is changing all aspects of life, its most revolutionary impact is probably the reversal of one of the main features of the industrial economy: its tendency to operate massively in both production and consumption. The massive nature of the industrial economy was one of the most glaring innovations of the Industrial Revolution. In feudal times, both production and consumption were individualized. Master crafters tailored their products to the specific needs of their consumers. This disappeared altogether with the development of industry and its economies of scale. Industrial companies reduced costs by producing enormous volumes of the same product and customers learned to consume standardized goods and services. Marketing became the art of designing products that could meet the average needs of millions of potential customers. The individual was not important. What mattered were the averages.

The lack of importance of the individual was manifest also in the production methods. For two centuries, individuals at the workshop level did not matter, except for their numbers. They were supposed to perform the same simple task endlessly, without applying any creativity, and without displaying any initiative. Quite importantly, they were not expected to communicate with each other. As an extreme example of the irrelevance of communication, in 1915 many of the workers of the famous Highland Park Ford car production plant—at the time, the most advanced industrial facility in the world—did not even speak fluent English.[7] Ford did not care if they could not talk to each other. They were human machines, perfectly replaceable by other people if they left the enterprise. Metal machines were more important. This was the key to success.

The massive nature of industrial operations was also visible in the way companies were organized. In the organizational paradigm inherited from the Industrial Revolution, enterprises coordinated their activities in a vertical way: information went up to the highest levels for decision, and commands came down for execution. This elevator system ensured that decisions were not only consistent with each other but also taken based on the broadest knowledge of the subject at hand. No one could manage averages better than the people at the top. Of course, the system had serious shortcomings. The richness of information needed to operate in personalized market niches is lost when summarized and conveyed to a central authority. The mood of the market can be inadvertently distorted in the long vertical chain. Moreover, there is a huge capital of ideas imbedded in the individuals in touch with the customers, a capital that is lost if decisions are taken by people disconnected with the clientele. Thus, in the old vertical structure, full coordination was achieved at the expense of knowledge of the particularities of specific customers, of speed of reaction, and of creativity. These problems, however, were not crippling in an age when the individual preferences of customers were not important, because everything was standardized.

Computers have changed the operation and coordination of firms in three main ways. First, they can cheaply convey and consolidate information that previously could only be gathered with extensive work and long delays at the top level of companies. Now this information can be made available to the people in the field, in real time. Second, computers and modern communications also make it possible to coordinate, also in real time, the decisions of many people in different locations, something that previously was impossible. Third, computers are making it possible for enterprises to operate massively and still produce highly individualized products, like the ones that the old artisans used to produce. Based on a subtler concept of standardization, the new technologies are taking advantage of standard methods to destroy standardized products.

These new opportunities have brought to center stage two aspects of business that were not very important in the industrial age: speed of reaction and creativity. Today, anyone can set up any productive facility in the place with the highest competitive advantage to produce it. The determinants of success are progressively linked to innovations that allow firms to differentiate their products and extract fleeting monopoly rents from the market. The key is producing something that no one else can produce. Inevitably, if one innovation is successful and commands very large rents, potential competitors will strive to copy it to share in those rents. When these competitors become successful, the rents shrink. They keep on diminishing until the product becomes standardized and the technology of its production becomes available to any entrant. At this moment, the product becomes a commodity and there are no excess profits left. To be successful, an enterprise has to keep on innovating, so that when one innovation is copied, another is ready to go into the market. Thus, companies must keep themselves in close touch with their customers, not just to discover new opportunities, but also to stay ahead of the competition in terms of satisfying the needs of the profitable customers in their portfolios.

This means that the individual—the only source of creativity—is becoming not just the focus of marketing but also the crucial factor of production.

The new technologies are also having a revolutionary impact on the optimal size of firms in many products. The Industrial Revolution was the epoch of the big firm. Bigger was always better in production because capturing economies of scale was the gist of development. Bigger was also better in marketing. To expand geographically, a company needed to establish a large bureaucracy to manage its sales in each place and to coordinate its activities in different places. Today, it is possible to gather and process data on markets, niches, and products anywhere in the world, at amazing speed. As much as the new technologies allow big enterprises to decentralize their activities globally and to innovate on the basis of connected creativity, they also allow enterprises to coordinate production, marketing, and financing of complex products without having to own or manage each of the stages of production, and without having to create a large corporate bureaucracy. They have also allowed firms to establish a presence in faraway markets without having to be there—in foreign countries or within the same country.

With the new lightning-fast coordination capacity of computers, firms can create alliances with other firms to operate globally without the deadweight of large bureaucracies. Rather than trying to produce a wide range of products, they can create alliances with other producers to offer such a range to their customers without having to invest in their production. These alliances bring about an advantage in flexibility. Frequently, profitable niches exist in combinations of products that require different technologies to produce. People are ready to pay a premium for packages of complementary goods and services that meet a specific, complex need for the sake of saving the complications of buying the complementary goods from different suppliers. Since individual corporations are well aware that they cannot possibly produce all these complementary goods and services, they are getting into limited alliances to sell the necessary packages. These alliances are limited either in terms of the scope of their objective, or of time, or both. This has given birth to the concept of the virtual corporation, another name for these temporary alliances, which work as a corporation only for some purposes, like developing a new product, or selling a package to a large niche or customer. Many observers have predicted that these virtual corporations could eventually kill the global and highly diversified corporations.

This is unlikely to happen. There are certain economies of scope that will remain in place. Even if this does not happen, however, the prominent role of alliances in the future seems assured. They are meeting the needs of customers shopping for increasingly complex mixtures of goods and services, which are not likely to arise again in the same shape. There is no doubt that this is a more efficient method of operation than centralized control in a big corporation for the solution of complex problems that require local attention. They are also a logical response to the high costs of research and development, which can be shared by many different enterprises. Since the needs of consumers are becoming more and more complex, these organizations will coalesce and dissolve with increasing frequency.

This is eroding one of the most important competitive advantages of big multinational firms in many areas. The large bureaucracies that gave the competitive edge to large organizations have become a deadweight that the small firms do not have in the increasingly fierce competition of the twenty-first century. Symmetrically, the new technologies have also allowed big enterprises to focus on small market niches. Size is no longer a decisive advantage or a disadvantage. The Connectivity Revolution is a great equalizer.

The possibility that these technologies open for both small and big firms to associate for accessing faraway markets or markets for goods and services they do not produce opens new dimensions of competition. Along with the possibility of selling directly to consumers through the Internet, it also opens the door to the international markets for firms in the developing countries. Contrary to what is so frequently said, connectivity and its associated globalization open more opportunities for the small companies in both developed and developing countries than for the multinationals. Actually, small enterprises are gaining this benefit at the expense of the latter, which are losing the exclusive niche they had enjoyed for centuries.

Through all these changes, connectivity is also shifting the basis for the competitiveness of countries in a subtle but very effective way, from the accumulation of physical capital and the skills needed for the old kind of industrial production to the sum of these plus the capacity to coordinate the new horizontal relations in an effective way. The shift is subtle because the accumulation of physical capital and scientific knowledge are positively correlated. The capacity to coordinate complex tasks is concentrated in the most advanced countries, too. This would seem to indicate that the Connectivity Revolution would not change the composition of competitiveness by country. Yet, the ability to organize complex tasks in a horizontal way, regardless of the use of computers or the nature of the task at hand, is not equally distributed across the advanced nations. Some European countries, like France and Germany for example, are more attuned to vertical structures than the Nordic and the Anglo-Saxon societies. The extremely complex social structure of Japan facilitates horizontal communication and coordination in some cases—as the invention of Lean Production shows—but makes it extremely difficult in some others, particularly when foreigners are involved. Since capital accumulation and knowledge are roughly similar among the advanced countries, this single ability to operate in networks will be the source of a new differentiation between countries in terms of competitiveness. Countries able to develop efficient horizontal networks will get ahead of the rest; those unable to do it will lag behind and could even decline.

As it happened during the initial stages of the Industrial Revolution, a country, in this case the United States, has overtaken all other countries in the development of the new economy. The advantage of the United States is not as pronounced as Britain's was in the mid-nineteenth century, but it is substantial in several important ways. First, American companies are dominant in the products spearheading the revolution. American companies almost exclusively carry out the design and production of the mass-market microprocessors, the brains of the computer. The mass-market software is also in the hands of a few American companies, and one single American company, Microsoft, dominates the market of operating systems. American companies also dominate the Internet server computers and the database software. This is similar to what happened during the first half of the nineteenth century, when most industrial machinery was produced in Britain.

The second area in which the United States is well ahead of the rest of the world is in the rate of creation of new enterprises, including not just those related to the new technologies but also in general. This gives it a capacity to adjust that far exceeds that of other advanced economies in the world. Third, the United States is ahead in the creation of an economy of services, developing a capacity to coordinate that is also unmatched in the world. Fourth and most importantly, the American society has been a melting pot of different cultures for centuries, anticipating the trends of globalization. All these advantages together are turning the United States into the central country in the world. As much as all roads led to Rome in the Ancient World, and as much as all roads led to London in the first half of the nineteenth century, all roads now lead to the United States.

The opportunities to catch up with the United States and other advanced countries, however, are much better than in the pre-connectivity times. The amount of capital needed to operate in the international market has collapsed to a minor fraction of what it was just 10 years ago. As we discussed in relation to the small enterprises, a person with a computer and a modem is potentially globalized. Enterprises in developing countries can also integrate themselves into the global chains of production through temporary or permanent alliances with companies with fully organized access to the international markets. They can get technology and become successful even if their products do not have a local demand.

This is radically different from what it was in the nineteenth century, when the only access that companies in the Third World had to the world markets was through their exports of commodities, which then returned to them in the form of industrial products. It is also different from what it was during the twentieth century, when the only contact that these countries had with the rest of the world was, in addition to their exports of commodities and imports of machinery, the presence of multinational companies that produced there to sell only domestically. Today, the opportunities are immense. While it is true that the new world that is emerging is based on knowledge, there are markets for all levels of knowledge and now it is easier to get it than in any other epoch in history. Governments can use the Internet and other new technologies to spread knowledge and skills throughout their societies, as well as to provide many social services to the poor and the population in general. Thus, while connectivity is giving additional advantages to the advanced countries in terms of privileging knowledge and human capital in general, it is also making it easier for poor countries to gain those advantages at a much faster pace. Connectivity has created the best opportunity that Third World countries ever had to catch up with the developed countries.

In this setting, the key to success in the near future will be, not just the ability to *organize*, but also that of *reorganizing* continuously the operation of enterprises, to keep them lean and focused on their evolving markets. This will be the source of competitive advantage. As expressed by Michael Porter:

The raising world standard for factors [of production] means that deriving competitive advantage from factors requires not just one-time investment but continual reinvestment to upgrade their quality, not to mention keeping the current pool of factors from depreciating. Advanced and specialized factors demand the greatest, most sustained investment in the most difficult-to-make forms.

Nations succeed in industries where they are particularly good at creating and, most importantly, upgrading the needed factors. Thus, nations will be competitive where they possess unusually high-quality institutional mechanisms for special-ized factor creation.[8]

The need for continuous renewal is already here. As new technologies sweep through the industrial countries, production facilities that were quite profitable and efficient just a few years ago become suddenly ob-solete, and enterprises that are a household name become threatened with extinction. The fate of professions that only 10 years ago were the wave of the future, such as mainframe computer experts, is becoming doubtful now that personal computers are as powerful as a large mainframe was in the 1970s. Changes are so fast that people will have to change profes-sions and skills several times during their lives. Today, when the revolu-tion is still starting, it is estimated that young people in the United States will change jobs 11 times and their basic skills at least three times over their lives.[9] Everything is in flux.

Connectivity is also increasing labor productivity in unprecedented ways in the country that pioneered it: the United States. It increased by an impressive 4.1 percent in the 12 months to June 2003, and by 3 percent a year since 1995, which is twice that rate of the previous two decades. Many economists believe that these rates of productivity growth can be sustained for another 5 to 10 years. This compares with the labor produc-tivity growth in the first few years of the Industrial Revolution in Britain, which averaged 1 percent per year, and with the productivity growth in the United States in the 1920s, when electricity was revolutionizing production, which averaged 2.3 percent. One of the main features of connectivity is that it is improving productivity in all sectors in the econ-omy—including services—while the technologies associated with indus-trialization mostly improved those of industry and agriculture. Moreover, the price of computers fell by 35 percent per year over the last three de-cades, while that of electricity fell by only 6 percent in a comparable period after its introduction. These gains have not been immediate. As it hap-pened during the Industrial Revolution, it takes a relatively long period for firms to master the productivity-enhancing aspects of the new tech-nologies. Thus far, only the United States is reaping the benefits of con-nectivity. In Europe, where the development of connectivity has lagged relative to the United States, and where the economies are more rigid and resistant to change, productivity actually declined in most countries while that of the United States increased. One by one, the economists working on the field are coming to the conclusion that connectivity is producing an explosion of labor productivity that is at least comparable to that of the Industrial Revolution.[10]

This brief discussion shows that the new technological revolution is not just changing the direction of economic progress. It is actually reversing itself into the opposite of what it was in the industrial age in many dimensions of life. I show some of these dimensions in Table 1.1. All of them have profound implications for the life of the average person all over the world.

What we see in this table is a big leap into the complex. The Industrial Revolution went from the complexities of individual production to the simplicity of standardized processes and streamlined chains of command. Now, we are going in the opposite direction, from the simple, standardized industrial world into the messy environment of horizontal interrelations in all dimensions of business. In a fundamental way—the turn toward more horizontal forms of social organization—this process is just a continuation of what started with the Industrial Revolution. The possibility of coordinating complex tasks at a distance in real time, however, shifts all the concrete conditions in which the next round of this transition toward a horizontal order will take place so deeply that what will be

Table 1.1
The Two Revolutions

Industrial Revolution	Connectivity Revolution
Aimed at multiplying the power of the muscle.	Aims at multiplying the power of the mind.
Aimed at optimizing the relationship of human beings with machines.	Aims at optimizing the relationships of human beings with other human beings.
Based on hardware: big machines, large smokestack factories.	Based on software, as imbedded in the knowledge of workers.
Bigger is better to access world markets.	Size is not relevant for that purpose.
Access to managerial abilities, natural resources, and closeness to markets crucial for choosing location of production facilities.	Almost everything can be produced almost anywhere in the world.
It concentrated industrial production in countries with managerial abilities, splitting countries in accordance with the availability of those abilities.	It spreads managerial and entrepreneurial abilities across the world, integrating the world economy.
Standardization reigned supreme in products, components, and processes.	Products are personalized, even if produced massively.
Workers were expected to repeat simple actions endlessly.	Organization techniques aim at empowering the creativity of the individual worker as the main engine of efficiency and profits.
Narrow specialization was the key to lifelong success.	People need to change their field of specialization several times in their lives.

emerging in the next several decades will be a society radically different from that of today. We can be sure that we are living through the initial stages of a true technological revolution.

By freeing economic activities from their geographical constraints, connectivity will eventually result in a more equal distribution of income around the world. By liberalizing information and putting it to the disposal of virtually everybody, it will also result in a higher standard of living across societies. Yet when doing that, it will disrupt the lives of most people, turning insecure positions, incomes, and privileges that seemed unassailable only a few decades ago. As economic activities move from one place to another, they leave many people unemployed in the original place and create competition in the place of destiny. As the relative prices of goods and services shift in accordance with their content of knowledge, the incomes of large parts of society go down while that of others increase fantastically. Events taking place on the other side of the world are suddenly becoming crucial for the political and economic environments of societies. And resistance to change is starting to rise.

I discuss all these consequences of the new revolution in the remainder of this part of the book.

NOTES

1. People tend to associate the so-called new economy with the firms that provide electronic connections. This is like believing that the impact of radio on society was limited to the success of RCA Victor in the 1920s. Among the innumerable examples of the behind-the-scenes role of connectivity we can pick the unveiling of the genetic code, which would not have been possible without the combined power of computers and communications. Another is the investigation of the most intimate features of matter. The Large Hadron Collider near Geneva will generate data in such huge quantities that its processing is possible only by combining the computer power of scores of computing centers linked together around the world. Also, online sharing of databases and blueprints has accelerated the design of innumerable products and processes. While the progress of the connectivity industries is astonishing and will continue to be so—independently of temporary setbacks that it might have, like the disastrous decline of the technology shares that started in 2000—the most far-reaching results of the new technologies will be manifest in their impact on the productivity of other sectors, a process that will take many decades to permeate the entire economy.

2. The discussion of Lean Production is based on James P. Womack, Daniel T. Jones, and Daniel Roos, *The Machine That Changed the World: The Story of Lean Production* (New York: Harper Perennial, 1990).

3. William Bridges, "The End of the Job," *Fortune,* 19 September 1994, 68.

4. The 16 countries are the following: Australia, Austria, Belgium, Canada, Denmark, Finland, France, Germany, Italy, Japan, Netherlands, Norway, Sweden, Switzerland, the United Kingdom, and the United States. See Angus Maddison, *Dynamic Forces in Capitalist Development: A Long-run Comparative View* (New York:

Oxford University Press, 1991), for comparisons in all major economic variables for these countries from 1820 to the late 1980s.

5. See Kevin H. O'Rourke and Jeffrey G. Williamson, *Globalization and History: The Evolution of a Nineteenth Century Atlantic Economy* (Cambridge: MIT Press, 2000), 215–16.

6. See Peter Drucker, "The Next Society, A Survey of the Near Future," *The Economist*, 1 November 2001.

7. Womack, Jones, and Roos, *The Machine That Changed the World*, 31.

8. See Michael Porter, *The Competitive Advantage of Nations* (New York: Simon & Schuster, 1989), 80.

9. See Richard Sennet, *The Corrosion of Character: The Personal Consequences of Work in the New Capitalism* (New York: W.W. Norton & Company, 1998), 22.

10. See "American Productivity, the New 'New Economy,' " *The Economist*, 11 September 2003; Robert J. Gordon, "Five Puzzles in the Behavior of Productivity, Investment and Innovation," 10 September 2003, draft of chapter for World Economic Forum, *Global Competitiveness Report, 2003–2004* (paper available in the author's Web site in northwestern.edu); Bart Van Ark et al., *ICT and Productivity in Europe and the United States: Where Do the Differences Come From?"* paper for the SOM Ph.D. Conference, 29 January 2003, De Niewe Academie, Groningen. This last paper can be obtained from the author in r,c.inclaar@eco.rug.nl.

CHAPTER 2

The Economic Disruptions

The picture that emerges from projecting into the future the trends of the Connectivity Revolution is quite exciting in the long run. The advance of science has created an enormous basis for innovations to appear, both in the form of new goods and services, and in new ways of producing the existing ones. Also, since the new means of communication are putting this scientific basis at the disposal of the entire world, there are opportunities for everybody to exercise creativity, and these will increase exponentially as new scientific discoveries are made.

It is difficult to believe that anybody would dislike living in a society providing so many opportunities to the average human being. Yet, there are two main dimensions in the effects of a deep technological revolution. First, there are the long-term transformations elicited in the shape of society. Second, there are the temporary effects of change itself—that is, the frictions that any process of transformation from one state to another creates in society. While the first offers a better future for everyone, the second poses difficult problems of adjustment across society. The immediate economic consequences of the transformation toward this new kind of society are creating severe tensions all over the world in terms of shifts in wealth and income distribution, increased unemployment and employment instability, human and capital migrations, and financial turmoil. Beyond that, it is already transforming social relationships in all dimensions in life, colliding with long-established mores and customs. This threatens to send several societies into chaos and potentially destructive reactions to it.

I analyze in the rest of this chapter the frictions that the development of connectivity is causing in our economies.

One of the most obvious implications of the new Industrial Revolution is that the prices of the services of the mind—creativity and the ability to organize and reorganize—are increasing relative to the prices of the services of the muscle. The signs of this shift are all around. The share of physical production and handling in the total costs of delivered goods is falling relative to the share of organizational and logistic services, showing that the most profitable opportunities are in the latter. Accordingly, the share of physical production in developed economies is falling, and that of services is increasing. The industrial basis of those countries is shifting toward highly sophisticated production of specialized items with high value added. Routinely organized massive production is becoming the territory of either developing countries or highly automated factories.

These facts, and their consequences, pose one of the biggest threats to the stability of developed and developing societies alike. People who cannot access the benefits of the Connectivity Revolution will see their incomes decline, while those taking advantage of the new technologies will prosper very rapidly. This will disrupt the income distribution between countries, and within countries, creating social tensions in developed and developing societies alike, very similar to those created by the Industrial Revolution.

The shift in the relative prices of the services of the intellect and those of the muscle is already apparent in the decline of the prices of the goods with the lowest content of intellectual services: commodities. Except for a brief boom during the 1970s, the prices of non-oil commodities have fallen substantially since midcentury. After deducting the inflation of the last four decades, their prices in 2001 represented 44 percent of their level in 1960 and only 30 percent of their exceptional peak in 1974. This means that today the producers of commodities have to sell more than twice the volume they sold in 1960 to buy the same amount of other goods and services. If, for example, they could get a truck with 100 units of commodities, now they need 225 to get the same truck. Some specific commodities are in a worse situation. Coffee prices, for example, are today a quarter of what they were in 1960.[1] This is not a short fluctuation in the prices; it has been the trend for forty years now.

Such decline is the result of both the direct and indirect effects of the technological revolution, in two dimensions. First, the increased efficiency in design and production methods and the invention of new synthetic materials are reducing the volume of traditional raw materials used in the production of other goods. Second, price competition in commodities is increasing because, having little knowledge embedded, they can be produced in any place with very low salaries.

The declining prices of commodities are negatively affecting the incomes of countries dependent on their production, which tends to increase the gap between rich and poor countries in a spectacular way. The average per capita GDP of the high-income countries—those producing goods increasingly based on knowledge—*grew* in 1980–2001 by three times the *total* per capita GDP of the commodity-producing middle-income countries in 2001 and by eight times that of the low-income countries in the same date.[2] Moreover, the median growth of per capita income of developing countries, which was 2.5 percent in 1960–79, fell to zero percent in 1980–98, while the developed countries, and particularly the United States, kept on growing.[3] Thus, a repetition of what happened with the Industrial Revolution—the sharp separation of the incomes of the countries adopting the new technologies from those that lag in such adoption—is in the making.

The transformation is already having a strong impact *inside* individual countries, including both developing and developed ones.

The methods of production of goods without much knowledge content have been simplified so much that low-skill, low-salaried workers in developing countries can produce them with the same efficiency as the much better paid workers in developed countries. Thus, people working in these activities in the latter have suddenly become overpaid. To justify the higher salaries they must do what Motorola did in the example of the previous chapter: produce something with a higher value, something that would require more education than that of the less skilled workers in developing countries. If not, the advantage in education that they have today over their counterparts in developing countries will become irrelevant from the economic point of view, and a decline in their income to the levels of their colleagues in the developing countries would be inevitable. Increased protection or higher social security contributions cannot change this fact. There is less income to be distributed out of these activities.

The way in which the redistribution of income away from the unskilled takes place depends mainly on the rigidity or flexibility of the labor markets. In countries where the labor markets are flexible—that is, where firing people is relatively easy and wages are mainly set on individual negotiations—the wages of the unskilled fall but unemployment either remains constant or falls. In countries where the labor markets are rigid—where firing people is very difficult and wages are set in collective negotiations between the enterprises, the government and the workers—wages do not decline but unemployment increases. The aggregate impact of these two alternative ways of adjustment is equivalent. At the individual level, however, unemployment is quite inequitable, for some workers keep their jobs at relatively high wages while others are left without any wage at all.

This process is already under way. In the United States, one of the most flexible labor markets, the real wage (by real it means the wage after deducting inflation) declined from their 1978 peak throughout the 1980s and then flattened during most of the 1990s. The wages of the unskilled started to increase again in the second half of the 1990s but only after unemployment had fallen to their lowest levels in history in an atypically long expansion of the American economy. Even so, wages flattened again under the impact of the deceleration of the early 2000s, so that the real wage of the unskilled in 2001 was the same as that of 1966, 35 years before, while the average income per capita had increased by 80 percent in real terms.

Unskilled workers are not the only ones suffering from this readjustment of incomes. The overall country's distribution of income has changed for the worse as the income of people better positioned to take advantage of the revolution increases very fast while the income of the rest stagnates or declines—negatively affecting not just the unskilled workers but also most of the American population. From the early 1970s to the late 1990s the income gap between college and high school graduates increased from 43 to 80 percent, while that of people with advanced degrees over high school graduates more than tripled, from 72 to 250 percent.[4] The deterioration of the distribution of income is also evident when measured in terms of the income of families. From 1977 to 1999, only the top two-fifths of the families in the country experienced an increase in their real incomes—the top fifth, which enjoyed an increase of 40 percent, and the second richest fifth, which experienced an increase of 7.5 percent. The income of all the other groups—comprising 60 percent of the American families—went down. If, rather than looking at the real income, we look at the shares of each group of families out of the total income of the country, we find that while the top 20 percent increased its share from 44 percent to 53 percent, all other groups—that is, 80 percent of the families—experienced a decline.[5]

This is not an exclusively American experience. The share of market income of the poorest 30 percent of the families deteriorated in all the 12 rich countries for which data is available from the mid-1980s to the mid-1990s. In 11 of these countries the middle class also lost income share. The only exception was the Netherlands, where the middle class experienced a gain.[6] These data refer to incomes obtained from the market, which includes salaries, interests on capital, and income from self-employment. Similar results are obtained when salaries alone are used. The losses of income diminish substantially if taxes and government transfers are taken into account and they level off or even become gains in some cases. Such transfers and taxes, however, are artificial mechanisms established by governments to compensate for what is happening in the market by redistributing income from the rich to the poor. It is a fact that market forces are causing a deterioration of income distribution in most, if not all, of the richest countries in the world.

The impact of unemployment and lower market incomes on the income distribution of continental European countries is dampened by their comprehensive social security systems. These, however, are in serious financial trouble precisely at the onset of a period when they will be more needed—particularly because continental Europe is now just starting the process of globalization that the United States started in the 1980s. One after the other, these social security institutions discovered that their revenues would be insufficient in the future to cover the benefits they are promising to their members. Some countries have initiated deep reforms of their systems to cope with this problem, mainly in the direction of reducing both the offered benefits and the certainty of them. In terms of unemployment benefits, the trend is toward reducing them. The combined effect is that of reducing the certainty of the population regarding their economic future just as the Connectivity Revolution is pushing exactly in the same direction.

Based on household data, Branko Milanovic found that the world's distribution of income worsened in 1988–93 in such a way that the ratio of the income of the top 5 percent to the lowest 5 percent went up from 78 to 114 times.[7] In a subsequent paper, the same author estimates that the share of total world's income of the lowest 70 percent of the population went down perceptibly during the same period.[8] These figures suggest that income distribution is worsening both within countries and worldwide. Evidence from the developed countries link this worsening with the distribution of skills and knowledge.

The same reasons that are leading to the skewing of income distribution also cause the financial instability of our times. As we already discussed regarding human skills, the new technologies turn obsolete the existing physical capital, shifting the relative prices in favor of the new activities and thus redistributing profits from the laggards to the leaders. This is the natural incentive that markets provide to induce a shift in the allocation of resources toward the new activities. Following such incentives, investment naturally moves from the low- to the high-profitability sectors and activities. If this could be done instantly, and if this had no implications for the people who had invested in the now obsolete activities, there would be an immediate adjustment and the economy would start expanding steadily by taking advantage of the opportunities offered by the new technologies.

The real world, however, is not like that. The premature obsolescence of the existing capital stock destroys the capital invested in the old activities, causing severe loses to investors and bankers. Just by itself, this mechanism is enough to generate financial crises. In addition, the level of uncertainty in new investments increases exponentially, so that investors moving fast to take advantage of the new technologies also run a high risk—higher, perhaps, than that taken by the laggards. This is so because the nature, strength, and other key characteristics of the demand for an entirely new product reveal themselves in the market only through time. New competitors entering an established market have all the advantages given by the experience of the firms operating in that market. They know what kinds of products have succeeded and which have not. There are established standards to ensure compatibility of one set of products with sets of complementary ones. Entrepreneurs entering a completely new field do not have any of those advantages. The possibilities are infinite and they have to make choices on assumptions about the way that markets will react to each of the features of their new product. The probability of making a mistake in one single crucial dimension, one that would lead to the failure of the enterprise is very high. Some of the opportunities that look bright turn into blind alleys, as it happened with the electric car in the early 1900s and the Wang dedicated word processor of the 1980s. Thus, connectivity increases the risk of both the existing and the new investments.

Of course, drastic shifts in relative prices can be produced by events different from technological revolutions. For example, the effects of market liberalization on financial stability are similar to those of technological revolutions because liberal policies open the economy to the influence of new methods of production, brought about by new domestic and foreign competition. Just like new inventions, the introduction of competition in hitherto closed and rigid economies results in drastic shifts in relative prices, which in turn, create substantial financial distress. In fact, the impact of liberalization on relative prices can be more dramatic than that caused by innovations because the latter tend to be more gradual than a sudden opening of the economy. In our times, the disruptive effects of the transition to connectivity have mixed with those of liberalization because, in practice, the former has led to the latter through globalization.

These direct and indirect effects generate ripples that go across the entire economy, increasing the uncertainty and, therefore, the risks of the financial system. For these reasons, the Industrial Revolution was characterized by deep and frequent financial crises. After the last of them, the Great Depression of the 1930s, the crises disappeared for almost 50 years. Then, they came back in force in the last two decades.

The modern crises started with Chile and Mexico in the early 1980s and continued with Venezuela and Mexico again in the early 1990s. At that time, Japan also went into a quiet but poisonous financial crisis. Later, in the late 1990s, there was a panic in East Asia and Russia defaulted on its debts. In 1999 Ecuador suffered a terrible crisis that wiped out most of its banking system and Argentina went into yet another crisis. The Russian crisis combined with the East Asian one threatened the stability of the worldwide financial system. For a few months, the prospect of a world-wide depression came back with striking clarity. It was averted only be-cause of the prompt coordinated action of the monetary authorities of the main financial centers.

Financial instability has also affected the developed countries. It has become manifest in the United States through the boom and bust of stock prices in the late 1900s and early 2000s. Thus far, the fall has been much smaller than that which started Japan's deep recession of the last ten years, sending the country's banking system into insolvency. There is no guar-antee that this would not happen in the United States as well. There is a price level at which, as it happened in Japan, the stock exchange crisis can turn into a full-blown financial crisis with unpredictable effects in the performance of the world's economy. Even if the trend in the stock prices is reverted, financial instability is likely to be with us for a long while because the uncertainty associated with the development of the new econ-omy will last for a long time. The shifts in relative prices and the conse-quent shifts in the absolute and relative profitability of sectors and firms will be a permanent feature of the economy in the next several decades, and this will be reflected in the varying prices of shares—both in absolute terms and in relation with each other.

Thus, the smoothness that characterized the adjustment to the first wave of the Connectivity Revolution in the United States in the 1980s and 1990s seems to be over.

The trends toward a concentration of income distribution and toward financial instability are also affecting the rest of the developed countries —even if their adjustment to the transformation is lagging. Certainly, German companies are moving parts of their production to East Europe; Britain, which became the first globalized economy during the Industrial Revolution, continues with its tradition of foreign investment and is moving away from the production of traditional industrial goods; Spain is investing heavily in Latin America; Japan has built factories all over the world. But, as we have discussed earlier, this is only half of a successful globalization process. The other half is spurring the creation of new activities that will take the place, in the local economies, of the lower-productivity ones that now are being parceled out. This is what is not happening as yet in most developed countries. As long as it does not happen, the rate of unemployment will tend to rise and the income distribution will tend to worsen, generating grave social problems.

This is quite worrying. Yet, the impact of the incipient connectivity on domestic economies has been much stronger on the formerly Communist and developing countries.

There is a common perception that the Soviet Union and the Communist regime that underlay it collapsed because the Soviet people wanted democracy and markets. This is not true. The Soviet Union was brought down by stark economic and military problems. The country was one of the most isolated and protected economic spaces in the world, comparable in its degree of economic seclusion only to that of the other Communist countries. It was known all along that the giant had severe weaknesses, particularly in agriculture, which was a continuous disaster. But its industrial power was not denied. And this power was the source of its military might.

Yet, while agriculture was ridiculously inefficient, the main weakness of the Soviet Union was in its industry. The symptoms of the inefficiencies of Soviet industry were apparent in the lack of demand for Soviet industrial products in the international markets, even at high discounts. They had awkward designs, were costly to operate, and broke down regularly. For this reason, the Soviet Union was forced to export commodities, like developing countries. In the international markets, the Soviet Union was not an industrial player. Still, the Soviet Union was a military superpower because, despite all its inefficiencies, it allocated enough resources to the military industries to produce enormous amounts of modern weapons.

Then, in the 1980s, something went ominously wrong. Up to that moment, the Soviet Union had been able to replicate the products that the West was turning out—either by industrial espionage or reverse engineering, the art of figuring out how to produce something produced by someone else. In the 1980s, however, the West was already producing something that the Soviet Union could not possibly replicate—connectivity—and this was resulting in a technological explosion that would eventually downgrade the superpower status of the Soviet Union.

Connectivity has a crucial military implication. For centuries, the fate of warriors has crucially depended on the ability to communicate fast, both before the battle and during it. One of the curses of soldiers has been what is called "the fog of war," the uncertainties that develop while a battle is going on. Even the best strategy may require revisions while confronting the enemy, which may do unexpected things. Opportunities not thought possible in the planning stage could become a reality; forces not identified by intelligence may turn around. Some people in the battlefield may see these developments but their knowledge is of no use if they cannot convey it to a central place and decisions revised to face them. Thus, connectivity has been always crucial in the battlefield. The combination of computers and telecommunications that was emerging in the West was allowing for an unprecedented capacity to eliminate the fog of war not just in a local battlefield but also globally, across battlefields scattered around the world. In the modern battlefield, and particularly when thinking of several battlefields thousands of miles apart—the likely shape of a war between superpowers—required computers of a power that the Soviet Union could not produce. This, however, was not the problem. They could steal some computers and learn how to produce them. In fact, this was the easiest part.

What the Soviets could not reproduce was the human element. Communist regimes could not possible replicate connectivity because it is based on increasing communications between people, something that a tyrannical government cannot possibly afford to allow. Tyrannies survive precisely by not allowing people to communicate among themselves. Moreover, connectivity is useful only when people can make decisions based on the ideas and information they are exchanging, and this was not possible in the rigidly centralized Soviet economy. The Soviet companies lacked incentives to innovate. It was clear that, without innovation and connectivity, the Soviet Union would lag behind the West in the new economy that was dawning. Watching how children in the West were connected through their computers even before the Internet was popular, the Soviets saw the emergence of a new generation of soldiers able to reduce the fog of war to a point they could not match because they could not allow their children or their adults to communicate with each other. They saw generations of scientists able to produce innovations in large teams connected around the world. And they saw western industry becoming more efficient and faster than anything in history. The Soviets could not compete.[9]

Andropov first and then Gorbachev realized that their system was in the losing end of history and that deep reforms were needed. Gorbachev focused on two of them. One was introducing incentives for enterprises to increase their efficiency and creativity by giving them autonomy, but without relinquishing the state ownership of the enterprises. The other was to gradually open society to freedom of speech, a precondition to introducing connectivity. The first led to *Perestroika* and the second to *Glasnost*, which literally means openness and can be interpreted as freedom of speech. The problem was that autonomy without an owner just destroys discipline. Perestroika crashed as the workers in the enterprises used their new autonomy to increase their own wages rather than to increase their efficiency and to sell their products in the black markets for personal gain rather than feeding the official chain of supplies. As most products went into the black markets, the official economy collapsed and, with it, the Communist system and the Soviet Union. The collapse spontaneously liberalized the Soviet markets. The black market became the only market in the country.

The brutal shift in relative prices that accompanied the spontaneous liberalization of Russia was one of the major sources of the instability that characterized the country after the late 1980s. As the economy opened in the post-Soviet period, it became clear that the distorted relative prices implicit in the Soviet production methods, as well as the attitudes of total unconcern about quality and other demands of customers, had created an industry that was hopelessly uncompetitive. Activities and enterprises that looked profitable under the old system of prices fixed artificially by the central planners suddenly became loss-makers under the new market prices. In fact, it became clear that, for many Russian industrial products, the value of the raw materials at international prices was higher than the value of the finished product. It made more sense to export the raw materials than producing the finished goods.

The problem has not been resolved as yet. Resolving it requires redesigning not just the final products, but rebuilding the machines that produce them, and the machines that produce these, and retraining all engineers and workers, and so on. In short, it requires the rebuilding of the entire industrial capacity of the country—a long and complicated endeavor.

The question could be posed that, if things are this way, why is it that Russia keeps on producing industrial goods for domestic consumption? The answer is that the market itself imposes a limit to the speed of the transformation of the Russian economy. The country cannot generate enough foreign exchange with its exports of commodities to pay for the imports that would terminate its industry. This is not as good as it sounds, because it tends to create a vicious circle. Without foreign competition, enterprises in Russia can survive even if being terribly inefficient, which, in turn, prevents them from exporting and generating the resources they need so badly to modernize themselves. Thus, the country teeters around a very fragile equilibrium, which any small event turns into the all-too-familiar crises.

Thus, Russia and the other formerly Communist countries are prime examples of how connectivity can bring down a society in two steps: first, by forcing its opening, and then, by disrupting all relative prices in one sudden sweep. With these two steps, connectivity generates a protracted instability that may last for several decades. Part of this instability is imbedded in the impoverishment of the population and the emergence of wide disparities in income and wealth. The World Bank estimates that the percentage of the Russian population living in poverty in 1987–1988, just before the Communist regime entered its final spin, was 2 percent. By 1993–1995, this figure had increased to 44 percent. The numbers for all the economies in transition are 4 percent and 40 percent, respectively. Only one country—the Czech Republic—kept this figure constant, below 1 percent, through those years. The number of people living in poverty in those countries increased from 13.6 to 147.1 million.[10]

This catastrophic social transformation cannot be attributed to the introduction of capitalism, however. It had already started in the early 1990s, when, still under the Communist regime, production collapsed in most industrial and agricultural products and the official distribution systems broke down. Poverty was already exploding in the winters of 1990 and 1991, when the world could see on TV screens how Soviet people scrambled for food and clothing in long lines in front of the official stores, leaving the weak and old behind.

Thus, the first few stages of the Connectivity Revolution brought about the collapse of the second superpower on earth. They also caused turmoil in the developing countries.

The case of developing countries is conceptually similar to that of the Soviet Union, although the level of distortion of relative prices present in the former is much lower than that of the latter. All developing countries pursued protectionist trade policies and interventionist government actions for at least six or seven decades during the twentieth century. Many of them were able to create an industrial sector. As in the case of the Soviet Union, however, these industrial sectors are terribly inefficient and uncompetitive in the international markets. As in the case of the Soviet Union, connectivity and globalization have forced many of these countries to liberalize and this has caused protracted instability and financial crises.

The mechanisms through which connectivity and globalization forced the opening of these economies can be exemplified with the case of Latin America, where most of the crises have taken place. During the 1970s, these countries reacted to the oil crisis of these years by expanding their economies artificially, financing it with money borrowed in the international markets. They were willing to pay higher interest rates than their developed counterparts and attracted the enormous amounts of liquid resources that flooded the international financial institutions in those years—the combined result of low demand for financing in the developed countries and the excess liquidity that was coming back from the oil producers in what was called the recycling of the oil proceeds. The boom in commodity prices that accompanied the oil crisis helped their borrowing spree by giving the impression that they would have the resources to pay back their increasing debt.

At the end of the 1970s, however, the prices of all commodities collapsed and these countries became insolvent. They could not diversify their exports to increase their foreign exchange earnings because their industries were not competitive on account of the comfortable degree of protection they received from the state. The lack of foreign exchange depressed their industrial sectors, which largely depended on imported inputs to keep on producing. Industrial production collapsed along with the prices of the commodities. Very gradually, the recognition that liberalization was needed to improve competitiveness and growth extended throughout Latin America. The crises of the 1980s brought a bonus in disguise, at least in Latin America: in addition to adopting liberal economic policies, the legitimacy of authoritarian regimes collapsed and, in the 1990s, practically all the countries in the region moved into democracy.

Yet, moving into democracy and economic liberalism did not bring automatic stability. The first country to liberalize economically was Chile under a still authoritarian regime, and it soon experienced a grave financial crisis, probably the worst of the modern sort of crises. Subsequently, other liberalizing countries, Venezuela, Mexico, Brazil, and Argentina principally experienced grave crises in the 1990s, both before and after they had moved toward democracy. Other countries in Latin America that moved toward liberal policies also suffered from crises as the dismantling of the terribly oppressive protectionist regimes of the previous years caused pronounced shifts in the relative prices prevailing in the domestic economy. Grossly inefficient companies failed, bringing about huge losses to the banking system.[11] Many governments tried to compensate for these problems by resorting to monetary expansion and devaluations, which, rather than resolving them, heightened the negative social impact of the transformation. Instability has continued and people are fast forgetting that economic liberalization started because state interventionism had taken them to a state of disaster.

Developing countries cannot resolve these problems by closing their economies because they need foreign exchange to pay for their imports, and the long-term decline of the prices of commodities inexorably reduces the flows of foreign exchange that their current exports can generate. They cannot increase their industrial exports because their still heavily protected industrial enterprises are too inefficient, and even those that are efficient are not competitive because they have to pay higher prices for their inputs as a result of the protection that other industrial and agricultural enterprises enjoy in their archaic regimes. Thus, these countries have to open further to improve the competitiveness of their industrial enterprises but the instability that accompanies liberalization is an obstacle for further liberalization. The same economic instability that eased the transition toward a new model of liberal economic policies and democracy is now threatening the new model. Venezuela, one of the few countries that remained democratic during the heyday of the authoritarian regimes in Latin America, has already voted into power a tyrannical regime that seems to have emerged from the 1950s.

Thus, modernization has also brought about instability to developing countries, directly and through the liberalization it forced on them. It is doing the same in developed countries.

The transition to the new world will not be easy.

NOTES

1. Data from International Financial Statistics, published by the International Monetary Fund, Washington D.C. The figures are published monthly in electronic form.

2. Calculations based on data from the World Tables, published by the World Bank on the Internet, worldbank.org. These figures have been adjusted for Purchasing Power Parity, which means that income estimations have been corrected for the differences in the cost of living across countries. In most cases, this adjustment results in increases in the estimation of the income of the poor countries, where the cost of living tends to be lower than in the developed ones.

3. See William Easterly, *The Lost Decades: Developing Countries' Stagnation in Spite of Policy Reforms 1980–1998* (Washington, D.C., The World Bank, 2001), p. 2.

4. W. Michelle Cox and Richard Alm, "The Good Old Days Are Now," *Reason*, December 1995.

5. U.S. Congressional Budget Office, *The Economic and Budget Outlook, An Update* (Washington, D.C.: U.S. Congressional Budget Office, 2000), Table 1.

6. Jean-Marc Burniaux et al., *Income Distribution and Poverty in Selected OECD Countries* (Paris: Organization for Economic Cooperation and Development, 1998), Economics Department Working Papers No. 189, Table 3.1, p. 37.

7. See Branko Milanovic, *True World Income Distribution, 1988 and 1993: First Calculation Based on Household Surveys Alone* (Washington, D.C.: The World Bank, 2000), p. 52.

8. See Branko Milanovic, *Can We Discern the Effect of Globalization on Income Distribution? Evidence from Household Budget Survey*, World Bank Policy Research Working Paper 2876 (Washington, D.C.: The World Bank, 2002), p. 7.

9. See Bruce Berkowitz, *The New Face of War: How War Will Be Fought in the 21st Century* (New York: The Free Press, 2003) for a glimpse of the difference that connectivity makes in war. A top Soviet economic advisor explained the military implications of connectivity to me back in 1990 when the former visited Washington to explore the possible integration of the Soviet Union in the Breton Woods system.

10. See *World Development Indicators on CD-ROM, Tables* (Washington, D.C.: The World Bank, 1999).

11. See Stephan Haggard and Robert R. Kaufman, *The Political Economy of Democratic Transitions* (Princeton, N.J.: Princeton University Press, 1995), 64.

CHAPTER 3

Riches and Stagnation

The economic effects of the transformation to a connected society present an uncanny similarity to those that led Karl Marx to announce the imminent collapse of capitalism. He identified two features of the society of his time as the harbingers of such collapse: the sharp differences in the distribution of income that accompanied the early stages of the Industrial Revolution and the financial crises that with almost predictable regularity devastated the economies of the newly industrializing countries throughout the nineteenth century and up to the last and worst of them, the Great Depression of the 1930s.

These problems disappeared for five decades after the end of World War II. Yet, right after the Soviet Union collapsed, the world economy started to show the same symptoms that Marx had pointed out. Marx's current followers are seeing those signs as proof that their master was right all along, and that the era of stable capitalism, mostly confined to the last 50 years, was just a fleeting stage in a process that inexorably leads to instability and growing exploitation. Some of them argue that this fleeting moment of stability was the result of the threat of Communism. Once this threat was removed, capitalism is going back to its natural tendency to concentrate incomes and generate crises.

Was Marx right?

Marx's main mistake in his historical analysis was to see the disruptions caused by the Industrial Revolution as the permanent features of capitalism and democracy and not as the temporary effects of a transformation from one form of society to another. Those who followed him found, to their chagrin, that the pains of adjustment were much bigger in the system that Marx envisioned, and that, after much suffering, they had to rebuild their countries along the principles of democracy and capitalism that their master had deprecated. Marx's current followers are making the same mistake as their antecessor: blaming on capitalism what is the natural disruption caused by a momentous technological transformation.

Marx also made predictions. History proved him wrong in at least two dimensions in this respect. First, capitalism withstood the convulsions he thought would bring it down. Second, the convulsions disappeared after World War II, and what emerged were not chaotic societies in which the rich exploited progressively poor masses, but stable societies where the distribution of income reached a measure of equality that had never been achieved in history. Actually, what collapsed in shambles was Marx's own creation, the Communist system.

In this chapter I show how the concentration of income and the financial instability of our times are the natural results of the ongoing technological transformation and are, therefore, due to disappear as all people and countries get access to the benefits of connectivity in a process that will be shorter the faster people integrate to the new connected world. Then I discuss why some countries are likely to do it faster than others, and why some may even be left out of the revolution altogether, repeating their dismal performance during the Industrial Revolution.

Knowledge has always been a crucial factor of production as well as the main vehicle for dissemination of economic development and wealth. In fact, as we will discuss in this chapter, the efficient use of knowledge is the main factor accounting for the difference between rich and poor countries in our current world. This role is increasing with the Connectivity Revolution, which privileges those activities that require more knowledge and coordination in their production over those that can be produced with lower levels of skill.

In the process, the emergence of connectivity is disrupting the distribution of income mainly though the increase of the prices of the services of the mind—creativity and the ability to organize and reorganize—relative to the prices of the services of the muscle. This fact poses one of the biggest threats to the stability of developed and developing societies alike. People who cannot access the benefits of the Connectivity Revolution—those whose incomes are tied to the activities with declining value—are seeing their incomes shrink, while those taking advantage of the new technologies are prospering very rapidly. The difference in the speeds of adjustment generates a gap between the incomes of the fast and the slow adjusters, which will initially increase fast, then will level off and finally decline as the slow adjusters catch up with the opportunities open by the new technologies. That is, at the beginning of the process, the fast adjuster grows much faster than the slow adjusters; at the end of the process, the opposite is true. This is what allows for the final convergence of the fast and slow adjusters. At the end of the process, the income of slow and fast adjusters becomes the same.

This is what happened during the Industrial Revolution. In the 1750s, the level of industrialization was about the same all over the world. Industries were mostly manufacturing activities based on handicraft and few companies organized on the capitalistic mode of production. Then, with the invention of the steam engine, the innovator, Britain, went ahead of the rest of the world in terms of industrialization and wealth. The differences in the speed of industrialization produced a differentiation in the income of countries and within each country. The income per capita of Britain grew much faster than those of the other industrializing countries at the beginning of the process did. However, many other countries, including the United States, Canada, continental Europe, Japan, Australia, New Zealand, and some countries in Asia eventually started their industrialization and grew faster than Britain in later stages.[1] They eventually caught up with Britain, and their domestic distribution of income, as it happened in Britain, improved dramatically from its dismal levels at the beginning of the process.

That is, the crippling concentration of income that Marx envisioned, both across countries and within each country, did not take place if we focus on the countries that adopted the new technologies and became industrial. All the capitalist countries that industrialized eventually became richer, in magnitudes that even surpassed the wealth of the pioneer, Britain. Domestically, they did not become enormous pools of poor people exploited by a few capitalists. On the contrary, their distribution of income became quite leveled.

Marx's misinterpretation of the initial differentiation of income and financial instability that accompanied the Industrial Revolution as the early signs of an impending collapse of capitalism could be understandable in his times. He had not seen the entire cycle of adjustment. It would not be understandable if we make the same mistake in our time, when we know more about processes of adjustment. Yet, this is what many people are doing at this moment, thinking that the current deterioration in the distribution of income and the recurring financial crises demonstrate the failure of free markets. As the experience of the Industrial Revolution proved, a mistaken diagnosis would lead to terrible results.

Moreover, blaming capitalism for what is a problem of adjustment distracts the attention from the true problem: how to accelerate the process of adjustment. The process of innovation is nonlinear, so that it can take several decades to close the gap created in the initial years of the process. A century passed before the Netherlands, one of the fastest adjusters in Europe, was able to close the gap with Britain in terms of income per capita. For Germany, France, and Japan, it took 150 years, although the data seem to suggest that the period would have been somewhat shorter—but still over a century—if World War II had not taken place.[2]

Thus, the key to catching up with the leaders was not to stage revolutions and discard capitalism. It was to adopt the new technologies, which, in the epoch we are discussing, was to industrialize.

Now we can turn to the next question. Why do some countries adopt the new technologies before others, and why do others not adopt them at all? The latter is the case of many Third World countries, which have not yet started industrialization. For them, the gap that opened in the nineteenth century became a permanent feature of their reality. As we discussed in the previous chapter, this gap would tend to increase as connectivity is increasing the relative value of knowledge.

Old and new critics of liberal ideas and free markets think that this gap was created and maintained by imperialistic designs of the industrial countries. Some other people think that the gap results from differences in the endowment of resources. Evidence, however, shows that it is *the efficiency in the use of the resources of a country*, rather than the endowment of those resources or imperialistic designs, which causes some countries to develop while others lag behind.[3] Differences in the general education of the population, saving and investment rates, and even in the absolute levels of the stock of human and physical capital, while explaining a small part of the differences in income that emerged in the nineteenth century, cannot explain most of them, even if all these variables are combined.[4] For example, if the time that society devotes to invest in human capital during a long time is increased from 6 to 48 percent the output by factor of production would multiply only five times, while the differences in income we want to explain is on the order of 27 times (the difference between the richest and the poorest countries in the world once the figures are adjusted for purchasing power parity).[5] Comparisons of savings and investment rates in physical capital produce similarly implausible results. Saving rates would have to be 8,000 times as big in the richest as in the poorest countries to account for the differences in income; going from 20 to 40 percent of income saved could result on an increase of just 25 percent in the basic level of income.[6] Moreover, some of the most advanced countries in the world, including most prominently the United States, have had notoriously low rates of saving throughout their histories. Furthermore, since the rates of investment in physical capital have been similar for long periods in countries with widely differing levels of income, and since some poor countries have invested a higher portion of their income than several rich ones, it is clear that such investment cannot be the source of the difference.

In contrast, in their book *Barriers to Riches*, Stephen L. Parente and Edward C. Prescott show that a country with a third of the United States' efficiency in the use of factors of production would have an income that is 1/27th of that of the United States. This is the order of magnitude that we are talking about.[7]

What makes for these differences in the efficiency in the use of resources? Parente and Prescott have shown statistically that *the most important variable making the difference in the efficiency in the use of resources is the efficient use of readily available knowledge.* Except for some very specialized activities, efficient methods of production are in the public domain, particularly in our times, when business and technical publications are plentiful and of high quality and when access to markets is only a computer and a modem away. Poor countries have not developed the capacity to acquire and apply such knowledge. When they do, they can grow faster than their predecessors in development because the stock of available knowledge increases with time, allowing countries to leapfrog over stages that took a long time to overcome, to the countries that developed earlier. This is what Hong Kong, Korea, Taiwan, and Singapore did during the twentieth century.

Why do people in underdeveloped societies fail to use available knowledge to increase their efficiency? The short answer to this question is resistance to change supported by the state. The economic backwardness of poor countries is self-inflicted.

Resisting change is a natural response to processes that render obsolete existing physical capital and skills, and entrepreneurs and workers having to lose from the introduction of such processes tend to oppose them. Such opposition, however, is ineffective in a competitive environment. Even if all the producers and workers in a country decided not to introduce an innovation that none of them like, the competition of foreign goods produced more efficiently because of the innovation would force the use of the new methods of production. Otherwise, the local firms would face extinction. If, however, entrepreneurs, workers, or both are able to convince the government that it should resist the innovation, they can stop progress.

Governments help entrepreneurs and workers stop progress through two main mechanisms. First, government policies aimed at protecting particular sectors in the economy by raising the costs of potential competitors to unaffordable levels. These policies include protection that discourages foreign competition; domestic market restrictions, such as price controls; subsidies to inefficient activities and monopolies granted by the government, all of them measures that discourage local competition; and barriers to fire workers that increase the costs of replacing them with machinery or other more efficient workers. In some cases, when these measures are not enough, governments issue regulations that explicitly or implicitly forbid the introduction of the new techniques. Second, governments also help the inefficient through the maze of bureaucratic regulations that keep costs of transactions in the economy at unreasonably high levels and make it even more difficult to establish competition. Such regulations, in addition to helping the bureaucrats themselves, help the entrepreneurs that can overcome them with their bribes or political connections.

The Peruvian economist Hernando de Soto has documented the high cost that these procedures impose on all producers.[8] Simple tasks like formalizing urban property take 168 steps and 13–25 years in the Philippines; to gain access to desert land and to register it takes 6–14 years in Egypt; to convert a house leasing to a sales contract takes 11 years in Haiti.[9] These procedures are the instrument through which bureaucrats and lawyers protect and foster their incomes, legally as a justification of their salaries and in many cases illegally through corruption. The seemingly irrational procedures also protect the status quo by discriminating against the small enterprises and the poorest sections of the population because bureaucracy weighs more heavily on the latter. In some countries in Latin America, for example, only lawyers can be notary publics and they charge fees that can go up to 2–3 percent of the value of the transaction when certifying the creation of a corporation, the transfer of a property or any simple procedure requiring their certification. Big companies reduce these costs by hiring lawyers that renounce these fees for a permanent salary. Small enterprises and citizens in general cannot afford this solution and have to pay the incredibly high prices associated with even the simplest tasks. Also, typically, there is a way to cut through the red tape but it requires spreading cash among bureaucrats and politicians, something that the small business cannot afford to do.

What governments do by taking these measures is granting monopolies to the suppliers of the inputs so that they can extract rents from their archaic skills and capital goods. Through this, governments effectively prevent the population from acquiring knowledge that is readily available in developed countries to improve the efficiency of production. While corruption is pervasive in these schemes, it is not the main motivation to create them. The problem is essentially one of resistance to change. People support these schemes because they think that through them they will stop the disruptions caused by competition, the main vehicle of technological advance.

An influential Massachusetts Institute of Technology (MIT) study on the car industry gives prominent attention to this phenomenon when discussing the large differences in productivity that have afflicted this industry since its inception.[10] Resistance to change has been incredibly strong in the two great revolutions in methods of production that have taken place in the sector. The first great revolution took place between 1914 and 1924, when Henry Ford and Alfred Sloan—the founder of General Motors—replaced the craft-based motor vehicle industry in the United States with the mass production car industry. The gains in productivity were immense, so much so that the number of companies operating in the field fell from more than 100 to barely 3, the reason being that all other companies failed to convert themselves with the new production methods and the mentality that drove them.

One could have expected that this revolution in production methods would be instantly adopted all over the world. Yet, it was only in the 1960s that continental Europe at last adopted mass production and gained from its productivity. That is, it took between 40 to 50 years for the European producers to adopt a technique that was obviously better. By that time, the technique was archaic because Toyota had already invented Lean Production and perfected it for more than a decade.[11] Such a lag had nothing to do with differences in education or capital between the American, Japanese, and European companies. They had nothing to do with industrial secrets, either. Both Henry Ford and Toyota had been quite open to show their methods of production to visitors from all over the world.

The most dramatic proof of the role of resistance to change in this sector is the failure of Ford to introduce mass production in its *own* factories in Europe for almost 50 years. When Henry Ford tried to replicate his American success in Britain in the early 1910s, he faced a solid opposition. At the time, car production in Britain was organized around highly specialized crafters who manufactured the most important pieces and supervised the manufacture of the rest. The point of mass production was the substitution of the crafters by standardized operations carried out by unskilled workers. Ford managers estimated that it took 5 to 10 minutes to train a worker to perform any of the operations needed in the plant. The crafters, who dominated the British trade unions, obviously opposed the substitution of a production method based on their skills by one that gave no advantage to such skills. It was a classic example of highly specialized skills that become obsolete overnight. The trade unions successfully prevented the introduction of the new methods with the help of government regulations and then, to ensure that this would not lead to the bankruptcy of the firms that kept the archaic methods in place, they succeeded in obtaining protection against competition from the United States. In 1915, Britain abandoned free trade and imposed a tariff of 25 percent on the importation of cars.[12] In this way, the trade unions stopped progress in car production in the United Kingdom by rejecting the use of readily available knowledge.

Then Ford introduced another innovation, this time with the design of a new engine that produced higher power with the same consumption of gas by shortening the distance that pistons had to run inside the cylinders. British competitors got the support of the government to stop Ford by introducing a horsepower tax, which counterbalanced the efficiency gain.[13] Thus, British producers could compete while producing less efficient engines than the American ones.

Society paid a high price for these actions. Cars remained scarce in Europe up to the 1960s, and this retarded social and economic progress in the region. For decades, cars were a luxury item in the region. In France in the 1930s, for example, a small nine-horsepower Citroen truck was more expensive than a house.[14] It was to alleviate this situation that Adolf Hitler asked Dr. Ferdinand Porsche to design a car that, like so many in the United States, could be the car of the people. Porsche designed the Volkswagen, but military priorities delayed the production of the car until after the war.

European governments extended protection to all parts and components used in the production of cars to force companies to buy their inputs from the inefficient local producers. This further insulated the European markets from progress, increasing costs, reducing the gains that could be attained with economies of scale, and retarding technological development. What happened with cars also happened in other activities, which were also using mass production techniques in the United States. Home appliances, for example, which in the United States became popular in the first few decades of the century, remained luxury items in Europe until well after World War II. Mechanical washing machines, moved by hand, were available in France since the end of World War I but electrical ones came on stream only in the 1950s, much later than in the United States. The price of refrigerators in the 1930s in France was equivalent to 1,200 hours of a cleaning woman's wages while the cost in the United States was between 300 to 400 hours.[15] Few people could afford to conserve perishable food in their homes. Telephones were also scarce. All these problems could be traced to the rejection of higher efficiency in the name of protecting the local workers and entrepreneurs.

The second great revolution in car production is that associated with lean production. This new technology is also advancing slowly all over the world, for the same reasons that delayed the adoption of mass production. The authors of the MIT car report are pessimistic about the speed at which the new approach can be diffused. High disparities in efficiency survive in the sector because governments compensate for these differences through protection, taxation, and subsidies that turn profitable operations that should go bankrupt as a result of their own incompetence.

Another telling example is that of breweries in Germany. American and Japanese breweries are much more efficient than those in Germany in terms of the value added per worker they produce. Surprisingly, they attain this higher efficiency by using *German* equipment that German brewers cannot use because rules and regulations forbid them in Germany.[16] A similar case of resistance, reported by G. Clark, is that of textile mills in the early 1900s.[17] In those years, there were conflicts all over the world because employers wanted workers to manage more looms. Yet, the conflict in England was between six and four; in France and Mexico, between four and three; in Russia, between three and two; and in India between two and one. The differences in productivity across all these countries had nothing to do with technology or education. They had to do with the power of the workers to enlist the support of the government to prevent the introduction of technologies that they thought would reduce their salaries per unit of output. Of course, the workers' opposition was suicidal. Applied to all sectors, these regulations repressed progress. While the Indian workers got the government support to produce less than their competitors in all sectors, competition spurred efficiency in Britain also in all sectors, creating more job opportunities in the economy in general. The textile workers that were displaced by the increase in productivity in England moved on to other activities and, in general, became vastly richer than their Indian counterparts—which remained trapped in their low productivity—and their children and grandchildren even more so.

Actually, the problem grew much worse in India after its independence in 1948, when the government decided to control "the commanding heights of the economy," that government permission was needed for practically all productive activities, including production runs in established factories.

Michael Fairbanks and Stacey Lindsay, the authors of a recent book on the subject,[18] have noticed how developing countries often manage to have lower productivity and growth in particular activities even if they have absolute advantages over the developed countries in those activities. For example, in the flower business a country with good soil, ideal sunlight, temperate climate, and low prices of land and labor failed to compete with a country with extremely scarce and expensive soil that freezes for long periods during the year, with deficient sunlight, and extremely expensive labor—the first country being Colombia and the other the Netherlands. They analyze scores of similar cases. Their conclusion is that companies in developing countries could extract much higher incomes from their existing resources if they only applied available knowledge and techniques in production, financing, and marketing. Those companies, however, do not do that, partly because existing regulations prevent them from doing it, and partly because they prefer to get another regulation from the government than improving their productivity when their business is not going well.

Of course, protection is at its worse as an agent to stop technological development when it is applied to the production of capital goods and other inputs of production. This forces all industries in the country to use machinery that is not just expensive but also obsolete, as the producers of capital goods do not have any incentive to improve the technologies imbedded in their products.

Protection also depresses technological advance by removing the incentives to hire top professionals to manage enterprises. Protected against foreign competition, there is no reason for enterprises to hire the first-rate managers and engineers they would need to remain competitive in a free market. The top professionals would only increase costs because of their high salaries. For the same reason, companies in protected countries do not invest in training their staffs. Even the low share of the total government budget allocated to education is related to this. People do not see the value of education and therefore do not press for expanding such share. One of the results of these realities is that developing countries, which are the ones that need more professionals, are in fact net exporters of professionals to the developed countries.

Government intervention in the economy, however justified on the defense of the defenseless, brings about another scourge of the developing countries: corruption. Clearly, the degree of corruption in a society depends not just on economic variables and systems. Also, there is corruption within the private sector, not just in deals with the government but also in deals among private companies and people, as the renowned cases of Enron and WorldCom made clear in 2001–2002. Yet, government intervention in the economy provides the opportunity for public corruption in a very obvious way. The more economic decisions the government makes, the more it commands the power of making or breaking enormous private fortunes by giving protection or withdrawing it, the better the opportunities for public corruption.

The two best-known indicators of corruption, those published by Transparency International and by the World Economic Forum, show that countries with freer economies tend to have lower levels of corruption.

One of the most dramatic cases of the stagnation resulting from all these manifestations of resistance to change is that of Argentina, a country that went from First to Third World status in the time it has taken other countries to accomplish the opposite feat. By 1913, the country's GDP per capita was $3,797, approximately equal to that of Germany, which was $3,833, both measured in 1990 US Dollars.[19] By the midcentury, Argentina had already stagnated enough to have its income at the level of Third World countries. At the beginning of the twenty-first century, poverty, before almost inexistent, is increasing fast in the country. The low rate of growth of the Argentine economy was largely the result of protectionist policies that populist governments put in place, avowedly to promote investment and preserve jobs for Argentine workers. Investment fell because those policies increased the prices of capital goods well over the international levels. With no competition from abroad, the domestic producers of machinery and equipment lagged well behind the advanced countries in the use of the available knowledge of the time. While the countries that were the peers of Argentina at the turn of the twentieth century progressed, Argentina got stuck in protracted labor, social, and political conflicts that blocked its opportunities for development up to this moment. As in all other cases, Argentina's problems can be traced to the ability of workers and entrepreneurs to manipulate the government politically to obtain protection against competition from abroad. As in all other cases, in the long run what seemed to be an advantage for both entrepreneurs and workers resulted in overall backwardness. The impact of these policies was deep. Argentina lost at least a century of development as a result of them.[20]

Another dramatic example of the impact that state-sponsored resistance to change can have in an economy is the long crisis that is currently affecting Japan. From the perspective of the 1980s, many people thought that this country would be the big gainer of the twenty-first century, for three main reasons. First, it had grown at astonishing rates for several decades after World War II, invading the world markets with thousands of products that were cheaper and better than those of its competitors. Japan seemed unstoppable. It was not the more export-oriented country in the world—the share of exports in GDP is far higher in the Netherlands, Germany, and Britain, for example—but it was perceived as the most successful international trader. Second, as we have already discussed, a Japanese company pioneered Lean Production, the administrative side of connectivity.

Lean Production was not a generalized technology in Japan in the 1980s, not even in the Japanese car business. In the years since, many non-Japanese companies have adopted the system so that it is no longer a Japanese system. But the fact that the approach was pioneered in Japan would suggest that the Japanese society was ready for the challenges of a more horizontal economy. This, however, has proven not to be true, mainly because of the rigidities introduced by what many people in the 1980s saw as the main competitive advantage of Japan: the close coordination between the government and the private sector in the planning and execution of economic strategies. This, the third reason why many people thought that Japan would dominate the twenty-first century, is in fact the main stumbling block for the Japanese economy to integrate successfully to the new world of connectivity and globalization.

During the decades after World War II, this coordination became the trademark of Japan. It was so tight and pervasive that people abroad felt that they were not competing against individual Japanese companies but against a powerful corporation called Japan, Inc. The MITI, the Japanese Ministry of Industry and Trade, was the institution in charge of such coordination. It became a legend of efficiency and foresight. It pointed out the next stage in the development of the country and arranged things so that the private sector moved in that direction using taxes, import tariffs, subsidies, and informal jawboning to accomplish its task. Externally, the government pursued international trade policies that supported the strategy defined by the ministry. This system allowed Japan to plan and execute its migration from light industry in the early years after the war to heavy industry in the subsequent decades and then to electronic goods in the 1980s—gaining market share with astonishing speed in all these products. Many western economists thought that this kind of social organization was the wave of the future, and wrote books urging the West to adopt the Japanese model in the twenty-first century.[21] They thought that this combination of private and public sector strengths would be as unbeatable during globalization as it had been during the previous five decades.

Lately, some observers have presented evidence that this close coordination had not been the source of the country's success. Rather, they found, the country achieved its feats not because but in spite of the heavy state intervention and coordination of the private firms' activities. In fact, the most successful companies were those that the government did not help, and in many cases, like Sony, they were among those that were penalized in the Japanese system of incentives.[22] These researchers concluded that the Japanese model might have been a liability all along. In any case, it is clear that, even if it were true that it worked in the linear world of the last few decades, the Japanese system is not going to work in the nonlinear times of connectivity and globalization. Rather than helping Japan to become the master of the new world, it has become a formidable obstacle for the progress of the country. The close coordination between the government and the enterprises introduced a uniformity of thinking that gave creativity a one-dimensional nature.

The failure of the Japanese system became evident in the collapse of the efforts that both the Japanese government and several powerful firms made to capture the world's software markets. In the early 1980s, the Japanese government correctly identified the computer industry as the wave of the future, and within it, the production of software as the component with highest value added. American companies controlled the market for software. In typical fashion, the government targeted one company—IBM—as the model to copy and beat. The government gathered several Japanese firms and asked them to develop both computers and software to overtake IBM, first in Japan, and then in the rest of the world. Consistently with their model of coordination, they told the rest of Japanese companies to buy Japanese computers and software. This would imply an initial cost for these companies, because Japanese software was still primitive and less efficient than the American ones. Later, however, it would become the best in the world and Japan would gain as a whole.

The dire effects of this one-dimensionality of thinking came quite un-expectedly, surprising not just the Japanese but their western admirers as well. For example, in the early 1990s, an American professor, Lester Thurow wrote these enthusiastic words in his book *Head to Head*, referring to what he saw as the successful Japanese assault on the American computer industry:

IBM, a firm that in the early 1980s was winning prizes for being the best-managed firm, is now similarly on the defensive. The Japanese press already talks of the Big Three [Japanese] Computer makers being ready to tackle "Big Blue" [IBM]. They are more than ready. Two of the three already have market shares larger than that of IBM in Japan. The third is also about to surpass the American giant. In 1990, IBM Japan's sales rose 1 percent while the total Japanese market was expanding 10 percent. Yet IBM is number one everywhere else in the world. Why is IBM incompetent in only one country? Other American companies in the computer business are doing no better.[23]

In fact, IBM was doing badly in 1990. Yet, the main architect of its pain was not the Japanese copiers but a host of small American companies. These companies, which did not even exist at the time when the Japanese decided to base their computer strategy on beating IBM, were shifting the direction of success in the computer business from the mainframes to the personal computers (PCs). Since the Japanese had copied IBM, these emerging companies, while bringing IBM to the brink of bankruptcy, also caused a crisis in Japan.

In *The Economist* of September 25, 1993, there was an article on Japanese software. Its title was *Crashed*. The article gave details that I quote at length because it shows the cracks on the surface of the juggernaut, and how these cracks can become holes in no time.

So far this year . . . 105 Japanese software companies have gone bust owing 10 million yens or more, compared with 68 in the same period of 1992 . . . Those firms that are not going bust are laying off employees . . . Japan's software industry is almost twice as labor intensive as America's. Differences between the two markets are to blame. Most American firms long ago started switching to networks of personal computers—and to the off-the-shelf software that goes with them. In Japan, by contrast, the software industry's bigger corporations stuck with their antediluvian mainframes. As a result, mainframe-based programs still account for 90 percent of Japanese software sales. And because most of this software is laboriously tailored to the needs of individual customers, it is unsalable elsewhere. So most software companies are highly dependent on a small number of clients. Indeed, around half Japan's software companies are at least partially owned by their biggest customers; and even independent firms usually have only two or three big customers.

Belatedly, this is changing. Japan's recession is forcing corporate computer users to cut costs—which means replacing elderly mainframes with networks. Unwilling to continue "subsidizing" the software industry, big corporate customers are severing their ties with Japan's software firms. With little in-house expertise in developing PC and networking software, and with the market dominated by Western (i.e., American) companies, Japanese firms have resorted to cutting the prices of mainframe software by 20 percent. Customers, keen on the new off-the-shelf software, have shunned them.

In May America's Microsoft, the world's largest software firm, launched a Japanese language version of Windows, the operating system now found in nine out of ten PCs sold in western countries. This has sharply increased the market for foreign applications-software packages . . . because most are designed to work only with Windows . . . [A]round 100 American software companies have now set up offices in Japan . . . To fight back, Japan's software firms are forging alliances with foreign rivals . . . Such deals may save many Japanese software companies from extinction. But it will also leave them as little more than distributors in a market they once controlled.[24]

This is the story of how Japan lost the leadership of the new world in the twenty-first century after seeming to be the leader during the last part of the twentieth century. It shows why the famed Japanese system has become a formidable obstacle for the country's integration to the new connectivity. The coordination of government and enterprises may be a strong asset in a static world but is a serious liability in times of innovation. One single mistake, as in the software example, causes the collapse of the entire structure. And, who can blame the government or corporate bureaucrats who made the decision to overtake IBM in mainframes? Who, in the early and even the mid-1980s, would have said that the PC networks—and even individual workstations—would be more powerful and flexible than the largest mainframes?

Many enterprises in the United States made the same mistake as the Japanese. IBM itself produced the first popular PC and established standards for them that have lasted up to this moment. The company, however, failed to see that the PC was the market of the future and tried to emphasize the mainframe in its marketing strategies because, at the time, they were more profitable by unit sold. Other American companies chased IBM in the mainframe business and they also suffered from it. But many others chased IBM on the emerging PC business, and succeeded in turning obsolete the mainframe. IBM managed to survive but many other mainframe companies went bankrupt. Diversity won over specialization in these early days of the personal computer.

This case also illustrates clearly the advantages of an open society in times of transformation. If, in the early 1980s, the American government had called for a meeting to decide on a research and development strategy in the computer industry, it would have invited IBM and other mainframe enterprises. It would have never invited the guys in blue jeans that were developing the PCs and their software. As in Japan, big enterprises belonging to the establishment would have shunned PCs to ensure the success of the agreed strategy. The PC companies would have died before they were born. We would not have the PCs. The next leap in information technology, the marriage of PCs, phones, and television, would not have been possible, its possibilities would not have been suspected. And it is precisely on this marriage that the fantastic technological and economic revolution of the twenty-first century is being launched.

Finally, the case of software also illustrates the suddenness of the changes produced by a technological revolution and the impact such suddenness has on the stability of a rigid economy. In the late 1980s and the early 1990s, as the impact of the new connectivity was becoming evident and the United States was emerging as the first globalized country in our times, Japan's economy stagnated, its stock exchange collapsed and its financial system became insolvent. For all the famed coordination of government and private sector that characterizes its social order, the country was unable to resolve those problems in the subsequent years. Today, the economy still refuses to grow 10 years after the problem became manifest. The gap between the United States and Japan, which was narrowing, had widened again. The income per capita of Japan, which was 90 percent of that of the United States in 1991, had receded to 78 percent of it by 2001.[25]

Traditional economists, particularly those with a Keynesian view of reality, think that the problem was lack of domestic demand, and have prescribed loose monetary policies, devaluation of the currency, and high fiscal deficits to revive it. Initially reluctant, the Japanese government tried all these courses of action. The economy did not recover even if easy money brought down short-term interest rates almost to zero if measured in yens. In addition, the government spent about one trillion dollars during the decade to stimulate domestic demand. This also failed to restart economic growth and in fact worsened the situation because the Japanese economy is still where it was in the early 1990s but now it has accumulated a huge debt, equivalent to 130 percent of GDP, more than twice what is considered acceptable in the European Union (EU) (60 percent). Many economists are still advising to loosen up monetary policy even further, even if the rate of interest is already zero. In any case, a more relaxed monetary policy would just inject more money in the economy, which is the same that the large investment programs and fiscal deficits have done to no avail. The problem is deeper and spending more cannot cure it. It has to do with the rigidities of the economy.

The real problem is that beneath the rosy image of a modern Japan projected by a relatively small number of efficient and creative companies, the country's economy is quite archaic, mainly because of the same structure of protection and privilege that many people thought was the source of its success. Agriculture, construction, many industrial operations with low productivity, utilities, and services in general were privileged into gross inefficiency by the government's tinkering with the economy during the last several decades, mainly to avoid the disruptions in employment that forcing the adjustment of those sectors would create. The result is a huge dispersion in the value added per worker across the Japanese economy. The problem in Japan is such that many of the companies in the low-productivity sectors are no longer viable if they do not introduce modern techniques that would force them to fire workers. Injections of liquidity cannot cure these ailments and in fact worsen them, because aimed at keeping in operation loss-making enterprises, they throw good money after bad, weakening the banking system, which continues to finance the bad performers. By 2001, the amount of bad and doubtful loans in the portfolios of Japanese banks was estimated at 1.23 trillion dollars.

Resolving these problems requires a complete restructuring of the Japanese economy, one that would replace the inefficient enterprises and activities with efficient ones. The market does it automatically through bankruptcies and financial crises. By distorting the economy in such a way that this does not happen, and by keeping alive banks that are already dead under the weight of bad loans, the Japanese government is effectively blocking the solution to the problem. The more money it injects to prop up the banks, the more the banks can refinance loss-making enterprises, allowing them to keep on making losses. In the next turn of the wheel, the bad loans are higher, more money is needed, and so on, in a vicious circle. Breaking this vicious circle would be difficult in any society, given the staggering volume that the problem has acquired by now. Breaking it in Japan is even more difficult, because the solution would imply breaking the social contract that underlies Japanese society: the compromise of enterprises not to fire workers. The government of Japan has already identified the problem. Yet, the political resistance to a true liberalization, which would wipe out the inefficient enterprises and would redirect the resources now used by them into more productive activities, is such that the government has been unable to resolve the problem.

There is a remaining question. If it is true that government intervention in the economy during times of fast economic transformations retards economic growth, how is it that Nazi Germany was so successful economically, and how is it that Stalin was able to industrialize the Soviet Union within a decade under Communism, if both of them controlled the economy to the last detail?

I turn to this question in the next chapter. The answer to it is intimately related to the main incentive that prevailed in those economies: terror.

NOTES

1. Paul Bairoch, "International Industrialization Levels from 1750 to 1980," *Journal of European Economic History*, 11 (1982): 294.

2. See Maddison, Angus, *Dynamic Forces in Capitalist Development: A Long-run Comparative View* (New York: Oxford University Press, 1991), Annexes A and B. Maddison calculated the figures of both GDP and population so as to eliminate the impact of shifting geographical boundaries. The calculations are based on the territories of 1989.

3. More strictly, it is the difference in the total factor productivity that makes the difference.

4. See Stephen L. Parente and Edward C. Prescott, *Barriers to Riches, Walras-Pareto Lectures, Ecole des Hautes Etudes Commerciales, Université de Lausanne* (Cambridge: MIT Press, 2000), and William Easterly and Ross Levine, *It's Not Factor Accumulation: Stylized Facts and Growth Models,* Preliminary Version, The World Bank, Policy Research Group, (Washington D.C., 2000).

5. Parente and Prescott, *Barriers to Riches,* p. 62.

6. Ibid., p. 39.

7. Ibid.

8. See Hernando De Soto, *The Other Path* (New York: Harper & Row, 1989).

9. Hernando De Soto, *The Mystery of Capital: Why Capitalism Triumphs in the West and Fails Everywhere Else* (New York: Basic Books, 2000), pp. 19–27.

10. James P. Womack, Daniel T. Jones, and Daniel Roos, *The Machine That Changed the World: The Story of Lean Production* (New York: HarperPerennial, 1991).

11. Ibid., p. 85.

12. Ibid., pp. 225–55.

13. Ibid., p. 230.

14. Eugen Weber, *The Hollow Years: France in the 1930s* (New York and London: W. W. Norton & Co., 1994), p. 66.

15. Ibid., p. 62.

16. Parente and Prescott, *Barriers to Riches,* p. 102.

17. See G. Clark, "Why Isn't the Whole World Developed? Lessons from the Cotton Mills," *Journal of Economic History* 47 (1987): 141–73.

18. Michael Fairbanks and Stace Lindsay, *Plowing the Sea: Nurturing the Hidden Sources of Growth in the Developing World* (Boston: Harvard Business School Press, 1997).

19. See Maddison, Angus, *Dynamic Forces in Capital Development* Annexes A and B.

20. See Alan Taylor, "On the Costs of Inward-Looking Development: Historical Evidence on Price Distortions, Growth and Divergence in Latin America from the 1930s to the 1980s," *Journal of Economic History* 58, no. 1: 1–28.

21. See, for example, Lester Thurow, *Head to Head: The Coming Economic Battle among Japan, Europe and America* (New York: William Morrow and Company, 1992).

22. A study by Richard Beason of the University of Alberta and David Weinstein of Harvard looked for a correlation between the support that the government of Japan has given to each of the sectors in the economy from 1955 to 1990 and the performance of these sectors in the same period. They investigated four kinds of support: cheap loans, net transfers, trade protection, and tax relief. They reached two important conclusions. First, they found that Japan Inc. was not as tightly coordinated as people thought. There was no clear, consistent policy behind the use of the different instruments of intervention. A sector receiving cheap loans could be receiving negative trade protection, for example. In several cases, some

of the privileges were compensations for costs imposed by the government in other dimensions of business. Second, and more importantly, they found that the correlation between the net support provided by the government and the rate of growth of the different sectors was negative for each of the instruments of subsidization. That is, the sectors that grew faster were those that had received no support from the government, and among the companies receiving privileges, the ones receiving less were the ones that grew faster. Thus, according to these authors, government intervention hindered rather than promoted the Japanese economic miracle. See *Growth: Economies of Scale and Targeting in Japan (1955–1990)* (Harvard Institute of Economic Research, Discussion Paper 1644). Michael Porter and Hirotaka Takeuchi reached the same conclusion in a more recent study. They found that the companies that did not receive help from the government were the ones that had led the success of Japan. See Michael Porter and Hirotaka Takeuchi, "Fixing what Really Ails Japan," *Foreign Affairs* May–June (1999): p. 66.

   23. Lester Thurow, *Head to Head*, p. 115.
   24. *The Economist*, 25 September 1993, pp. 76–79.
   25. Author calculations based on data from The World Tables, published by The World Bank. They are available on The World Bank's Web site, worldbank.org.

CHAPTER 4

Cold-Blooded Destructiveness

Explosions of destructiveness have been common in history. Yet, the destructiveness of the Nazis and Communists was special in four respects. First, its magnitude was extraordinary by any standard of measure. A new word, genocide, had to be invented to describe the enormity of the crimes. Second, its crimes were perpetrated in cold blood over long periods. Most of its victims were killed not in the spur of the moment but in sustained efforts aimed at wiping out entire races or social classes from the face of the earth. This allowed the destructive regimes to take an institutional approach to murder, which resulted in a chillingly efficient organization of destruction. Third, the victims had no possible escape. They were accused not of having *done* something, but of *being* something—either Jews or bourgeois. Fourth, genocide was a legitimate step in their pursuit of a state of social perfection, the Communist Paradise or the One-Thousand-Years Reich of Nazism.

There was no precedent for this kind of destructiveness. It was an original contribution of the twentieth century to the annals of humankind.

As it was done with the French Revolution, the process that culminated in this explosion of destructiveness has been glorified in our texts of history as the heroic struggle of the masses to liberate themselves from the poverty and political oppression that small minorities imposed on them under the old regimes. Two reasons have been advanced to explain the inconvenient fact that all these glorified struggles ended with terrible explosions of destructiveness. First, a popular theory says that the revolutionaries were misguided into electing as their leader a psychopath, who then diverted the originally humane objectives of the revolution into mad exercises of destructiveness. Second, other people maintain that the revolutionaries engaged in violence to remove the obstacles that small minorities placed on the path of irresistible social change. There are several versions of this second explanation. According to these, destructiveness

- was natural in the bloody battles that the revolutionaries had to fight against the ancient regimes, both to take over power and to defend it once they had succeeded;
- was the consequence of the generalized poverty, or impoverishment, of the revolutionary society;
- was a manifestation of resentment about wide income differences; and
- was the only course available to open the road for progress against the obstacles posed by the ancient regimes.

In the remainder of this chapter, I claim that destructiveness was not exercised by a mad dictator acting alone but by the entire society. Further, I claim that such violence was not necessary, was not aimed at bringing about freedom from poverty and political oppression, and, naturally, did not attain these pretended aims. Then I show that contrary to what these theories say, *revolutionary* violence was aimed at *stopping* the autonomous change that was moving society in the direction of freedom. This violence was supported by the majority of the population, in processes that resembled the ancient art of witch hunting. The exorcised devils were precisely the social forces pressing for change: trade, finance, and democracy.

Socialists easily dismiss the genocide perpetrated in the 1920s and 1930s in Russia as the action of one single madman, Stalin. The Chinese blame their genocide on Mao. Germans blame their Nazism on Hitler. And so on.

People in general accept these explanations for the horrible destructiveness of Communists and Nazis. It has become part of the conventional wisdom around the world. Yet, the view that the terrible destructiveness of the twentieth century was the result of the chance emergence of psychopaths as the leaders of the Soviet Union, Germany, China, and so many other countries is hard to accept. There is no doubt that sinister characters like Lenin, Stalin, Hitler, and Mao played a crucial role in the establishment of a reign of terror in their countries and abroad. It is also true that the application of terror cannot be explained without reference to the personalities exercising it, and that, by definition, a psychologically healthy person cannot apply terror. Yet, it does not make sense to attribute the deaths of so many millions of people to one, two, or a thousand individuals. Pathological killers exist in all countries, and they do not become the national leaders. They are sent to mental health institutions. Furthermore, one person cannot kill millions of individuals. He needs the cooperation of the population. Lenin, Stalin, Hitler, and their likes were able to dominate their countries because their terror was consistent with what their countries wanted. There is no doubt that these countries suffered terrible pains in the rampages of destructiveness they engaged in. But they brought it unto themselves. As expressed so well by the popular saying, all countries have the government they deserve. This includes not just the countries that elect their leaders democratically, but also those that are governed by terrible tyrannies. This is so because all societies base their social order on ideas.

Societies are like magnetic fields directing their members toward the achievement of a set of common goals. The features of this field—the nature of the magnetic ideas, their strength, and their direction—is what gives societies their identity and life. The basic ideas are not necessarily spelled out in their entirety, and may be vague. Even so, they produce what is called national character and very precise behavioral expectations. This is evident in statements like "this would never happen in England," "everything works in Germany," or "this is the American way." Such statements are the result of comparing a potential course of action or an event with the collective mind's concept of itself. This national character is what gives predictability to societies, well beyond any political statement of governments.

The laws of a society are reflections of this magnetic field. Yet, the shape and strength of the magnetic field go well beyond the laws. It is only those commands that lay down procedures that are not obvious in the social milieu that needs to be written. The most important of the features that give shape to a society—such as the pragmatism of the British, or the German penchant for obedience, or the predisposition for action of the Americans—are never legislated. They are transmitted from parents to children in uncountable informal and formal ways, along with the values that underlay the social order. The laws then translate these basic attitudes and values into fields that are too complex to be comprehended without a written statement. Even so, the oldest constitution in the world, the British, has never been written even if it is exceedingly complex for an outsider. It lives in the bones of the British subjects, who know instinctively if something is constitutional or not.

This subtle uniformity is what makes societies governable. The power of a government depends on people *believing* that it has power, which ultimately depends on its legitimacy, understanding the latter in the sense that, to be obeyed, commands must seem reasonable to the people, and must be in harmony with their conception of how the world is and how it should be. It is only when commands are in harmony with this conception that people obey them. People living in societies where the social order is based on principles obey because the commands are consistent with the prevailing social values. In societies where social order is based

on the savage logic of power, people obey because they *think* that everybody else will obey, so that if they rebel they will be easily caught and
punished.

The mechanism also works in reverse when the commands are not legitimate in the mind of the population. It is for this reason that the power
of previously redoubtable governments can collapse in one moment—as
was the case in the fall of the French Capetos, the Russian Tsars, the
crowned heads in Central Europe at the end of World War I, and the
Communist tyrannies in the Soviet Union and East Europe in the early
1990s. In all of these cases, and many others, the regime collapsed when
people stopped believing that the government was legitimate, and, therefore, powerful. There was no army, or police, or KGB large enough to stop
the collapse. In fact, as a manifestation of the dissolution of the power of
the government, in all cases these repressive institutions stopped defending the regime, even to the point of joining those calling for its demise.

Oswald Spengler, a famous writer of the early decades of the twentieth
century, expressed this very clearly with the following words:

The destiny question, for states that exist in reality and not merely in intellectual
schemes, is not that of their ideal task or structure, *but that of their inner authority,*
which cannot in the long run be maintained by material means, but only by a
belief—of friend *and* foe—in their effectiveness.[1]

What Spengler calls the *inner authority* is the invisible magnetism that
links the ruler and the ruled, passing through a common vision of the
world and the way it should be ruled.

One of the most successful absolute rulers in history, Catherine the
Great, Empress of All Russias from 1762 to 1796, expressed the same idea
when somebody told her that she had the advantage of enjoying blind
obedience from her subjects:

It is not as easy as you think. In the first place, my orders would not be carried
out unless they were the kind of orders which can be carried out; you know with
what prudence and circumspection I act in the promulgation of my laws. I examine
the circumstances, I take advice, I consult the enlightened part of the people, and
in this way I find out what sort of effect my law will have. And when I am already
convinced of general approval, then I issue my orders, and have the pleasure of
observing what you call blind obedience. But believe me, they would not obey
blindly when orders are not adapted to the customs, to the opinion of the people,
and if I were to follow only my own wishes not thinking of the consequences.[2]

Thus, legitimacy is essential for the workings of government in both
societies based on principle and those based on naked power. For this
reason, all countries have the government they deserve—not just in democratic regimes but in tyrannies also. What varies across societies is the

set of unifying ideas that constitute the national character, and from it, the particular society's concept of legitimacy.[3]

That is, destructiveness established its reign in those countries where people thought that destructiveness was legitimate. Then, we can turn to ask why was destructiveness legitimate in those countries?

The idea that massive violence erupted in the course of the bloody battles that the revolutionaries had to fight to dethrone the ancient regimes does not fit with the facts. It was the revolutionaries once in power who staged the massive, cold-blooded regimes of destructiveness, not the old regimes or the revolutionary mobs during the struggle for power. Mobs, acting impulsively, cause and suffer surprisingly low numbers of casualties. In revolutionary France, very few people died in the confrontations between the population and the royalist troops. The real massacre started when the revolutionary authorities imposed the Terror. By this time, a Constituent Assembly elected by the people had enacted a Constitution, a National Assembly had been elected under such Constitution, and the King had been deposed. The purported objectives of the Revolution had already been attained, and the population had even lost interest in politics. Only 10 percent of the population voted in the elections of the National Assembly.[4] Moreover, the victims of the Terror included as many revolutionaries and common citizens as royalists and nobles.

In Russia, the number of people killed up to the Bolshevik take over was infinitely smaller than that of the victims that fell in the subsequent decades of Communist regime. In Germany, the events that led to the demise of Kaiser Wilhelm II at the end of World War I, the Bolshevik Revolution that exploded after his abdication and the turmoil of the Weimar Republic that replaced him, traumatized the country. The number of victims in those events, however, was nil when compared with that of those killed by the Nazis years after their accession to power.

Thus, the bloodiest events of the Industrial Revolution did not take place during the revolutionaries' accession to power.

Massive terror was not a mechanism that the revolutionaries had to use to wage a war against the dethroned oppressors and their allies, either. Certainly, France was at war with Austria when its revolutionaries imposed the Terror, and the Red Terror raged when Russia was at war with the White Russians. Nazi Germany was at war when Hitler decided to apply his diabolical Final Solution. However, terrorizing soldiers into battle and civilians into supporting war efforts were not sensible strategies. On the contrary, they demoralize both the population and the armies. The martial efficiency of the French did not diminish when the Terror was ended with the beheading of Robespierre and his allies. It actually improved. Rather than introducing order, Lenin's Red Terror during the Civil War against the White Russians led society into a frenzied chaos that eventually threatened the survival of the Communist regime. Lenin acknowl-edged this and justified, precisely on these grounds, a temporary reduction in the level of terror in early 1921. Then, Stalin killed most of the victims of Soviet Communism more than a decade after the revolution, when the White Russians were long gone and the leaders of the ancient regime were either dead or impoverished nobles living abroad. The Jews did not pose any threat to the Nazi regime, either.

Thus, destructiveness did not arise in violent battles to take over power and it was not justified as a mechanism to improve the military efficiency of the revolutionaries in power.

Stating that cold-blooded destructiveness was the result of generalized poverty does not fit with the facts, either. The worst manifestations of destructiveness in Europe took place in two completely different coun-tries, Russia and Germany. While the former was one of the poorest coun-tries in Europe, with wide differences in income across its population, the latter was not only among the richest, but also among those with the most equitable income distribution in the Continent. Germany never suffered from the widespread poverty and the appalling urban living conditions that accompanied industrialization in other European countries. Otto Von Bismarck invented social security in Germany, many decades before Na-zism, and the German trade unions were the strongest in Europe. More-over, the Nazis took power away from the Weimar Republic, a democratic regime created by the Social Democrats, an offshoot of the trade unions. It cannot be argued that the German poor were not represented in this regime.

Furthermore, there is no clear correlation between the direction of change in the standards of living of the population and the explosions of cold destructiveness. Some of the worst of these explosions took place when the economic conditions of the population were improving sub-stantially. This is clear in the case of Russia. While the standard of living of the Soviet population declined sharply in the years immediately after the Revolution—when Lenin was applying his Red Terror—it recovered its pre-Revolutionary levels 10 years later, just before Stalin started the second wave of massive killings. That is, terror ravaged Russia when the economic fate of the population was declining and then again after it had improved.

The lack of correlation between major eruptions of destructiveness and shifts in the economic lot of the population was also evident in Germany. The country went through a failed Bolshevik revolt in 1918–19, when the population was at the brink of starvation as a result of the wartime block-ade imposed by the Triple Entente. Yet, the destructiveness unleashed by this revolution pales when compared with that of the Nazi years. Fur-thermore, even if the Nazis started their evil processes right after gaining power—when Germany was going through the Great Depression—their destructiveness went into full blast only in the late 1930s and early 1940s, when the country had already staged an impressive economic recovery. This recovery improved not only the overall GDP but also reduced unemployment, thus improving the distribution of income.[5] German destructiveness became worse as the economic lot of the population kept on improving. If poverty, or the aggravation of it, were the causes of destructiveness, the worst explosions of Nazi destructiveness would not have taken place in Germany. The forces leading to it would have been defused by economic growth.

The correlation does not hold geographically, either. Karl Marx predicted the imminence of revolutions based on the dismal fate of the British masses, probably the worst in all industrializing countries. Yet, his ideas were never put in practice there. The impact of the world depression of the 1930s was as devastating in Britain and the United States as in Germany. France and other European countries suffered from similar problems. Yet, none of these countries fell prey to either Nazism or Communism—even if there were Nazi and Communist Parties in all of them.

Reality also contradicts the idea that wide income distribution differences were the cause of the cold-blooded destructiveness of revolutionary regimes. As I mentioned before, income distribution in Germany was better than that of many countries that did not fall prey to destructive regimes. Furthermore, in both Germany and the Soviet Union, the people that perpetrated the worst episodes of cold-blooded violence could not be distinguished from their victims in economic terms. Certainly, the Bolshevik Revolution and the repression that followed were carried out on the pretext of economic and political equality. But the number of victims—in excess of 20 million in a country with about 130 million inhabitants— belies such ideas. There have never been so many rich people in Russia. Moreover, the immense majority of the killings took place when the state was already the owner of all the assets in the country and controlled the incomes of all citizens. There were no rich people left in Communist Russia when the worst rampages of Communism took place. In Germany, there were no economic differences between the killers and the killed. In revolutionary France, many of the victims were of noble origin, but they had already lost their economic and political power when they were killed.

Were the revolutionaries opening the road for progress? The French revolutionaries portrayed the French Revolution as a breakthrough in the history of freedom and modernity that accelerated progress not just in France but also all over the world. The socialists extended this myth to the Russian Revolution, and they succeeded in portraying Marxism as a progressive ideology. Intellectuals saw socialism as the next step in history, and labeled as reactionary any tendency opposing it. The myth that bloody revolutions open the road for progress was built on these assertions.

We do not have to believe what the revolutionaries said about themselves, however. To understand the true nature of historic movements, we should see what they really accomplished, not what they claimed to be doing. As Marx wrote:

Whilst in ordinary life every shopkeeper is very well able to distinguish what somebody professes to be and what he really is, our historians have not yet won even this trivial insight. They take every epoch at its word and believe that everything it says and imagines about itself is true.[6]

When we apply common sense to analyze what the revolutions did, not what the revolutionaries said and imagined about themselves, we realize that the revolutionary mythology is a reversal of the truth. To analyze this point we first have to define what progress in terms of social organization is. That is easy. History has proven that a social order based on individual freedoms is the road to such progress, both because freedom is the only social objective that makes sense from the individual point of view and because it brings about creativity, the mother of material development. The logic of industrialization also pushed in that direction. The complex nature of an industrial economy requires a decentralized shape of social organization, which is consistent only with free markets and a decentralized, democratic political regime. Thus, from both a human and a practical point of view we can say that the measure of progress is the extent to which societies become able to manage themselves in freedom.

Now we can turn to notice that free, democratic regimes meeting this criterion did not emerge from bloody domestic revolutions. The American Revolution and the evolution of the British Constitution during the last two centuries, the midwives of modern democracy, were born out of peaceful processes. Certainly, there was a War of Independence in the United States. But this was not the result of domestic conflicts but of the new country's desire to become independent. No domestic war was needed to write the American Constitution. There was no violent revolution in Britain, Switzerland, the Nordic countries, Holland, Belgium, Australia, Canada, or New Zealand, all of them societies that, along with the United States, created the model of the modern industrial state.

In contrast, looking at violent revolutions as historical processes that continued after the ancient regime was overthrown, we find two common factors pointing in the direction of stopping progress.

First, the main features of the regimes that emerged after violent revo- lutions resembled those of the regimes that had been displaced by the revolutions, but taken to extremes. In this way, the French Revolution dethroned a king only to enthrone an emperor a few years later. The social order built by Napoleon was quite similar to that established in the sev- enteenth century by Louis XIV. The process initiated by the German Rev- olution, which dislodged the kaiser in 1918, ended with the elevation of a super kaiser in 1933. This new super kaiser did not go back to the au- thoritarianism of the Second Reich that collapsed in 1918—which had coexisted with a certain measure of popular consultations through the Reichstag and the Landtag—but to something much worse. Hitler aban- doned any pretensions of popular participation in the government and reasserted the darkest quasi-religious autocratic values of the Middle Ages. The Russian Revolution, which ended the autocratic Romanov dy- nasty, established a new and more autocratic Bolshevik dynasty eight months later. In all three cases, the new regimes went back to the author- itarianism that had been the basis of the regimes they dethroned.

Second, in all cases, the new order established by the revolutionaries was not conducive to social or economic progress. On the contrary, it led to disastrous consequences. After the Revolution, France lagged behind Britain and even behind Germany—then a collection of small states—in terms of industrial development. Based on repression, the economy of the Soviet Union was unbelievably archaic and inefficient. The hatred un- leashed by the Communists generated divisiveness among the popula- tion, the opposite of what is needed for progress. The economic revival of Nazi Germany was built on an unsustainable military buildup. To main- tain the growth of the economy, Nazi Germany needed what Hitler called the *Lebensraum*—conquered territories exploited under a regime of slav- ery. The Nazi society was racist to the point of exterminating the depre- cated races. No one can say that these were features of the modern, cosmopolitan society required by industrial development. Furthermore, the new vertical order eventually destroyed the possibilities of sustained progress through either a mad confrontation with superior enemies or social sclerosis. The clearest example of the first kind of destruction was Germany's economy, which was devastated by World War II—an inevi- table consequence of Nazi values. The spirit of conquest of Napoleonic France also led it to a disastrous defeat. Russia was destroyed by sclerosis.

The regimes that the Communists established when in power were truly archaic in many other dimensions. The peasants lived in collective farms.[7] In these farms, they earned a miserable wage or no wage at all. In com- pensation, they had the right to cultivate a small plot of land individually. Since the peasants tended to work more in their individual plots than in the collective, the government passed a law in 1939 forcing them to ded- icate a compulsory minimum of workdays to the collective.[8] Thus, the socialist agricultural structure became an exact reproduction of the feudal sharecropping system. It consisted of tenant peasants that worked almost in slavery for the master in exchange for the right to plant small pieces of land.

The collective farm, however, was worse than the most exploitative landlord. The amount that was left for the peasants' own consumption, adding up the payments they received in the collectives plus the production of their own plots, left them close to starvation. The peasants lived in destitution for decades to come, and, to this day, they live in dire conditions. In 1935, the average member of a collective earned 247 rubles per year. This was the price of a pair of shoes. Many of the peasants did not receive any pay for their work in the collectives. A Pravda correspondent in Ivanovo, for example, wrote in 1936 that 998 of the 5,401 collectives in the region were paying nothing to their peasants.[9] This was the situation even in the 1950s, when an authoritative author estimates that the workers in the collective farms, at the time accounting for 40 percent of the population, worked on annual salaries that were just enough to pay for one kilogram of bread.[10]

The industrial workers also lived and worked in appalling conditions. As it had been in the feudal times, the Communists tied the industrial workers to their factory. They did that with the introduction of the workbook, a booklet that everybody had to carry. These booklets contained the entire working record of the individual, including the place where he was supposed to be working at. Nobody could get a job if not properly discharged from the previous one, so that this document effectively tied the worker to his present job. The Communists also reintroduced the internal passport, a Tsarist device that the Tsars had abolished 100 years before. The Soviet citizens could not leave their cities or farms without the permission of the state. To obtain such permission they had to justify the need for the trip and give exhaustive details of their itinerary—which was monitored by the authorities in the destination places. Thus, the workers in both the urban areas and the countryside effectively became feudal serfs, tied to their place of work.[11] This was a reproduction of the system that Peter the Great had introduced in Russia in the early 1700s. Living conditions were even worse in the enormous public works projects undertaken in Stalin's times. In order to meet the targets imposed by the government, people worked sixteen-hour shifts for years on end, lacking even proper clothing for the unmerciful Russian winters.[12]

Like Lenin in Russia, Hitler established a truly archaic regime in Germany, using the remnants of the feudal system that had survived in the country through the Second Reich and the Weimar Republic. For the rural areas, he inaugurated a program called "Blood and Soil" that reduced the peasants to serfdom not just in fact but also by law. As part of this program, Hitler promulgated, in 1933, two basic laws that effectively re-created the old feudal structures. The Hereditary Farm Law of September 1933 prohibited selling, dividing, mortgaging, or foreclosing farms up to 125 hectares (308 acres). These lands could be transferred only through inheritance, which by law could only be received by the oldest or youngest son, depending on the customs of the locality, or to the nearest male relative. The heir had to provide a living and an education for his brothers and sisters until they were of age. As in the feudal times, the law also tied the peasants to their landlords. To balance the system, the law also vested on the landowners the responsibility for the well being of their peasants. This was an exact replica of the old feudal legislation. It also had a racial twist. To own land, people had to prove the purity of their German blood back to 1800. The second basic law created the Reich Food Estate, a giant organization in charge of controlling agricultural prices and production to attain self-sufficiency in food.[13]

The labor shortages created by the rearmament of Germany had an unintended result: they subverted the agrarian laws, which were not fully enforced. As industrial labor was becoming scarcer, the government allowed peasants to migrate to the cities.[14] This, however, did not lead to an abandonment of feudalism. The peasants were liberated from their bondage to their landlords only to be thrown into an equally demeaning bondage to the industrial enterprises.

On the urban side of the economy, Hitler used the pre-industrial organizations that had been traditional in Germany to impose a tight economic tyranny. He took over the national organizations that both the employers associations and trade unions had created to fight against each other, and put them under the service of the state. The industrialists could not be happier because Hitler took the restrictions on competition to their feudalist extremes. For all his populist speeches, Hitler had not time for the small enterprise, which was more difficult to control than the big cartels. In 1937, the government issued a law dissolving all corporations with a capital under US$40,000 equivalent and forbidding the creation of new ones with a capital of less than US$2 million equivalent. This effectively blocked the entry of new competitors in most areas of business. Another law issued in the same year empowered the Ministry of Economics to organize new compulsory cartels and to order firms to join existing ones.

With these measures, all businesses became members of the state-controlled system. The old employers associations served as the mechanisms that conveyed the commands emerging from the government and monitored their implementation. On top of the German private sector was the government-appointed head of the Reich Economic Chambre, who controlled seven national economic groups, 23 economic chambers, 100 chambers of industry and commerce, and 70 chambers of handicrafts.[15] These comprised the entire entrepreneurial private sector. There was, however, another institution on top of it, the Labor Front, which consoli-

dated the entrepreneurial associations with an organization containing all
the workers in the country. The Labor Front, with its all-encompassing
membership, was the guild of all guilds. In this way, the vertical structures
that had been evolving in industrial Germany reached their logical conclusion: they became one single organization, controlled by the government. Economic and political power was one. German society had
perfected its one-dimensional structure.

The industrialists and big businessmen did not lose their privileged
positions, however. The government was mostly interested in orienting
the country's production toward military purposes and did not care about
other dimensions of private activity. The Hitler years were actually highly
profitable for the private enterprises and their owners, particularly the big
ones. They benefited from the large military contracts and from Hitler's
racial policies, mainly by buying, for a pittance, the properties of the Jews
in Germany and every place that the German armies conquered.[16] The
entrepreneurs were happy also because the government did not tolerate
demands for wage increases, much less strikes. The aim of the Labor Front
was to "create a true social and productive community of all Germans. Its
task is to see that every single individual should be able . . . to perform
the maximum of work."[17] This was socialism in Hitler's definition.

The situation worsened with time. As the military buildup accelerated,
unemployment declined. Employers tried to steal good workers from
other entrepreneurs by offering higher salaries. The government stopped
this by forbidding the movement of workers without permission from
their current employers. In February 1935, the government introduced the
workbooks—the hellish device that the Communists also introduced at
about the same time in the Soviet Union. The workbook contained the
entire working history of the individual. Nobody could get a job without
showing his or her workbook with the required signatures of the previous
employers. Employers could retain the workbooks, thus preventing the
worker from changing jobs. This was not sufficient. After June 1935, the
state employment offices were given total control of employment. Employers could not hire or fire without the authorization of these offices. In
June 1938, the government imposed the labor conscription. The state offices decided who worked and where. Nobody could refuse to work, and
had to do it where the state office told him or her. They could not be fired.
If they did not go to work, they were punished with fines and prison. As
in Russia, the workers became the slaves of the state.

That is, what emerged from domestic violent revolutions were archaic,
repressive regimes. They went against the grain of the true revolution that
was taking place in their times: the creation of the modern, democratic,
horizontal society based on individual rights. Rather than making their
societies more horizontal, they re-created vertical structures of state power
that controlled the life of their citizens to extents unknown before. Rather

than empowering their citizens with the freedoms of modernity, they restricted such freedoms through the imposition of harsh tyrannies of the old style. They did not seduce societies into progress; they raped them into destructiveness.

The backwardness of the regimes emerging from revolutions was so catastrophic that one cannot but remember Edmund Burke's words about the French Revolution:

By following those false lights, France has bought undisguised calamities at a higher price than any nation has purchased the most unequivocal blessings! France has bought poverty by crime! France has not sacrificed her virtue to her interest, but she has abandoned her interest, that she might prostitute her virtue![18]

Simon Schama, a distinguished historian of the French Revolution, made the same point with words that could be applied to the Nazi and Communist revolutions:

In fact it might even be argued that the Revolution drew much of its power from the (ultimately hopeless) attempt to *arrest,* rather than hasten, the process of modernization. And in many respects it was all too successful.[19]

But, can we say that the authoritarian regimes that emerged from revolutions were manifestations of the will of the people? Certainly. They elicited strong popular support. Napoleon was the most popular of all French rulers ever. When Stalin died, the Russians cried as if they were left orphans. Hitler was immensely popular in Nazi Germany. Germans fought fanatically his wars and cooperated enthusiastically with his macabre racial policies. The leaders of Napoleonic France, Soviet Russia, and Nazi Germany embodied what the population wanted. People revealed their preferences through them.

So much for the mythology that romanticizes revolutions. We need a different approach to understand why did it happen and why did it lead to the restoration of archaic regimes.

The preferences that people revealed in revolutions and the terrible events that followed them demonstrates that the aim of the population in the wake of revolutions was not opening the road for new trends, but filling a more urgent social need: reestablishing order in the midst of chaos.

To understand why archaic regimes emerge in the wake of revolutions we have to look at something I already mentioned in the introduction: profound social changes, including those arising from rapid technological changes, are terrifying. Radical technological advances render obsolete the capital accumulated in physical assets, in human knowledge and skills, and, even more fundamentally, in the shape of the institutions linking together the fabric of society. This brings about all kinds of economic and social disruptions, including unemployment, bankruptcies, frequent financial crises, and depressions. Life becomes unstable, the future unbearably uncertain. Through these effects, rapid technological progress threatens the very foundations of social life. There is nothing that people fear more than the collapse of the social structures that frame their lives. And this is precisely what waves of rapid technological changes do to their host societies.

This fact is crucial to understand the dynamics of social transformations. The sources of destructiveness and creativity in the behavior of different societies during the Industrial Revolution were all related to their attitude toward change, or, what is the same, to the way they managed the anguish of deep social transformations.

Looking at revolutions from this perspective we can understand the archaism of the regimes they installed. We can also understand the mechanisms that the prophets of these regimes used to make their destructiveness legitimate: materialistic religions promising worlds where the anguish of institutional dissolution would never come back because they would be so perfect that they would never have to change.

The ideologies of destructiveness sublimated resistance to change by disguising it as its exact opposite: a hunger for progress. These ideologies performed this trick by devising utopias that resembled what the industrializing societies were losing, the social order of the past, and then portraying those utopias as the order of the future.

The utopias played a crucial role in both Nazism and Communism. Hitler got his power by promising to reestablish the stability and predictability that the Germans had lost in the short-lived democratic Weimar Republic. He promised his utopia, the One-Thousand-Year Reich, based on the archaic values of absolute authority that had been the basis of the feudal world. The Marxists had done the same a few years earlier in Russia, assaulting power on the promise of the Communist Paradise.

The two utopias shared two important features. First, they reinstated a social order that was quite similar to the old order that the liberalizing trends of industrialization had destroyed. They reversed the sense of progress, leading societies back to their past. Second, these societies, being perfect, would not be liable to change. The success of these utopias taking hold of the imagination of Russians and Germans was a direct consequence of these features. People loved the idea of creating a society that would be organized under the rules that they had been accustomed to and enthusiastically supported the idea that the new regime would stop the source of their anguish: rapid social change. This, the promised absence of change, was the most crucial feature of the perfect world they embraced. With these motivations in mind, these countries went back to their most savage past. They, however, were able to build economic miracles based on illiberal tyrannies.

The perfect societies were never created. Yet, the unity of purpose produced by the search for it, strengthened social bonds, producing tremendous outbursts of energy that allowed these countries to perform feats that were considered undoable—ranging from Communist Russia building a world superpower out of an unworkable economic system, to Nazi Germany fighting against almost every other major power in the world. The bond tying together those people was the faith that, through these feats, they would achieve perfection.

There is no better example of the magnitude of the transformation that a strong unity of purpose can produce in a society than a comparison between the German Weimar Republic of the 1920s and the Nazi Reich of the 1930s. Before the Nazis arrived, Germany was a demoralized country, torn by internal dissension, always in the brink of repeating the 1918–19 failed Bolshevik revolution, with an economy that performed badly in terms of its previous and subsequent achievements. The self-confidence that had propelled the country to the fast industrialization of the last decades of the nineteenth century seemed to be gone. Just a few years later, under Nazism, the country was solidly unified and staging another economic miracle. Carl Jung, one of the founders of modern psychology, wrote the following lines in the 1930s describing this new unity:

If thirty years ago anyone had dared to predict that our psychological development was tending towards a revival of the medieval persecution of the Jews, that Europe would again tremble before the Roman fasces and the tramp of legions, that people would once more give the Roman salute, as two thousand years ago, and that instead of the Christian Cross an archaic swastika would lure onward millions of warriors ready for death—why, that man would have been hooted as a mystical fool. And today? Surprising as it may seem, all this absurdity is a horrible reality. Private life, private aetiologies, and private neuroses have become almost a fiction in the world of today. The man of the past who lived in a world of archaic *"représentations collectives"* has risen again into a very visible and painfully real life, and this is not only in a few unbalanced individuals but in many millions of people.[20]

Jung's words are quite disturbing. They portray a collective mentality taking over the private will of millions of individuals, giving them a unified purpose like a magnetic field aligns scraps of metal spread on a surface. It was as if, as a result of a perverse act of alchemy, the flesh of all these Germans—who had been unable to create a sustainable political and economic system for more than a decade—had been melted down and then molded into gigantic machines of destruction. A Nietzschean Idea— the creation of a world dominated by a pure race—performed this alchemy. While Jung wrote his observation on sight of the Nazis, he could have written the same lines about the Communists who, also organized in a machinery of destruction, were killing people by the millions in Russia to achieve an equally mad idea—the creation of the Communist paradise.

It was these unifying, religious ideas that the Communists and the Nazis provided to their populations. They both identified an absolute evil—the social disruptions that were taking place as a result of the Industrial Revolution—and an army of devils causing those disruptions—the traders and financiers that were threatening the state control of economic activities that had given stability to the pre-industrial society. They both promised redemption from the absolute evil, which required an act of social exorcism—the elimination of the devils from the face of the earth. The Communists eliminated traders and financiers as a class; the Nazis almost succeeded in wiping out the race most identified with these activities, the Jews.[21]

This answers our question regarding the legitimacy of destructiveness. As perverse as it may seem, destructiveness emerged as a socially unifying force, as a way to renew the social bonds that the Industrial Revolution had been dissolving. The destructive ideologies provided this new unifying force by splitting the world between "we"—the destroyers—and "them"—the destroyed. Communists and Nazis did so by first creating an artificial divisiveness in society, and then by unleashing all the fear and anguish that change had created in the population against the people on the wrong end of the division. The majority of the population supported these persecutions.

The processes in Germany and Russia were similar to those that took place in Japan, which sank in a ruthless tyranny of the military during its industrialization and then went into a spree of aggressiveness that led to the Pacific episode of World War II. They were also similar to the terrible events that took place in China during the Revolution and the Cultural Revolution, and in Cambodia during the Communist regime of Pol Pot, and in all other countries that fell under the grip of Communism. Furthermore, they are similar to those taking place currently in most of the Middle East. Resistance to change took over rigid countries that could not live in the liberal environment of a modern society. As in the cases of Russia and Germany, the fundamentalists, once in power, are using the perverse social cohesion of fundamental destructiveness to carry their war against progress to the rest of the world.

We can draw a mold of the behavior of the countries that fell prey to the doctrines of destructiveness during the Industrial Revolution based on the previous analysis:

First, in all cases, destructiveness took hold of societies in a moment of uncontrollable dissolution of social ties, which had turned domestic political conflicts into bloody struggles. That is, destructiveness appeared after a period of social chaos.

Second, the installation of the destructive regime unleashed outbursts of organized energy so powerful that they amazed the world. Napoleon, Hitler, and Stalin carried their countries to unprecedented feats, impossible to forecast only a few years before, when the three countries were consuming themselves in internecine struggles.

Third, similar to the Spanish Inquisition, the cold-blooded destructiveness that unleashed these outbursts of energy was the means to build a pure society, at home and abroad, based on perverse, or perversely interpreted, religious ideas.

Fourth, in all cases, the crucial feature of the pure society that the doctrines of destructiveness aimed at creating was its imperviousness to change.

Fifth, while the revolutionary dogmas were advertised as gigantic leaps into the future, they were in fact violent, authoritarian re-assertions of the old ideas that had provided the basis for social relations in the past.

Sixth, the ultimate result of these regimes was self-destructive. By attacking diversity, the source of change that was threatening their existence, they introduced an even stiffer rigidity that eventually led to their demise, either through sclerosis, or a mad confrontation with the rest of the world.

The former conclusions can be enveloped in a final one:

The tendency to revolutionary violence, the dogmatism that accompanied it, and the destructiveness of subsequent regimes, emerged as a perverse cure for the social dissolution caused by rapid and uncontrollable change in societies too rigid to handle it in a harmonious way.

Naturally, the probability of a collapse of social order increases with the speed of change of social relations. However, speed of change is not the only factor explaining why social orders collapse. Some vessels sink in particular stretches of turbulent waters while others fare well in the same ranges. In the same way, some societies transform themselves harmoniously under the same challenges that lead others to dissolution. Given a certain speed of social change, the probability of failure depends on the resilience of a society to change, which, in turn, depends on the rigidity or flexibility of its institutions.

All the now-industrialized countries were subject to the same transformation during the Industrial Revolution and all of them had radicals in their midst. Britain, the United States, along with many other countries, adjusted harmoniously to such transformation. Radicalism disappeared with time in those countries. France, Germany, and Russia resisted the changes that this process was causing in their social order until they became overwhelming. When they collapsed in chaos, these societies turned toward the radicals and their destructive ideologies as the way to restore the social order they had lost. *That is, they got their revolutions and their subsequent periods of destructiveness not because they were poor and oppressed but because they were rigid.*

Now we can turn to examine the question we posed at the end of the previous chapter: how is it that Nazi Germany was so successful economically, and how is it that Stalin was able to industrialize the Soviet Union within a decade under Communism, if both of them controlled the economy to the last detail?

The common thread that explains the economic success of both economies was the repression of the resistance to change in the labor force, which was attained in the Soviet Union by giving all the power to the owner of the enterprise, the government, and in the case of Germany by transferring such power to the private owners but still under the tyrannical authority of the government. Private owners were just proxies for the all-powerful state.

Companies did not sink in the complacency normally produced by monopolies because the government forced them to improve their efficiency continuously, regardless of what the workers could say. This was the way Nazi Germany worked. In the Soviet Union, companies eventually fell into complacency and corruption but this happened only when the reign of terror that had driven the industrialization of the country subsided. At their height, Nazis and Communists were able to achieve growth in their enormous industrial economies—the former with high efficiency and the latter with much less success—only because they crushed the workers. In countries where governments have not been willing or able to do that, the policies of government intervention have resulted in the stagnation and decay of developing countries. There, government and industrial entrepreneurs and workers have joined hands to stop competition and progress.

It is important to emphasize that it was the crushing of the workers, not of the entrepreneurs that was common to Communism and Nazism. This was what allowed Stalin to industrialize the Soviet Union with slave labor and Hitler to spur technological progress without competitive markets. Finally, it was the capacity to repress the workers' movements that made the difference between, for example, Nazi Germany and Peronist Argentina.

That is, *the policies of government intervention that the radicals are proposing in this very moment to ensure a better life for the workers can elicit economic growth only if they are combined with a harsh repression of the freedoms and rights of the same workers they are supposedly defending.* This is what the workers joining in the demands for government intervention have not understood. If they succeed in their demands, there are only two ways open for them: stagnation or slavery. The choice, however, is not just for the workers. The vertical regimes prosper in destructiveness but eventually collapse on their own destructive dynamics, leaving a legacy of devastation in their wake.

The main mechanisms through which destructive regimes destroy themselves are corruption, military defeats, and the lack of incentives for innovation.

Corruption was always a serious problem in the Soviet Union and all Communist countries. In fact, terror was needed to contain it because, in a country where people manage capital goods for an abstract entity, the state, there is a natural incentive for managers and bureaucrats to use the companies' assets for their own benefit. Terror kept the managers relatively honest during Stalin's times. When terror subsided with the death of Stalin in 1953, however, discipline weakened progressively until the economic regime became a market economy of corruption. Everything had a price and people collected it using government property and positions as the mechanisms of collection. In this way, Party and government bureaucrats charged for the services they had to provide for free in accordance to law; for hiring newcomers in their bureaucracies; for deliveries of goods produced in state-owned facilities. Companies lied to the central planners and sold increasing proportions of their production in the black market. A chain of imaginary production developed and became strong. Companies charged the central planners for production that did not exist and delivered it to other companies, which reported receiving inputs they had never received but, in turn, reported delivering the imaginary products they had produced with the imaginary inputs, while the real production was delivered to the black market. Trains leaving a factory with real goods arrived empty to their destinations. Pilfering became a systemic problem.[22] By the late 1980s, corruption was so pervasive that the official chain of supplies broke down. The long lines of people trying to buy food in empty official stores that the world saw on TV coexisted with a thriving black market where goods were bartered for other goods or exchanged for dollars. Communism collapsed when it had become a total lie.

Nazism collapsed militarily before it could collapse economically. Yet, it was also a corrupt regime. Hitler was not motivated by economic wealth and, therefore, he was not corrupt in the economic sense. Still, corruption was rampant among his lieutenants and the government and party bureaucracies. They lived in stolen mansions furnished with stolen things, including art pieces taken from the houses and museums of their vassals. They compromised for money even with their most sacred principles, like that of finishing with the Jews. Many of the latter were able to escape from the Nazi hell by bribing officers of all levels. Regarding creativity, it might sound inaccurate to say that Nazism was incapable of innovation—after all, they invented or improved many things. However, it is enough to ask if Nazi Germany would have been able to invent the Internet and connectivity to realize that this would have been impossible. As we already noted, tyrannical government cannot allow its subjects to communicate with each other. Thus, a Nazi regime would have frozen the world into their perverse version of the industrial age, tainted with the blood of slave workers. Well before that, however, the regime would have collapsed by the internecine fights that would have taken place after Hitler's death.

In summary, most of the differences in income between countries are attributable to the barriers to progress that those in the lower end have imposed on themselves. This happens to poor countries for two main reasons. First, these barriers are manifestations of the political power enjoyed by the small groups that would lose from the introduction of more productive methods. Second, these small groups get political power mainly because they cover themselves with the mantle of "social progressiveness." In the long-standing tradition of the opponents of free markets, they portray as progressive what in reality is resistance to change based on the defense of their own private interests. They get support from intellectuals because advocating the creation and maintenance of these monopolies is an easy way of showing social concern without having to work for it. The result is extremely damaging for society. Measures aimed at protecting existing activities against the more efficient that are emerging in the markets actually retards growth and are at the core of the reasons why some countries develop fast while others lag behind, creating and deepening the gaps in the international distribution of income and wealth.

The impact of institutionalized resistance to change on the prospects of economic growth and development is always negative. Yet, such impact is even more negative, by many orders of magnitude, when, as it happened during the Industrial Revolution and as it is happening today, the entire structure of production is being transformed by a technological revolution. Each year of protection to politically important groups creates enormous gaps in the income per capita of developed and developing countries—gaps that then take decades to close, or, possibly, that will never be closed. The symbiosis between the political and the economic circles benefiting from protection is so strong that it tends to linger forever through mechanisms that, more often than not, involve corruption. Certainly, globalization is making it more difficult for this symbiosis to survive. The old system cracks under economic realities. Yet, as the experience in many countries in Latin America is showing, the legitimacy of protection is so deeply imbedded in the mentality of many of these countries that it comes back after a few years of liberalism. This is particularly tragic because, as we discussed earlier, connectivity offers unprecedented facilities for poor countries to integrate to the international economy and, through it, the opportunity to grow and develop.

This runs contrary to what the radicals of today are proclaiming, that the only way to deal with globalization is to increase the government intervention in the economy to protect the population against the disruptions of the process. The economic problems we are facing today are not the result of liberalism but of a technological transformation that cannot be stopped except with measures that would lead to stagnation, corruption, destructiveness, or a combination of all of them. In countries where technological development is a domestic activity, the measures that would be needed to stop the transformation are even more radical than in the developing countries, where technologies are imported. While closing the borders to trade would stop the transformation of the latter, more restrictive measures would be needed in the former, because domestic creativity would have to be repressed to prevent the further differentiation between the fast and the slow adjusters. Nothing short of a tyranny would achieve such feats.

Corruption and stagnation are very common in our times. Destructiveness is reemerging. I turn to this subject in the next chapter.

NOTES

1. Oswald Spengler, *The Decline of the West*, (New York: Oxford University Press, 1932), p. 360.

2. Catherine the Great, quoted by Isabel de Madariaga, in *Russia in the Age of Catherine the Great*, (New Haven and London: Yale University Press, 1981), p. 580.

3. Plato had Socrates making the same point in Republic VIII. See "Republic VIII" in John M. Cooper, ed., and D. S. Hutchinson assoc. ed., *Plato: Complete Works* (Indianapolis/Cambridge: Hackett Publishing Company, 1997), 544e–d, p. 1157.

4. See Simon Schama, *Citizens: A Chronicle of the French Revolution* (New York: Vintage Books, 1990), p. 581.

5. See Thelma Liesner, *Economic Statistics 1900–1983* (London: The Economist Publications Ltd., 1985.

6. Karl Marx, "The German Ideology," in *The Marx-Engels Reader*, ed. Robert C. Tucker, 2d ed. (New York and London: W. W. Norton and Company, 1978), p. 175.

7. There were two kinds of farms in the Soviet Union: the collective and the state farms. In practice, there was no difference between them.

8. Alec Nove, *Economic History of the Soviet Union* (London: Penguin, 1989), p. 233.

9. See Robert Tucker, *Stalin in Power* (New York and London: W. W. Norton and Company, 1990), p. 549. Medvedev estimates that millions of peasants worked without pay after the collectivization. See his *Let History Judge* (New York: Columbia University Press, 1989), p. 799–800.

10. Tatyana Zaslavskaya, *The Second Socialist Revolution: An Alternative Soviet Strategy* (Bloomington and Indianapolis: Indiana University Press, 1990), p. 23.

11. See Carrére D'Encausse, *Stalin* (London and New York: Longman, 1981), pp. 24, 70–71 and Medvedev, *Let History Judge*, pp. 246–47.

12. See Stephen *Kotkin, Steeltown, USSR: Soviet Society in the Gorbachev Era* (Berkeley and Los Angeles: University of California Press, 1991), pp. 208–9.

13. William L. Shirer, *The Rise and Fall of the Third Reich* (New York: Fawcett Crest, 1992), pp. 354–56.

14. The government enforced those aspects of the agrarian legislation that did not restrict the mobility of labor to industry. For example, only farmers could buy farms. Franz Schlegelberger, who acted as Minister of Justice in 1941–42, required a special permission to buy a farm in 1944 because he was not a farmer. See Raul Hillberg, *Perpetrators, Victims, Bystanders: The Jewish Catastrophe 1933–1945* (New York: HarperPerennial, 1992), p. 29.

15. William L. Shirer, *The Rise and Fall of the Third Reich*, pp. 361–62.

16. See David S. Landes, *The Unbound Prometheus* (Cambridge: Cambridge University Press, 1997), pp. 416–17.

17. Shirer, *The Rise and Fall of the Third Reich*, p. 363.

18. Edmund Burke, *Reflections on the Revolution in France* (1790; Indianapolis/Cambridge: Hackett Publishing Company, 1987) p. 33.

19. See Simon Schama, *Citizens* (New York: Vintage Books, 1990), p. 185.

20. Carl Jung in *The Archetypes and the Collective Unconscious,* and in Joseph Campbell, *The Portable Jung* (New York: Penguin Books, 1981), p. 66.

21. The perception that trade and finance are unproductive activities aimed at dispossessing the true producers of material wealth was common in preindustrial European societies. In Germany and other countries of the region, these activities were identified with the Jews. See, for example, Eva G. Reichmann, *Hostages of Civilization: A Study of Anti-Semitism in Germany* (Boston, Mass.: The Beacon Press, 1951), pp. 42–46. Also, see Arnold Toynbee, *A Study of History,* Abridged vol. 1 (Oxford: Oxford University Press, 1946), pp. 303–5.

22. The tendency to corruption in the Soviet society is described in many books dealing with the industrial organization of the country and with general aspects of Soviet social life. For example, see Hiroaki Kuromiya, *Stalin's Industrial Revolution: Politics and Workers, 1928–1932* (Cambridge: Cambridge University Press, 1990); Helene Carrere D'Encausse, *Stalin: Order through Terror* (London and New York: Longman, 1981); Hendrick Smith, *The Russians* (New York: Ballantine Books, 1976); Hendrick Smith, *The New Russians* (New York: Random House, 1990); Dusko Doder, *Shadows and Whispers: Power Politics Inside the Kremlin from Brezhnev to Gorbachev* (New York: Penguin Books, 1988); Jan Winiecki, *The Distorted World of Soviet-Type Economies* (Pittsburgh: University of Pittsburgh Press, 1988).

CHAPTER 5

The Resurgence of Fundamentalism

The impact of a technological revolution on the shape of society is not limited to the economic effects we have examined in the previous chapters. Even more deeply, technological innovations erode social cohesion, the subtle web of interpersonal attitudes, mores, customs, and laws that keep society together. This might be the most dangerous of all of the destabilizing effects of the transformation. Actually, the economic effects threaten social peace because of their effect on social bonds and the legitimacy of the existing social order.

The relationship between change and social order is extremely complex. We associate order with steadiness and permanence, and chaos with change. Yet, the single most important factor determining the existence of order in a society is its ability to organize itself in the pursuance of common goals—which is, in itself, a dynamic process, a process of change. Development starts when societies acquire this ability, and progress proceeds as it matures. Thus, *change is the source of social order.*

Societies introduce order through institutions, which may take the form of rules and regulations—such as the constitution and the body of laws—or that of organizations in charge of performing certain duties—such as the court system, the government, and business enterprises. These institutions facilitate social and economic growth mainly because they take care of all routine transactions in society, establishing rules to perform them and allocating clear responsibilities for the people in charge of applying them. Because of the existence of such institutions, people do not have to worry about the means to send communications to other people, or ponder on whether stealing is good or bad, or worry every day on how to organize the distribution of food. This liberates the energies of society for the pursuance of goals related to growth, taking advantage of the routines embedded in the existing institutions. With growth, activities that had been challenging in the past become part of the routine of society, and institutions take care of them. In this way, for example, a matter that is the subject of scientific speculation at one stage of the process, becomes engineering knowledge in the next, and from there it becomes production techniques. The wider the institutional basis, the more a society can apportion its energies to grow.

Thus, growth builds on the stock of order already established in society, and results in higher, more complex levels of order. Expressed in another way, the existing social order is a stock, which was built with the flows of the creative activity of the past. *Order, the ability to organize on top of organizations already in place, is a capital asset, it has an economic value, it is the foundation of the wealth of a country.*

It is common nowadays to think of social capital as the ability of a conglomerate to associate in civil organizations. I use the term with a meaning that differs from this in two important ways. First, in the meaning I am giving to the term, it is formally similar to the economic capital, referring to what already exists, not to the capacity to create new organizations—which would be the capacity to invest in a certain kind of institution. Second, its scope is wider. It includes not just the civil society organizations but also the Supreme Court, the legal system, the enterprises, and in general, all the rest of the social organizations in place. This is what is really the capital of a society. This is, for example, what modern immigrants from the Third World look for in the developed societies.

Like any capital asset, social order must be renewed continuously. Social changes of any kind—such as the introduction of new technologies or improvements in the educational level of the population—pose challenges to existing institutions because they modify the relationships and transactions these institutions were set to regulate and channel.

In normal times, institutions struggle to adapt themselves to these new relations, redefining their objectives to broaden their scope. Successful adaptation results in stronger institutions, and in a sense of accomplishment that generates more energy, focusing it in the direction that has proven successful. Under the right environment, change is like blood, which pushes and expands the veins and arteries, strengthening a living body. Within some boundaries, the higher the level of activity channeled through the institutional setting of any given society, the stronger these institutions become, and the more complex the challenges that such society can take and overcome.

This process, however, is nonlinear. As much as change can lead societies into order and progress, it can also destroy institutions and, with them, the fabric that holds society together. This happens when the pace of change overwhelms the existing institutions' ability to adjust. People start to create relationships that bypass those institutions, disrupting the social order and threatening the stability of society. Social relations overflow the institutions created to channel them, producing results that people consider chaotic, unfair, or both. When a regime's institutions are turned into carcasses, the regime loses legitimacy. The adjustment to the changing conditions then tends to take place in a catastrophic fashion, and society sinks in chaos.

Such erosion takes place in all societies, including the most developed ones. Actually, it is a precondition for the process of creation of a new, superior form of social order that would be consistent with the opportunities opened by the new technologies. Yet, in some societies the erosion of the old bonds may lead not to a renewal of social order but to chaos. It is in those societies that fundamentalism, the obsessive desire to go back to the past, emerges, easily leading to destructive regimes. Not all countries where fundamentalism appears are led to destructiveness. However, it creates severe problems in all of them.

I discuss this problem in this chapter, starting with a brief review of the ways in which technological revolutions erode social bonds.

In a book called *The Corrosion of Character: The Personal Consequences of Work in the New Capitalism*,[1] the sociologist Richard Sennet argues that the transient nature of the interpersonal relations produced by the human mobility and speed of the new economy of connectivity—which he calls the new capitalism—is corroding our character. "Character," he says, "is expressed by loyalty and mutual commitment, or through the pursuit of long-term goals, or by the practice of delayed gratification for the sake of a future end."[2] But, how, he asks, could these long-term goals be pursued in our societies? Things are changing too fast. Interpersonal relations are too short to create a sense of loyalty and commitment with our friends and coworkers because of the constant migrations and the temporary nature of work teams. Moreover, more people are working at home and their personal contacts with other people are very scant.

In such an environment, Sennet argues, there are no incentives to assume responsibility, to be accountable in the long term. Furthermore, the possibility of feeling empathy for our fellow human beings is blunted by the temporary nature of our relationships with them. People do not want to get involved with people they just have met. And in the new world we tend to be in touch mostly with people we have just met. Thus, the result of the new technological progress is a weakening of both social bonds and the moral character that can give permanence to them. As he wrote, "This is the problem of modern capitalism. There is history, but no shared narrative of difficulty, and so no shared fate. Under these conditions, character corrodes . . . "[3] In the long run, Sennet believes, this would lead to a breakdown of social life. The strong social cohesion that was the basis of the success of the modern industrial state would disappear from the most advanced societies and these would retrogress to the indifference for the common good that is characteristic of both underdeveloped and destructive societies.

Sennet is only one of the many social observers that are worrying about these developments. Another of them, Allan Bloom, noted the same point from a different perspective in *The Closing of the American Mind*, a book he wrote about the changes he had perceived in his students during his long career as a professor in elite universities in the United States. He also traces the isolationist attitudes to the possibility of separation from the people who are close to us, much more common today than some decades ago.

The aptest description I can find for the [current] state of student's souls is the psychology of separateness.

The possibility of separation is already the fact of separation, inasmuch as people today must plan to be whole and self-sufficient, and cannot risk interdependence. Imagination compels everyone to look forward to the day of separation in order to see how he will do. The energies people should use in the common enterprise are exhausted in the preparation for independence . . . The goals of those who are together naturally and necessarily must become a common good. But there is no common good for those who are to separate. The presence of choice already changes the character of relatedness . . . This continual shifting of the sands in our desert—separation from places, persons, beliefs—produces the psychic state of nature where reserve and timidity are the prevailing dispositions. We are social solitaires.[4]

Benjamin Disraeli, Prime Minister of Britain in 1868 and in 1874–80, expressed similar concerns about the dissolution that the Industrial Revolution was causing in his country in a political novel, *Sybil or the Two Nations*. He wrote it in the 1830s, when Britain was becoming conscious of the deep changes that industrialization was eliciting in its social relations. The following dialogue summarizes Disraeli's concerns:

"As for community," said a voice which proceeded neither from Egremont nor the stranger, "with the monasteries expired the only type that we ever had in England. There is no community in England; there is aggregation, but aggregation under circumstances which make it rather a disassociating than a uniting principle."
. . .
"It is community of purpose that constitutes society," continued the younger stranger; "without that, men may be drawn into contiguity, but they still continue virtually isolated."
And is that their condition in cities?
It is their condition everywhere; but in cities that condition is aggravated. A density of population implies a severer struggle for existence, and a consequent repulsion of elements brought into too close contact. In great cities, men are brought together by the desire of gain. They are not in a state of cooperation, but

of isolation, as to the making of fortunes; and for all the rest they are careless of neighbors. Christianity teaches us to love our neighbor as ourself; modern society acknowledges no neighbor.[5]

More than 80 years later, in 1926, Hermann Hesse, a famous Swiss novelist born in Germany, wrote an article called *The Longing of Our Time for a Worldview* in which he expressed his distress at the dissolution of social bonds that the Industrial Revolution was eliciting in Central Europe— where, as we know, industrialization started about 80 years later than in Britain. In this piece, he wrote the following words:

The new image of the earth's surface, completely transformed and recast in just a few decades, and the enormous changes manifest in every city and every landscape of the world since industrialization, correspond to an upheaval in the human mind and soul. This development has so accelerated since the outbreak of the world war that one can already, without exaggeration, identify the death and dismantling of the culture into which the elder among us were raised as children and which seemed to us eternal and indestructible . . . Destroyed and lost for the greater part of the civilized world are, beyond all else, the two universal foundations of life, culture and morality; religion and customary morals. Our life is lacking in morals, in a traditional, sacred, unwritten understanding about what is proper and becoming between people.

One need only undertake a short journey to be able to observe in living examples the decay of morals. Wherever industrialization is still in its beginnings, wherever peasant and small-town traditions are still stronger than the modern forms of transportation and work, there the influence and emotional power of the church is quite essentially stronger as well. And in all of these places we continue to come across, more or less intact, that which were once called morals. In such backward regions one still finds forms of interaction—greeting, entertainment, festivals and games—which have long since been lost to modern life. As a weak substitute for lost morals, the modern individual has fashion. Changing from season to season, it supplies him with the most indispensable prescriptions for social life, tosses off the requisite phrases, catchwords, dances, melodies—better than nothing, but still a mere gathering of the transitory values of the day.[6]

The similarity of Disraeli, Hesse, Bloom, and Sennet's pieces is striking. All of them regret the destruction of the old values that gave society its stability and moral strength in the recent past. All of them express doubts that morality can be maintained in the new environment that new methods of production are creating. All of them worry that social cohesion— the mainstay of a humane and flexible society—is weakening in our times.

There is something that could lead us to readily dismiss Sennet's concerns. The old social order that Sennet longs for today is the one that Hesse thought was incompatible with a moral life three generations ago. One could express Sennet's worries about the disconnection with neighbors with Disraeli's words, "Christianity teaches us to love our neighbor as ourself; modern society acknowledges no neighbor." Sennet feels nostalgia for the structures that framed the lives of people under the industrial order—the routine work, the repetition of the same tasks day after day, the trade unions, the massification of the individual—which, in his opinion, even if restrictive, gave people a structure in which to insert their lives. That is, the things that Sennet laments are disappearing are the ones whose apparition caused anguish to Hesse and Disraeli, who were longing for the old rural order of the pre-industrial society. The exact coincidence of those worries would easily lead to labeling those writers as alarmists because, today, we know that it was not impossible to give a sense of community to industrial countries and that, in fact, the modern industrial countries are more humane than the feudal communities. The bonds are also broader because they tie entire countries rather than only the small feudal localities.

This, however, does not invalidate their concerns. What these three thinkers pointed to is the problem generated by the dissolution of the social bonds that support one existing order while the new social order has not yet emerged.

The fact that a few societies were able to go thorough the transformation without falling into the dangers that Disraeli and Hesse saw does not turn them into alarmists. In fact, only a few countries were able to regenerate the social bonds that were weakening in their times. Several other countries, including Hesse's native Germany, were not able to do it. They fell in the social dissolution that both Disraeli and Hesse identified and, from there, to chaos, revolutions, and destructive regimes. The problems that Sennet points to in our times are also real and we still do not know whether they will be resolved. Sennet, in fact, has fingered one of the main problems of the current transformation.

While the problems these thinkers identified in two different technological revolutions affect all countries in the world—in fact, they all wrote about highly developed countries—they are at their worse in rigid, less developed societies, where social bonds are so weak that social unity can be held only by vertical shapes of organization. It has been there, when connectivity and globalization started to erode those vertical institutions that fundamentalism erupted with utmost violence. The ideas that the fundamentalists are embracing have been there for generations. The fact that today they have become the basis for fanaticism after having been dormant for centuries is the key point to explain. The explanation is that it is today that connectivity and globalization are threatening the integrity of these societies.

Fundamentalism, the extreme form of resistance to change, is the urge to force the return of society to mores and social structures of an idealized past, when things did not change and people could plan their lives within a predictable structure. It emerges in all processes of radical transformations. It becomes strong, however, only in the last stages of dissolution of a society, when people think that they are veering into chaos. People try to escape the present by going to the past, thinking that nothing could be done with the existing society except destroy the forces that are dissolving it.

There are, however, two varieties of fundamentalists. Some of them preach for a return to the past in a straightforward way, while others portray their vision as a futuristic one. As Arnold Toynbee wrote:

Futurism and archaism are both attempts to break away from an irksome present by taking a flying leap out of it into another reach of the stream of time without abandoning the plane of mundane life on Earth ... They differ from each other merely in the direction—up or down the time-stream—in which they make their two equally desperate sorties from a position of discomfort.[7]

The first kind of fundamentalism is that which looks at the past. It is the driving force of the religious fundamentalism. It includes the Muslim fanatics who have declared war on the liberal principles of Western civilization as well as terrorist groups that have emerged in the last several decades in all the main religions, including Christianity. The second variety is secular and is the driving force for most of the groups that today oppose globalization in the west. It was the driving force of both the Communist and the Nazi regimes; while being western in origin, it also declared war on liberal principles. Even if the secular fundamentalists like to think that they represent the wave of the future, they are as archaic as the religious ones in the dimension that matters most, the shape of social organization. All of them are intolerant defenders of vertical shapes of social order and all of them want to create a state of society that would never change.

In the aftermath of the terrorist attacks of September 11, 2001, the attention of society turned to explain the aggressiveness of Islamic religion. As I discuss later in this chapter, there are plenty of paragraphs in the Koran that can be interpreted in an aggressive way. Yet, the question is why aggressive interpretations of religious texts are back not just in Islamism but in every other important religion as well and precisely when aggressive secular doctrines are also re-emerging. In the rest of this chapter, I discuss the emergence of both kinds of fundamentalism and examine the consequences it may have beyond the wave of terrorist attacks that started on September 11.

Adjustment in Islamic societies is difficult because modernization easily contradicts religious precepts. This is so because their religion establishes strict rules on almost all aspects of human relations. Some of them are in the Koran and some of them have developed from tradition. Some of these refer to form while others refer to substance. Many of them, however, even those referring to form, go against the conception and the realities of a modern society. An example of these are the rulings that proclaim and enforce the inequality of men and women, which materialize in many regulations of behavior, including those that forbid the transit of women unaccompanied by men beyond certain hours and those that impose the use of veils to cover the faces of women outside the intimate quarters of home. For many Muslims, just seeing an uncovered woman is an insult. Equally, seeing a woman joining the men in a house party, even if she is the hostess, is a violation of morals. Thus, westernized Muslims create conflicts with their traditional fellow citizens just by behaving in what for them is a normal way.

These and other prescriptions are inserted within the ultimately intolerant notion: Islamic law prescribes that the government has to be subservient to the Islamic religion, so that there is no room for the infidels in any dimension of life except that of submitting economically and politically to the precepts of the religion. Life in Islamic societies is one-dimensional: everything is prescribed by religion.

Customs and activities that contradict these and other similar precepts were introduced in the Muslim countries during the western colonial period. In some countries, like Saudi Arabia, the westerners living in the country were (and still are) confined to special districts to prevent the clash of lifestyles. In other countries, they mixed with the population and many Muslims adopted their lifestyles. Moreover, all countries established banks even if the Koran banished lending with interest, and established governments that were effectively separated from the church, even if the Koran also condemned this.

Such deviations from the Islamic law were seen as fully justifiable in view of the changes that society had gone through since the law had been first written. The idea that rules had to change with the times and that some of the precepts of the Koran and Islamic law had become obsolete became the mainstream. However, the numbers of western or westernized people living in these societies were relatively small and their visual impact was slight. Only a small elite had access to the operation of the westernized portion of the economy and such elite was mainly pragmatic in its interpretation of the Islamic law. The immense majority of the population remained poor and sticking to their Muslim traditions. It was only when the interaction with the West increased quickly and innovations coming from there started a serious transformation of the Islamic societies that a serious resistance to change began to emerge.

Naturally, the more westernized parts of society were the ones that would take advantage of the economic innovations brought about by the introduction of industry, bank financing, and modernization in general.

This led to the shifts in income distribution and the instability that accompanies liberalization. It was very easy to identify the western ideas as the sources of these problems and the westernized Muslims as the agents that were importing them from the West. It was then that fundamentalism was born.

Islamic fundamentalism is a movement aimed at bringing back to Muslim countries the social order that had prevailed in the premodern times. It emerged in the 1970s, precisely when one could have expected that the high prices of oil and the increased contact with the West would propitiate a faster rate of modernization in those countries. In fact, the movement started in the countries that were most integrated to the western ways of life. In the words of an expert in the field,

Ironically, its most potent manifestations of the Islamic resurgence both in the 1970s and in later decades, occurred in those societies regarded as the most "modern" or modernizing, those possessing a well-trained, Western-oriented, secular elite: Iran, Egypt, Lebanon, Tunisia, Turkey, and Algeria.

From Cairo to Kuala Lumpur, the resurgence of Islam manifested itself in personal and public life, in piety and politics. Many became more religiously observant in prayer, fasting, dress and behavior . . . At the same time, governments and opposition in countries as diverse as Egypt, Pakistan, Malaysia, and Indonesia increasingly appealed to Islam to enhance their legitimacy and mobilize popular support. Islamic ideology, rhetoric, symbols, actors, political parties and organizations became prominent fixtures in Muslim politics and society.[8]

The concentration of Islamic fundamentalism in the countries that were most modernized was not the result of an irony of history, but the natural consequence of the disruption that the new ways of life was introducing in the midst of traditional societies. Countries where the traditional way of life was not threatened could live without fanaticism; it was those where people saw that the world was changing in ways they did not understand that fell prey to fundamentalist preaching. Not all the countries listed in the quotation went into fundamentalist revolutions. The emerging movement, however, rocked all of them.

The first flare of serious religious violence emerged in Lebanon, the country where westernization had gone deeper and where social fragmentation was worse in the region. In the 1950s and 1960s, Lebanon was the financial center of the Middle East and the hub of all its communications with Europe. Educational levels were the highest in the region as well, and the economy was growing faster than in any other neighboring country, even if the country did not have oil. By the early 1990s, the country was totally destroyed by internecine fights. The events that led to such destruction were extremely complex. They, however, can be summarized in one sentence: the rapid westernization of Lebanon created insolvable problems between those who had integrated within the new environment

88 The Triumph of the Flexible Society

and those who were out of it. While there were some economic dimensions to this cleavage—the westernized Lebanese tended to go up faster in the middle classes and the lower-class Muslims stagnated—the issues were not primarily economic. The point of contention was the change in the mores of the country, which many if not most of the Muslims saw as demoralizing and contrary to the dictates of their religion.

Though the Lebanese conflict was the first manifestation of fundamentalism, it did not go beyond chaos. Fundamentalist revolutions started in the Muslim world with the overthrow of the Shah of Iran. For most of his reign, the latter had struggled to introduce modernity in the Iranian society. He liberated women, promoted industry and trade, and adopted western commercial and financial customs. The rapid modernization of the country elicited by these measures brought about the same kind of distortions that we have already discussed: a modern elite concentrated mainly in the urban areas progressed faster while most of the country lagged behind. The idea that the former were exploiting the latter became common, and Iranians came to identify them as the local representatives of foreign exploiters who were introducing reforms to better exploit the Iranians. As the old mores that had kept the country together weakened and the new mores were slow to penetrate beyond a small elite, the country veered into chaos. Communists, anarchists, socialists, democrats, and other activists agreed on dethroning the Shah without agreeing on what should be done afterwards. All of them attacked the Shah and the latter attacked them back in fits and starts, alienating all sectors in sequence without being able to find a clear enemy to destroy. The Shah lost legitimacy as it was plain to everybody that he was unable to keep society in order. When watching the increasing problems faced by the Shah, people in the West misunderstood the nature of what was happening in Iran. They thought that the problem was that the Shah's regime was too archaic and was not modernizing the country as fast as it should. The subsequent events showed that the problem was that the Shah had been modernizing the country too fast, against the will of the majority of its population. Eventually, people went back to what had given order to society in past times, and gathered around the mullahs, the Shiite Muslim clerics. The mullahs then led the country into a total return to the past, reestablishing the discrimination of women, banning western dresses, eliminating the separation of state and religion, and making calls to fight the unbelievers abroad—echoing the calls made, 1,300 years before, by the Muslim leaders of the day. This restored order in the country. While it was tyrannical, much more so than the Shah's, the new government was legitimate because it embodied the population's resistance to change.

A third case was that of Afghanistan. The Soviet Union invaded the country in 1979 to support the local government, which was aiming at turning the country into a Communist satellite of the Soviets. The invasion strengthened the *mujahideen*, the Muslim militias that were opposing, for religious reasons, the Communist regime. They called for a sacred war against the invaders. After 10 years of a terrible conflict, the mujahideen expelled the Soviets and established a new revolutionary regime in Kabul. They, however, could not agree on the shape that a Muslim government should take or on the person that should lead it and they split into several factions warring against each other. The country veered into chaos. In 1994, a new force appeared unexpectedly. They were the *Taliban*, the students of the colleges of Islamic law, and the mullahs, their professors. Within two years, they gained control of the country and re-established order based on their interpretation of the Koran. They proscribed the contact of sexes outside home; closed girls' schools; imposed full coverage of the face on women in public places; expelled women from the workplace; and forbade television, movies, and music.[9] Under the Taliban, the country recovered its social order. The Taliban attained worldwide notoriety for their support of terrorism abroad. They were eventually deposed by the American invasion in the aftermath of the September 11 attack.

As globalization is spreading western customs and practices across Muslim countries, fundamentalism is also spreading, although not necessarily in its aggressive dimension. Recently, for example, pressures to abolish lending and borrowing are on the rise in many countries. Concerned governments are discussing the creation of what is called "Islamic finance," which tries to get around the prohibition by concealing the payment of interests through repurchase agreements—selling and buying something between lender and borrower with the difference in prices equaling the interest. Some theologians, however, object to this trick, which in any case, greatly complicates the operation of the financial system and increases the risks of its operation. The only thing that Islamic law allows is full participation in the business of the financed party, the equivalent of a venture capital arrangement. The system is unviable when large numbers of operations are involved. Governments worry that introducing it would result in a financial disaster and retardation or even reversal of growth. But they cannot resist the pressures of the population. Ironically, the introduction of western-style democratic institutions is accelerating the process. In Pakistan, for example, the independent Supreme Court decreed that Islamic finance should be imposed on the country and has set specific dates to do it. The court has been clear that the system should be as Islamic law prescribes, without tricks to meet the letter but not its spirit. Doing so could send the country back to the pre-financial times.

These problems are worsened by the terrible fragmentation characteristic of Muslim countries. Governments have only a tenuous control over the societies they rule, which are split into scores of different groups and sects, many of which have in common only one view: that the current regimes are usurpers or apostates. The danger of having suicidal infighting as in Lebanon or chaotic revolutions as in Iran and Afghanistan is very high. These could come about as a result of any motive, be it the refusal of governments to abolish the banking system, or their refusal to support fundamentalist movements in the current war against terrorism. The rapid modernization that accompanies connectivity is a mortal threat to these regimes, both directly and because it elicits a strong resistance to change. The growing confrontation between the two may lead to even more destructiveness.

Religious fundamentalism is not exclusive to Islam. The Western civilization has produced episodes of terrible religious destructiveness. Christian violent fundamentalism erupted in the last quarter of the twentieth century with the bombing of abortion clinics in the United States. While this fundamentalism was based on a specific issue, a broader one soon developed, one that like its Muslim counterparts aims at overturning the separation of state and religion, and aims at making of the United States a Christian nation—meaning that all other religions should be proscribed as well as all secular institutions. These fundamentalist movements developed into two branches, one in the political right and one in the political left. Among the former, the most notable have been the movements based on the Dominion Theology, articulated by famous preachers such as Jerry Falwell and Pat Robertson, and the Reconstruction Theology, which aims at creating a full-fledged theocratic state similar to those of the Muslims. More advanced in terms of radicalization, we find the Christian Identity movement, which defines such identity in terms of the superiority of the white race.

Certainly, these groups are small and thus far they have not declared a full-fledged war against liberal principles. Yet, violence is just one step ahead of some of their activities. Identity groups run camps where they train followers for the day when the war between good and evil that is already taking place behind the scenes will become open warfare. Moreover, some individuals belonging to these groups have already engaged in terrorism. Terrorists emerging from them include Buford Burrow, accused of shooting into a Jewish day care center on August 10, 1999; Timothy McVeigh, who bombed the Oklahoma federal building; and Rev. Michael Bray, who bombed abortion clinics in Delaware and in the Washington D.C. area.[10]

On the left side of the ledger, Christian fundamentalism created the Liberation Theology, which played a prominent role in the bloody revolutions and civil wars that plagued Latin America in the 1980s. This theology adopts the Marxist view of life, seeing capitalism and democracy as instruments of oppression and substituting the Divine Providence for Marx's laws of history as the mechanism that will inevitably lead society into Communism. Believing that Jesus was a member of a guerrilla group called the Zealots, many of the followers fought for the establishment of Communist regimes in several countries in Latin America in the 1980s, participating in uncountable terrorist acts, kidnappings, and guerrilla warfare. These groups mixed religion with secular radicalism.

Islamic, Christian, Zionist, and Buddhist fundamentalist movements are straightforwardly religious and openly propound returning to the past. These features are unacceptable to the majority of the people in the secular West, even if western fundamentalists are carried away by a religious fanaticism and want to go back to social structures of the past. To accommodate western tastes, the secular fundamentalists profess a materialistic religion and pretend that they are reaching out for the future, not the past. In this way, the Communists rejected the modernizing trends of trade, finance, and democracy pretending that they had invented something more modern—the archaic tyrannical system that they imposed on the Communist countries, which was based on the most primitive of all mechanisms of social control. The same can be said regarding Nazism.

The similarity between religious and secular radical movements is the product of the influence of the vertical, one-dimensional thinkers that created the intellectual foundations of the leftist and rightist secular *vertical* societies. Those thinkers perceived reality as linear confrontations of opposed interests that could be resolved only if one of the contenders imposed its will over the others. This confrontational attitude was only logical. Compromise is impossible between two forces opposing each other in one single dimension of life. In a vertical world, one has to be on top of the other, so that one gives the commands and the other obeys them. To decide who will be on top of the other, a bloody struggle is needed. This is the same in religious societies in which one is either a believer or an infidel.

Karl Marx and Friedrich Nietzsche were the secular popes of this one-dimensional view of society during the Industrial Revolution. As a manifestation of the inadequacy of the right-and-left classification of regimes and ideologies, their ideas cannot be classified in those terms. Even if both of them split the world in two opposing camps, we cannot say that Nietzsche was on the right and Marx on the left. Certainly, Marx split the world in terms of right and left and positioned himself on the latter. Nietzsche, however, split it in terms of above and below.

Marx thought that people had one overriding motivation in life, fulfilling their economic self-interest. They could be interested in political power but only as a mean to fulfill their economic ambitions. Nietzsche also thought that people had one overriding motivation in life, but such motivation was the will to power. People could be interested in economic power, but only as a means to satisfy the overriding will to power.

For Marx, the one-dimensional confrontation took place because, in their insatiable pursuit of economic well being, some people inevitably ended exploiting other people, in a process that split the world into a class of exploiters and one of exploited. This essential fact did not change through history. What changed was the shape of the exploitation, which evolved into more sophisticated forms as a result of the evolution of the methods of production. Thus, the world had gone from slavery to feudalism and then had reached capitalism, the most advanced and sophisticated method of exploitation ever invented. Marx then prescribed that the exploited in the capitalist system, the proletarians, should engage in a violent class war to dethrone the exploiters and establish a Dictatorship of the Proletariat, which in turn, after ridding society of the exploiters, would lead into a classless society, the Communist Paradise. That is, the liberation of humankind passed through a period of one-dimensional destructiveness.

For Nietzsche, destructiveness was an end in itself. Different from Marx's, his ideal social order was not an immutable state of bliss. To the contrary, the optimal state of the world was a constant struggle between the powerful to dominate the weak, which strengthened humankind as a whole. Nietzsche reckoned that this struggle left only desolation and suffering among its participants. The pursuit of happiness, however, was not the prime motivation of humankind, but the exercise of the will to power.

This was the social order that had prevailed in the best period of humankind: that created by the blonde beasts of prey that populated the primeval forests. The world had decayed since those times because the weak had dominated the strong in the confrontation of wills to power, using morality as their instrument. The domination of the weak had been the most terrible disgrace that could have happened to humankind, because the race had lost the natural mechanism to improve the perpetual competition to be the strongest. This terrible perversion had been the result of what could be taken as the largest, most consistently carried out and most terrifying conspiracy the world had ever known: the conspiracy of the Jews to destroy the Aryans in revenge for the leveling of Jerusalem two thousand years ago. It was them who, by incredible cunning, had imposed the morality of the weak on the rest of humankind, while they themselves still ruled their behavior by the morality of the strong. The instrument that they had used in this revenge had been Christianity.[11] A superman would liberate humankind from its mediocrity by devolving power to their natural holders, the blond beasts of prey, who would then reshape the world with blood and fire, reaffirming the superiority of their race.

Since for both Marx and Nietzsche, politics and economics could only act together—for one was only a means to attain the other—their theories can be encompassed by one saying that life is the enactment of the permanent confrontation of people moved by the desire of obtaining a composite substance—economic and political power, the essence of the one-dimensional society. The confrontations predicted by both Marx and Nietzsche had to be violent, for only violence can remove an impasse in a one-dimensional world. At this level, Marx and Nietzsche were not opponents. They were one and the same. They were on the same side, the side of one-dimensional interpretations of reality.

The main difference between the two philosophers—the opposition between Marx's state of bliss and Nietzsche's state of permanent struggle—was removed by the Nazis, who took Nietzsche's ideas and enhanced them with a proper state of bliss that would be attained after the long struggles of the ultimate superman and his following supermen. This state of bliss was the One-Thousand-Year Reich.

The destructiveness that the coming heroes would engage in was justified with a new concept of morality, one that attached moral virtue to all acts that were in accordance with the ideas and predictions of these two philosophers, even if they contradicted the longest-held moral precepts of humankind. This is the same morality that encourages the religious terrorists of today. It is the morality that naturally emerges from one-dimensional views of reality, in which the gains of some must be the losses of others. In such vision, one has the power or is enslaved; one exploits the others or is exploited by someone else. Within that asphyxiating conception of life, there is no alternative but violence.

Lenin expressed this conception of morality with chilling clarity in the following words:

For us there do not, and cannot, exist the old system of morality and "humanity" invented by the bourgeoisie for the purpose of oppressing and exploiting the "lower classes". Our morality is new, our humanity is absolute, for it rests on the bright ideal of destroying all oppression and coercion.

To us, all is permitted, for we are the first in the world to raise the sword not in the name of enslaving and oppressing anyone, but in the name of freeing all from bondage ... Blood? Let there be blood, if it alone can turn the grey-white-and-black banner of the old tyrannical world to a scarlet hue, for only the complete and final death of that world will save us from the return of the old jackals.[12]

This brand of morality, which underlay the actions of the Communists and the Nazis, is the one that the fundamentalist terrorists of today use to justify their actions. They are as one-dimensional as the Communists and Nazis.

The people who created the institutions that became the basis of the modern horizontal society, in contrast, perceived reality in all of its multidimensional diversity. For this reason, they could conceive of multidimensional solutions to conflicts, as costs in one dimension could be compensated with benefits in other dimensions. To ensure that this multidimensionality would survive, all of them emphasized the separation of economic and political power.

We can classify the new groups that have emerged in the developed countries to radically oppose globalization in two kinds. The first comprises chaotic subgroups that see life through a single political issue, like feminism, homosexual liberalization or racism; the other includes less chaotic subgroups seeking in a more organized way economic advantages for themselves. Both kinds of groups have become convinced that globalization and liberal ideas are their enemies. Groups of the first kind oppose globalization because they see it as a manifestation of the system and they are anti-system. Groups of the second kind, while appearing to attack the system, are actually defending its current shape—a system where they had an advantageous position that is becoming obsolete.

The arguments that the radicals of the first kind present to support their opposition to globalization are convoluted and parochial but they have one factor in common. They see the disruptions of globalization as manifestations of capitalism, which for them is the source of everything that is bad in society—from imperialism, to white supremacy theories, to sexism, and cultural chauvinism. They do not stop to think that capitalism cannot explain the imperialistic history of the Soviet Union or that white supremacy theories cannot account for the terrible Japanese imperialism in the 1930s and early 1940s, or explain the fact that non-white people have also tried to dominate other people, white or non-white, throughout history. Mimicking the posture taken by Friedrich Engels in *The Origin of the Family, Private Property and the State*,[13] the feminist side of this new radicalism argues that the oppression of women is a manifestation of capitalism and concludes that globalization can only worsen such oppression.

In all these and similar assertions one finds not attempts at understanding social problems but only tortuous justifications for a prejudice, that capitalism, liberal democracy, and globalization are bad. This trend is the more dangerous because one of the segments of society that radicalism is taking over is academia—a phenomenon not known in the United States, which was instrumental in the legitimization of destructiveness in the industrializing Europe. While many of the intellectuals in academia do not see themselves as Marxists, their ideas show the traces of the old master: the ideas that everything in society is determined by economic phenomena; that capitalism is naturally oppressive; and that all the institutions of the democratic capitalistic state have been created to defend the existing oppressive system. Starting from these premises, they analyze society with a method that they call deconstructing, which purportedly aims at finding the reasons why institutions—including social mores and customs—are what they are. Given their premises, in reality they aim at showing how sexism, white supremacism, and other chauvinistic institutions are the result of capitalism.[14] For them, as it was for Marx, liberal economic ideas are just an instrument that the capitalists have invented to oppress the world. Globalization, for them, is just the most recent invention of the oppressors and, therefore, it should be stopped. If this is achieved, and liberalism is defeated, the world would be free of sexism, racism, and exploitation. Politically, they have also copied Marx. Claiming to defend tolerance, they have created an environment of intolerance in the shape of political correctness. They preach militancy and see compromise as treachery. It is Marx again, in disguise. Marxism, however, is reemerging in a more open fashion as well.

History is full of ironies. One of the most marked of them is that Marxists would take courage to reemerge from the very trends that brought about the demise of their ultimate creation. The neo-Marxists see the Connectivity Revolution—the technological advance that sealed the fate of their Soviet Union—as the harbinger of the collapse of capitalism and the blooming of the Communist Paradise. As in the past, they are calling for a class struggle and revolution. As in the past, they are using the tensions of the transformation to attack democracy and capitalism.

While there are many different Marxist interpretations of today's reality, they all share some fundamental features. First, they see the development of connectivity as yet another instrument of exploitation invented by the capitalists to keep the rest of the world society in economic bondage. Second, they see that the social turmoil caused by connectivity, and particularly by its associated globalization, will mark the last stage of capitalism. Third, they see class struggle, insurrection, and the banning of private ownership of means of production as the way to seal the fate of capitalism and establish the foundation of a new paradise on earth that is none other than the old Communist Paradise.

The idea that connectivity and globalization are inventions of the capitalists to exploit the rest of the world has many shades, going from the straightforward conspiracy theory—there are some dark characters managing the whole process through the World Bank, the International Monetary Fund, the World Trade Organization, and the Internet—to more sophisticated theories where faceless capitalists are taking advantage of the technological revolution to keep on exploiting the population. Those more knowledgeable of Marx's theories even believe that the Connectivity Revolution is good both because the problems it poses for the survival of capitalism are insurmountable and because the new technologies establish a good basis for the Communist Paradise.

Thus far, the most sophisticated exposition of a Marxist version of the Connectivity Revolution is that contained in *Empire*, a book written by a professor of Duke University and an inmate of an Italian prison, published by Harvard University Press.[15] The authors, Michael Hardt (the professor) and Antonio Negri (the inmate) have a clear perception of the shift from vertical to horizontal forms of social organization that has taken place with the Connectivity Revolution. Looking at this shift from the Marxists' perspective of power, they call the vertical shape the *disciplinary society* and the horizontal one the *society of control*. The society of control functions based on what they call "biopower," which they define as the "form of power that regulates social life from its interior. . . . "[16] With connectivity that power has been organized in networks. Thus far, this seems to be a conventional view of our reality. However, they say that, lurking behind what we see of connectivity, there is something they call *Empire,* the most sophisticated instrument of exploitation that human minds have been able to invent. This is not a group of specific people but an impersonal social order that grows on its own impulse to enslave humankind—presumably with the exception of some unmentioned capitalistic monsters benefiting from this growing menace. Different from the capitalism of Marx's times, this new Empire has no nationality. It is global in the sense that it exercises its power not only internationally but also domestically, in all countries in the world.

In typical one-dimensional fashion, the authors say that the existence of Empire makes possible the existence of the counter-Empire, which would then lead the proletarians into their insurrection. Such an insurrection is more likely now than ever before because the proletariat has grown explosively with the Connectivity Revolution. In the new world of connectivity everything—not just industrial machinery but also computers, telephones, multimedia, CD players, knowledge—is an instrument of production and therefore an instrument of exploitation. Thus, almost everybody is a subject of exploitation, so much so that a new term, "multitudes," is needed to name the exploited, replacing the more limited term "proletarians," which referred only to industrial workers. The multitudes can now revolt under the leadership of the counter-Empire, dethrone the Empire and use the network for the advance of humankind.

Like Marx, these new Marxists are very vague regarding what would be the shape of the society that would emerge from their revolution. They have, however, some proposals. First, there would be a global passport, which means that all frontiers would be open for everyone to cross. Second, this would not create a gigantic migration to the rich countries because there would be a *social wage* for everybody in the world, which would guarantee equality of income to all people in all places. Third, the private ownership of means of production would be banned in a process that they call the *reappropriation* of capital by the multitudes. Since the authors insist that one of the features of the new society is that everything is a means of production, this presumably means that the counter-Empire would prohibit the private ownership of everything. We would expropriate ourselves. It is as if, paraphrasing the popular saying, the authors are urging us to say that we have discovered who the exploiter is and the exploiter is us. We could carry out this revolution by saying simultaneously "we are expropriating ourselves" to "reappropriate" our capital and then going back to work. The authors, however, are not proposing this. They leave no doubt that they are talking about establishing a regime similar to that of the Soviet Union, where the state would own everything and would use instruments immensely more powerful to reduce the population to subservience.

They also do not leave any doubt regarding the methods that should be used to eliminate private ownership and the putrefaction of capitalism. In the final section of the book, called *Militant*, they describe what a militant Marxist should do:

Here is the strong novelty of militancy today: it repeats the virtues of insurrectional actions of two hundred years of subversive experience, but at the same time it is linked to a new world, a world that knows no outside . . . This is a revolution that no power will control—because biopower and communism, cooperation and revolution remain together, in love, simplicity, and also innocence. This is the irrepressible lightness and joy of being communist.[17]

In reality, there is nothing new in this exposition of Marxism. What the authors of this piece call the Empire is just an extension to the global level of what Marx called the superstructure—the set of values, principles, and institutions created by the dominant class to fool the exploited into obedience. The denunciation of this Empire as the last stage of capitalism sounds quite similar to Lenin's denunciation of the nineteenth-century imperialism as the last stage of capitalism. Even the name evokes Lenin's piece on imperialism.

Like Marx, his current followers are inconsistent in the projection of Marx's laws of history to the future. Marx always insisted that revolutions do not happen just because the exploited are unhappy. For a true revolution to happen, he repeated frequently, the methods of production should have changed in such a way as to automatically give the power to the new exploiters—as it happened, for example, when the capitalists replaced the feudal lords as exploiters because their methods of production were superior to those of feudalism. The substitution of regimes came just naturally, imbedded in the new methods of production. Thus, in a Marxist sense, the natural rulers of industrial capitalism were the industrial capitalists—something that history proved right, because the Communists could not manage their industrial states without terrorizing the population. To predict, under the Marxist logic, that everybody would control the new connectivity economy, the authors should assume that effectively, the new economy leads everybody to control it, in a natural way. This is actually happening in the liberal states. The Internet is a great equalizer. But, then, why call for the revolt of the counter-Empire? Why call for the 200 years of insurrectional experience, in a clear reference to violence? This is because at a deeper level their movements are manifestations of the Will to Power of Nietzsche. They are looking for power.

Conceptually, the neo-Marxists are right in pointing out the grave social problems that the Connectivity Revolution is posing to the survival of democracy and capitalism. They are wrong, however, in their diagnosis of the situation. They are making the same mistake that Marx made when blaming the social turmoil of his times, not on the deep technological revolution that was changing all social relationships but on capitalism. The neo-Marxists are taking the disruptions caused by the development of connectivity as the natural consequences of capitalism, not as a temporary phenomenon. Following the proposals for action that the neo-Marxists derive from their faulty analysis would lead to the same destructive results that the followers of Marx generated in real life.

This, however, is not a mistake. As in Marx, one can see through the neo-Marxists' claims that the new networks of the multitudes would be controlled by the state, which, obviously, should be managed by people as smart as they are. As it was true with Marx, we are seeing here not a scientific approach to understanding reality but an instrument in the struggle for power. This is one of the quotations that the authors of Empire chose to put at the beginning of the book that says in very clear words: "Every tool is a weapon if you hold it right."

Marx's and Lenin's vanguards of the proletariat and Nietzsche's supermen are back. Now, however, they are called *Militants*. As the authors of Empire say, they don't have to be representative. "Political militancy," they say, " . . . must rediscover what has always been its proper form: not representational but constituent activity."[18] They only have to be creative artists, as Nietzsche would have called them, to create a new world with blood and fire. As in Marx's time, the solutions that the neo-Marxists propose can be summarized in two: stop change and go back to the vertical orders of the past. The word *resist* is repeated many times in the Empire book when referring to what the multitudes should do. This is what Marxism is all about: resistance against change.

One can easily understand the enthusiasm of the Marxists in the current world. In a sinister way, the new technologies are ideal for the creation of a truly Marxist social order. A central state can use Internet as a means of propaganda and a way to spy on its citizens and control their actions (making true the definition of connectivity produced by the authors of Empire, *the society of control*). The new technologies even make possible the insertion of chips that could report on the actions and words of every citizen in a society and scanning methods make it possible to give an alarm when someone approaches some particular individual or place, or pronounces certain words. Of course, creativity would stop in such a world. But that is not important if the Communist regime takes over the world—which is the dream of these neo-Marxists.

All this is nonsensical. It would be easy to dismiss these calls for violence as intellectual gibberish hidden in books that few people will read. Even if many try, not many will finish reading them. None of the neo-Marxists inherited the powerful, concrete style of Marx, much less the startling passion of Nietzsche.

However, we must remember that traditional Marxism was also nonsensical and still attracted millions of people, including many of the so-called intellectuals. This was so because some people look for destructive ideas as a means to give legitimacy to purposes or emotions they cannot confess and some others because they want to believe in something that will give a sense to their lives in the confusing world of a radical social transformation. If the Marxists repeat that the problems of the transformation are the result of the weaknesses of democracy and economic freedom rather than the natural result of a technological revolution many people will believe them, particularly as the tensions of the transformation become stronger.

Providing philosophical legitimacy to destructive actions is the prologue to destructiveness, even if the underlying philosophy is flawed. As for the number of readers that these philosophers can reach, we have to remember that only a minuscule minority of all the Communists that have existed ever read Marx's books. But they heard that a famous philosopher supported their destructive actions and this was enough to give legitimacy to their destructiveness.

Ironically, the leftist intellectual radicals are in the company of extreme rightists who oppose globalization based on a vision of reality that is directly opposite to that of the academic intellectuals. For them, globalization is not a vehicle for the whites to dominate the non-whites—something that they would see with sympathy—but a vehicle for the non-whites to corrupt and dominate the whites. Like the intellectuals, however, they attack globalization as the last manifestation of something bigger: liberal ideas. The notorious National Alliance, one of the groups that have emerged in the United States to proclaim these ideas, says in its statement of principles that "we need an economic system which, in contrast to Marxism, allows individuals to succeed in proportion to their capability and energy, but, which, in contrast to capitalism, does not allow them to engage in socially or racially harmful activity, such as eliciting competition or importing non-white labor."[19] Some of these groups are indistinguishable from the religious fundamentalists that we have already discussed, defending what they see as the essentially white Christianity against the attacks of the non-whites, non-Christians.[20]

Even more ironically, the leftist intellectuals are also allied with some of the people they despise the most: the entrepreneurs in the developed and developing countries that are trying to stop globalization purely to defend their economic interests, and the trade unions that work for them. Thus, opposition to globalization in the developed countries has brought together strange allies—people who want to keep the existing system in place with people who want to go back to the times of intolerance and vertical assertion of a social order.

The mechanism most proposed by the rightists in both developed and developing countries is protection against imports. In the developed countries, however, protectionism is being mixed with increasingly xenophobic feelings, motivated by the idea that it is foreigners who are causing all the problems of the modern world, both in their countries and through immigrations to the developed countries. In *The Death of the West: How Dying Populations and Immigrant Invasions Are Threatening Our Country and Civilization*,[21] Patrick Buchanan traces a sharp line that is very similar to that traced by one of the intellectual ancestors of Nazism, Oswald Spengler, in *The Decline of the West* and by Samuel Huntington in *The Clash of Civilizations and the Remaking of World Order* in our days. Spengler thought that the enemy of German society, the carrier of decline, was civilization, the urban and Jewish invention that threatened the German rural Volk culture. Huntington and Buchanan think that the enemy is the mass of people in the developing countries, which are debasing civilization from the outside with terrorism (Huntington) and from the inside through immigrations (Buchanan). Following Nietzsche, Spengler also added the need for the Caesar-man who would come to fight the invaders and reaffirm Volk culture. Buchanan and Huntington do not even suggest something like that. Instead, Buchanan proposes policies aimed at increasing the birth rate of the proper people in the developed societies and restricting immigrations. This means isolation and reversing globalization and the resurging liberalism.

Quite worryingly, these ideas tend to split society and therefore go against the mainstay of stability in the societies that adjust more harmoniously to deep social transformations—their social cohesion—and, not by chance, are coming out precisely when cohesion is weakening in the most advanced countries. Moreover, the problems that must be resolved to revert this disintegration are worse than those faced by the industrializing societies of the past, because in their times, what had to be integrated was a society defined within the confines of a nation state with common history and customs. Today, in these times of globalization, the sense of social cohesion must be expanded to include immigrants with different history, race, and customs, and even to include people in other countries. As the history of Nazism and Communism clearly show, ideas that trace a line between "us" and "them" and then portray a conflict between those on the different sides of the line run counter to what is needed. Moreover, as I discussed in the introduction regarding Huntington's portrait of the problems of our times in terms of a confrontation between the West and the rest of the world, and as an analysis of Buchanan's ideas about racial demographic policies shows, such lines do not bear any relation with the reality of our social problems—least of all when we discuss the dangers posed against the shape of social order in the developed countries.

Finally, these isolationist ideas, which built obstacles for progress all along history, are likely to lead to even more negative results if they are implemented in these days. Given the development that connectivity has already reached, protection is not likely to produce its avowed benefits—maintain employment and income in the protected sectors. On the contrary, it is likely to accelerate the decline in both magnitudes, aggravating the problems of adjustment. With the world economy taking the costs of the unavoidable adjustments, while refusing to take the full benefits of connectivity, social disintegration would become a real possibility, and the threats of chaos, terrorism, and destructiveness would loom large in our future.

The worst of the possibilities that we might face is that, in reaction against the threats coming from countries and societies already trapped by destructive ideologies, the most civilized countries in the world would fall prey to protectionist, isolationist, and racist ideas, reversing the liberal principles that gave birth to them. If such thing happens, the societies that today are democratic and capitalist may survive in the more violent world they would be contributing to create, but they would lose their essence because democracy and economic liberalism would die in the process. In a tragically perverse way, the savagism of those who, today, oppose progress would lead civilization to commit suicide by deleting the liberal ideas that gave birth to it. This could lead the world into a nightmare worse than that we lived in the twentieth century.

NOTES

1. Richard Sennet, *The Corrosion of Character: The Personal Consequences of Work in the New Capitalism* (New York and London: W.W. Norton & Company, 1998).

2. Ibid., p. 10.

3. Ibid., p. 147.

4. Allan Bloom, *The Closing of the American Mind* (New York: Simon & Schuster, 1987), pp. 117–18.

5. Benjamin Disraeli, *Sybil or the Two Nations* (New York: Oxford University Press, 1981), pp. 64–65.

6. Hermann Hesse, *The Longing of Our Time for a Worldview*, eds. Anton Kaes, Martin Jay, and Edward Dimendber, *The Weimar Republic Sourcebook* (Berkeley: University of California Press, 1994), pp. 365–68.

7. Arnold Toynbee, *A Study of History* vol. 1 of D. C. Somervell's abridgement (Oxford, U.K.: Oxford University Press, 1957), p. 515.

8. See John L. Esposito, "Contemporary Islam: Reformation or Revolution?" ed. John L. Esposito, *The Oxford History of Islam*, (Oxford, U.K.: Oxford University Press, 1999), pp. 656–57.

9. Ibid., pp. 658–61.

10. See Mark Juergensmeyer, *Terror in the Mind of God: The Global Rise of Religious Violence* (Berkeley: University of California Press, 2000) for an analysis of the groups of Christians connected with terrorism.

11. Friedrich Nietzsche, "On the Genealogy of Morals: First Essay, Sections 7–8," in Walter Kaufmann, *Basic Writings of Nietzsche* (New York: The Modern Library, 1968), pp. 470–71.

12. Lenin in an article written for *Krasnyi Mech (The Red Sword)*, a weekly published by the Cheka, the original KGB. Quoted in Clark, *Lenin: A Biography* (New York: Harper and Row, 1990), p. 378.

13. See Friedrich Engels in "The Origin of the Family, Private Property and the State," in Tucker, *The Marx-Engels Reader* (New York and London: W. W. Norton and Company, 1978), pp. 734–59.

14. For an exposition of these ideas, see for example, Mark Rupert, *Ideologies of Globalization: Contending Visions of a New World Order*, RIPE Series in Global Political Economy (London and New York: Routledge, 2000), pp. 5–10.

15. Michael Hardt and Antonio Negri, *Empire* (Cambridge and London: Harvard University Press, 2000).

16. Ibid., p. 23.

17. Ibid., p. 413.

18. Ibid., p. 412.

19. Quoted in Mark Rupert, *Ideologies of Globalization, Contending Visions of a New World Order*, RIPE Series in Global Political Economy (London and New York: Routledge, 2000), p. 107.

20. See Mark Juergensmeyer, *Terror in the Mind of God: The Global Rise of Religious Violence* (Berkeley: University of California Press, 2000).

21. Patrick Buchanan, *The Death of the West: How Dying Populations and Immigrant Invasions Are Threatening Our Country and Civilization* (New York: Thomas Dune Books 2002).

CHAPTER 6

The Inversion of Reality

As Arnold Toynbee wrote in the quotation at the beginning of the previous chapter, societies and groups that cannot deal with the blast of change are liable to react to them by creating a chimera, which may take the form of futurism or archaism. As we have seen before, however, futuristic doctrines of this kind tend to be inversions of reality: what the people propounding the abandonment of economic freedoms are demanding as a way to modernize our social structures is in fact a return to old and archaic forms of social organization. Today, they celebrate the people who protest against the opening of the economies to foreign competition, against privatization of inefficient state-owned enterprises, and against economic freedom in general, as the heralds of the emergence of this new social order, where the state would introduce rationality into the chaotic functioning of the markets. They say that this would be modern and fair, and people believe them. In fact, they are repeating what Marx, Lenin, and Hitler said, and they are going against the grain of social progress: the creation of societies progressively able to function within a horizontal social order, one that would function not on the basis of vertical commands but on the basis of a strong social cohesion.

In fact, this is the trend that technological progress has made possible in the last 200 years, which is the period in history in which the concept and reality of technological progress was invented. The societies that preceded industrialization were rigid and vertical; industry allowed for, and actually demanded, the functioning of more horizontal forms of social organization. This is what the countries that today lead the world created during the last 200 years. Those that went the way of government intervention were left behind, and those that did so to the extreme collapsed.

Connectivity is making possible, and actually demanding, the creation of a still more horizontal society, based more firmly on social cohesion than the one we are living in today. Hierarchies are becoming obsolete in many dimensions of our economic and social life under the impact of the Internet. Even borders are becoming obsolete in many ways. The way of the future is horizontal, not vertical; the symbol of the new society is not a pyramid, but a network.

This trend toward a more horizontal way of life is what people tend to resist the most, however. Vertical structures constrain freedom but give the illusion of security. In this chapter, I trace a parallel between the resistance to horizontal ways of organization at the very beginning of the Industrial Revolution and the resistance to change that is emerging in our times. I do that by focusing on the process that, as an example of the inversion of reality that accompanies resistance to change, is portrayed as the big leap into democracy and economic freedom, while in fact was a terrible convulsion of resistance to change: the French Revolution. The similarity between the great protests that preceded the Revolution with those that we are seeing today is remarkable in their opposition to a more horizontal world.

The history of the French Revolution is surrounded by thick myths. According to these, the terrible events of 1789–92, which made the words *terror* and *terrorist* applicable to governments, were prompted by the people's strong commitment to freedom, and their success set France firmly in the path of democracy and economic modernity. None of these assertions is true. The Revolution was started by the nobles to perpetuate the privileges they were losing as a result of the modernization of French society. The success of the Revolution brought about a reign of terror, worse than any absolute monarchy, and then the rule of an Emperor that reestablished the main features of the regime that the Revolution had toppled. Then, for a century, France lagged behind unrevolutionary Britain in terms of both economic and political development, and even behind the politically archaic Germany in economic terms.

It is a historic fact that the nobles started the Revolution. They, however, were not the only unhappy group in pre-Revolutionary France. Practically all the rest of the population was discontent with the instability brought about by the transition to modernity and opposed modernization. In comparison with the population, Louis XVI looked progressive. Contrary to what is normally asserted, he made many efforts to remove the obstacles to progress that were ingrained in the old order. But these invariably made him increasingly unpopular and brought him closer to his downfall. The rigidity of France was more ingrained in the minds and hearts of its people than in those of its rulers.

Ironically, the problems that led France to its Revolution came from what it was considered, at the time, its claim to modernity: the political and economic structure that Louis XIV had put in place in the seventeenth century. Even today, the Sun King is deemed as a great statesman because he concluded the unification of France and created the first centralized state in Europe under professional bureaucrats, chosen by their capacity rather than by right of birth.

To accomplish this feat, which required the neutralization of the feudal nobility, Louis relied on both brute force and enticement. He resolved his conflicts with the most elevated nobles by separating them from their fiefdoms and bringing them to Versailles to a life of ease and luxury. Other nobles he bribed with increased privileges, which allowed them to live in splendid idleness. In the economic field, he substituted the tight control that the feudal institutions imposed on the local producers with even tighter controls imposed by the central government. Thus, different from the process in Britain, the nobles did not lead the unification of the country. This was led by the central state. The nobles were either bribed or forced to accept it. This process weakened the intermediate stratum that existed at the time in other European countries between the central power and the population, an event that would have momentous consequences in the development of France.

The man who helped Louis XIV to centralize political and economic power was Jean Baptiste Colbert. The King appointed him as his Comptroller-General, the equivalent to Minister of Finance, and charged him with the task of creating a unified economy, geared to producing the industrial goods that France needed to keep for its position as the most powerful military power in Europe. Colbert first focused on the basics. He decided that cheap food was needed to sustain large armies, and established a thorough system of controls on the price of grains. To ensure enforcement, he ruled that only people with licenses issued by the government could trade in grains, effectively giving monopoly privileges to license holders over certain regions. On the industrial side, he decided to promote the creation of new industries by granting them monopolies until they were well established. Enforcing this also required the establishment of a system of licenses in the industrial sector. He also granted tax exemptions and state financing to industrial firms, at interest rates lower than those prevailing in the market.

To ensure the harmonious functioning of this system, Louis XIV created an all-encompassing corporative state that would be the envy of modern supporters of state intervention. For each industry, the government regulated product design, quality of output, production methods, sales volume, prices, finances, wages, and recruitment and promotion practices.

Colbert made work obligatory, granting 38 days of rest per year in addition to Sundays. To give an example of the standards that the private industries should aim at, Colbert nationalized the famous Gobelin factory in Paris and turned it into a model of efficiency and quality. He absorbed several of the feudal guilds, which controlled production at the local level, into a national system of guilds that enforced his production controls. He, however, failed in carrying out one of the most important reforms required to unify the country: the removal of the domestic trade impediments erected by the local guilds and other local institutions to protect themselves against competition from other parts of France. This hindered the formation of a national market until after the Revolution.[1]

The French statesmen of the eighteenth century identified the problems that the mercantilist policies of Louis XIV had created. While Colbert's strategies had allowed Louis XIV to be a more absolutist king than his royal colleagues in neighboring nations and to establish a more centralized national bureaucracy than those emerging in other European countries, they had also introduced a fatal rigidity in the country. His economic regulations, while initially successful in promoting the creation of incipient industries, choked economic growth.[2] Price controls on agricultural products and the high rents that the government guaranteed to the intermediaries discouraged production to the point that large extensions of fertile land were left idle. The system of licensed monopolies encouraged complacency in the few individuals that were fortunate enough to get a license and discouraged the economic creativity of the rest of the population. Altogether, the mercantilist policies killed the entrepreneurial spirit of France.

Seeing across the Channel, the French statesmen of the eighteenth century realized that France was trailing well behind liberal England in economic terms even before the Industrial Revolution began in earnest in the British Islands. Britain was the main exception to the rigid social order of Europe, which largely resembled that of France. There, the state intervention in the economy was nonexistent; new enterprises were not funded by the government but by private investors, directly or through the stock exchange; and people did not need government permission to engage in any productive activity. French visitors—including Voltaire—were surprised at the ease with which individuals could move up and down the social ladder in Britain. They also admired the absence of privilege. They noted that aristocrats paid the same turnpike tolls as common people. The Peers had the right to be tried by the House of Lords but, if condemned, they were publicly sent to the same gallows as any other criminal. In 1760, Lord Ferrers was executed for murdering his servant, something unheard of in continental Europe. Also importantly, trade and finance were not deprecated in England as it was in most of continental Europe. Business success competed with nobility of origin as a source of social respect. As much as traditions in the continent legitimized government control of the economy, the British had a long tradition of economic freedom. These trading traditions were the source of British progress. They were also the source of a deep contempt for Britain in continental Europe. Expressing this contempt, Napoleon later called Britain "a nation of shopkeepers." But it was this nation of shopkeepers that carried in its womb the Industrial Revolution and this showed in the economic dynamism of the British Isles, which established a stark contrast with France's stagnation.

Looking at the British, many Frenchmen understood that the underlying trend of the Industrial Revolution was a push for a more horizontal society. Industrialization increased the complexity of economic relations to a point that the centralized control of the feudal and mercantilist ages was no longer practical. A web of contracts between private parties became the natural mechanism to introduce order in both the economic and political domains, replacing the strict commands of both feudal lords and guilds. All the dimensions of economic life that had been controlled in the previous decades and centuries—prices, wages, production volumes, imports, hiring, and firing—came under pressure to be liberated for the simple reason that they could not be controlled any longer. It became impossible to tie peasants to the land. In the more dynamic industrial economy that was emerging, people had to change jobs, move to other places. The size of industrial production and transactions also pushed for the elimination of barriers to trade, not just between the petty localities of the feudal world, but across countries as well. Politically, democracy—also the result of a contract among equals—became the logical response to the complexities of the life of this new society.

Belying their image of useless mummies, the French statesmen of the eighteenth century realized that free markets were essential for the development of industry and devoted substantial energies to try to catch up with Britain. The most thorough efforts of modernization were carried out by a series of comptroller-generals who served under both Louis XV and his successor and grandson, Louis XVI. These functionaries were members of a group called the *physiocrats,* who believed that the progress of France was being hindered by the pervasive intervention of the state in the economy. The physiocrats prescribed fiscal prudence, economic liberalization, and policies aimed at developing an independent private sector.[3] These policies were truly modern and progressive, consistent with the Industrial Revolution that was about to take place. People resisted them strenuously.

In the 1760s, the physiocrats removed the regulations imposed on the transshipments of grain—which included price controls, licensing requirements for the people trading on grains, as well as restrictions on trading across regions and on the places where transactions could take place. People rioted, ransacked granaries, and prevented barges containing grain to depart to other regions. The political problems became so grave that the government was forced to restore most of the restrictions, granting again monopolistic licenses to traders and limiting their geographical scope.

In 1774, Louis XV died and his grandson became Louis XVI. The new king revamped the government. He appointed as comptroller-general the most determined of all the physiocrats, Anne-Robert Jacques Turgot, Baron de l'Aulne. The new comptroller-general obtained the new sovereign's approval for a thorough reform of the economy, which had it been implemented, would have turned France into a liberal economy similar to Britain. Turgot wanted free trade, free labor, free capital, and no government intervention. He emphasized the importance of educating the population with the latest industrial techniques, which the government supported with the publication of wonderfully illustrated manuals. He also sent deputations to study the British industries. He appointed his friends Condorcet and d'Alembert to a committee aimed at improving river navigation and, an additional touch of modernity, reducing pollution. He wanted to decentralize power to local assemblies. It is impossible to think of a more progressive program, even today.[4]

Turgot started by dealing with the problem of agriculture. The production of food, particularly grains, was not keeping up with the population growth, while there were large tracks of idle land. People blamed the landlords for this problem, which in reality was the result of Louis XIV's policies. Idle lands were not cultivated because it was not profitable to do it, both because the prices of grain were controlled by the state, and because a lion's share of these prices were kept by intermediaries enjoying the monopolistic powers also granted by the state.

Following on the track of the earlier physiocrats, Turgot liberalized again the prices of grain and its derivatives, including bread, in all parts of France except Paris. Knowing that this measure would lead to uncertainty in the price of these products, encouraging hoarding and excessive prices, he arranged beforehand the importation of grain from abroad. He also removed the local tolls imposed on the product, abolished the monopolies, and disbanded the administrative bodies that granted them. Pierre Samuel Dupont de Nemours, a physiocrat who eventually established the famous American firm bearing his name, wrote an introduction to the edict. Voltaire was elated and sent Turgot a letter congratulating him.

As in the 1760s, the people revolted against the liberalization of the prices of grain. In a dramatic defense of the people who exploited them, they burned farms, emptied granaries, threw their contents to the Seine, and blocked the way of the imported grain coming from Le Havre to Paris. More ominously, a mob 5,000 strong marched on Versailles and would have stormed it had not Louis restored the price controls on the spot. Turgot protested and prevailed. Louis raised the controls again when the mob went away; the imported grain arrived; the grain prices fell; forcing hoarders to sell; and the crisis ended.

Turgot took advantage of this victory. He abolished the monopolies of chandlers, merchants, and porters. Then he disbanded the powerful *Bourse of Sceaux and Poissy,* which set the prices of meat and fish, and abolished the regulations that forced the sale of certain parts of the animals through special guilds. Encouraged by the speed of his reforms, he then proposed to finish feudalism altogether. He wanted to abolish all trade guilds and their monopolies, and the restrictions they imposed on nonmembers who wanted to work in their activities. Finally, he wanted to eliminate the *corvee,* the forced labor that the state imposed on the commoners to build roads. Instead, Turgot proposed to finance public works with a tax on property paid equally by all sectors of the population, including the nobility.[5]

This was too much. The new measures encountered a solid wall of opposition. They caused, or threatened to cause, the same response as the liberalization of grain prices had. Most local authorities chose not to enforce them, with the support of the people who would benefit from these measures, including the reduction of their tax burden caused by the taxation of the lands of the nobles. Turgot reacted by sending opponents and procrastinators to the Bastille. When Louis hesitated, Turgot told him unceremoniously that he (the King) was not only a bad judge of men but also a weakling. This was another mistake. Louis dismissed him and restored the guilds and other restrictions on free enterprise, to great contentment of the nobility and the population at large.[6]

While this was going on, the French nobility was in the last stages of a decline that had started under Louis XIV. Most of the nobles had lost touch with the people, either because they lived in Versailles or because, even if living in their own localities, they had withdrawn from any economic activity different from collecting rents. Their political functions having been largely superseded by the bureaucracy, they had no clear reason to exist. While many nobles participated in the creation of modern businesses and increased their wealth in the second half of the eighteenth century, most of them looked for bureaucratic positions in the centralized government as the sinecures that would afford them a living. However, the competition of a growing middle class for these positions reduced drastically the probabilities they had of getting them. Being part of the centralized apparatus of government, those that succeeded in getting bureaucratic positions lacked credibility to mediate solutions between the king and the population. The French nobility became a weak anachronism, incapable of mobilizing the people of their localities to the defense of the old order—or of their own skin. France had lost the intermediate stratum that could give stability to society.

The majority of the nobles tried to shape up their declining economic basis by demanding additional economic privileges from the crown—such as increased tax exemptions and the exclusive right to occupy lucrative positions in the national bureaucracy. They wanted to eliminate the competition of the middle class. In the late 1780s, as France was going down under the weight of the unsustainable fiscal deficits created by a war against England that started with strong popular support, the nobles forced Louis XVI to call the Estates General, believing that they would be able to negotiate new privileges against some immediate taxes and contributions. Instead, as everybody knows, the convocation of the Estates General was the beginning of their own end.

These are the facts. They show that the old regime broke not because most of the people wanted to change and a minority wanted to keep things as they were, but because *most of the people did not want to change,* and things were changing by themselves. Louis XVI fell and lost his head because he tried to accommodate change and because, in the view of his subjects, he was a weak ruler. He destroyed the legitimacy of his dynasty because he was unable to stop change.

When seen from this perspective, there is no contradiction between the supposedly democratic nature of the French Revolution and the emergence of the autocratic Napoleonic Empire only a few years later. Napoleon was popular with his and subsequent generations of country fellows not only because he gave France a dream of military superiority, but also because he was able to restore predictability to the social and economic relations in his country. He reestablished absolutist power while keeping in place a pliant National Assembly. Democracy would come back to France in a sustainable way only in the 1870s, almost one century after the Revolution, when many other countries already enjoyed democratic regimes and had been doing so for several decades—a fact that makes one wonder what did the Revolution accelerate. Economically, Napoleon protected local production from foreign competition, granted state credit to industries, controlled wages, and regulated the operations of bakers, butchers, and manufacturers in general. With these policies, he restored Louis XIV's regime, the one that the revolutionaries supposedly had aimed at dethroning. Napoleon was so successful in France because, *through him, the Revolution reestablished the Old Regime.*

Resistance to change had the same retarding effects in the economic dimension. The restoration of Louis XIV's policies delayed France's industrialization and its economic progress in general throughout the nineteenth century. After having been, without dispute, the most powerful economy in Europe, it slipped well behind other countries after the Revolution. It took France more than a century to catch up with other countries in Europe and the United States in terms of industrial development. France was one of the latecomers. The companies that led the Industrial

Revolution were not those enjoying the paternalistic protection that the Napoleonic regime copied from Louis XIV and then legated again to France, but the free enterprises that flourished in Britain, and then in other countries that enjoyed economic freedom.

France, however, was not the only country that exploded in chaos and then in revolutions and destructiveness. After the defeat of Napoleon in 1815, countries in most of Europe started to liberalize gradually, following the lead of Britain, which, after a long process, went into full trade freedom in the midyears of the century. It was, like our times, a time of free trade agreements, of progressive liberalization of the domestic economies. However, liberalization started to be reversed in the 1870s. State intervention in the economy and protection against foreign competition spread all over Europe and the countries adopting it progressed very fast, particularly Germany. This was the time when the second stage of the Industrial Revolution—that led by chemicals and metallurgy—was raging. The German government intervened to foster the creation of cartels, which helped German industrialists to attain the large economies of scale that these industries offered. British producers, by contrast, found it difficult to consolidate their operations with those of their competitors. In terms of size, the median member of the German cartels was four times as big as its British counterpart. The same happened in terms of standardization. In 1900, German steelmakers met the needs of their customers with 34 different products, while their dispersed British competitors needed 122. The result of these developments was that the British products lost their competitive advantage. Around 1914, the Germans were able to sell steel plate at prices 20–25 percent lower than their British competitors.[7]

Germany and its imitators, however, shared a common trait: they had begun their industrialization within archaically vertical political and social forms of social organization. While some of them grew very fast economically, the very speed of their growth posed tremendous pressures on those vertical structures. In Germany, for example, which was an absolutist regime with some pretenses of parliamentary democracy, the predominance of the feudal lords was transferred to the new industrial lords, who used their political power in the Reich to keep the workers repressed. Bismarck tried to resolve the contradiction between modern methods of production and archaic institutions by creating the first state-managed social security system, and protecting the enterprises against foreign and local competition to enable them to pay for the additional costs. In exchange for the new security brought to the workers, he restricted the powers of trade unions, giving absolute authority to the entrepreneurs in all labor matters. He even prohibited the participation of trade unions in political parties. To keep this system in place, and to extend the already excessive authority of employers, the industrialists in league with the

large landowners, created industrial associations that effectively managed
the economy. To counterbalance this enormous combination of economic
and political power, the workers built their own countrywide labor organizations. By the 1890s, when, with the fall of Bismarck, the prohibition
of political participation by the trade unions was lifted, the country was
already set for a one-dimensional fight for political and economic power
that would lead to the failed but extremely violent Bolshevik Revolution
of 1918–19, to the brief experience of democracy with the Weimar Republic
of 1918–33, to the radicalization of politics in the late 1930s, and then to
the accession of Hitler.

The conflicts that led to Hitler had begun with the logic of vertical
organizations established by Bismarck, which in turn, was just a revitali-
zation of the mercantilist regimes that had existed before the industrialization. All the countries that fell into these destructive regimes shared this
feature: all of them tried to insert the new forces of industrialization within
the archaic economic and political institutions of state control—including
Russia, Spain, Japan, and the countries of central Europe.

On the other hand, all the countries that went along to adjust peacefully
to the Industrial Revolution and create the modern industrial and democratic state—including all the Anglo-Saxon countries plus Belgium, the
Netherlands, Switzerland, and the Nordic countries—kept and extended
their economic and political freedoms throughout the period. Even countries that, like Sweden, created the welfare state later in their histories,
worked under total economic freedom during those years and beyond,
and relied on civic organizations, rather than on state-managed social
security systems, to resolve their social problems.[8] They became horizontal
societies based on economic freedoms and self-reliance.

The tradition of portraying opposition to change as a drive to accelerate
progress survived through the nineteenth century. The strength of this
tradition flared again in the second decade of the twentieth century, at the
end of World War I. It is flaring again in our times. TV news is full with
demonstrations against globalization, against the dislodging through privatization of exploitative bureaucracies entrenched in state-owned monopolies; against the elimination of price controls that ultimately prevent
the growth of supplies; against free trade agreements that would cheapen
the goods and services of the population and open new markets for the
local producers—although not for the inefficient ones that now finance
parts of the opposition. When one sees these people throwing stones and
listens to the reporters saying that they are protesting against that horrendous devil, globalization, one cannot help but remember those people in
France that succeeded in stopping the progress of their country for almost
a century, fighting against that equally horrendous devil, the modernization of the economic structures that was essential for progress in the

new industrial age that was dawning. And when intellectuals portray this as the fight of the masses against exploitation, one realizes that one is, again, watching a tragic inversion of reality. They want to keep in place the vertical structures of a gone past.

NOTES

1. See Will and Ariel Durant, *Rousseau and Revolution* (New York: Simon & Schuster, 1967), pp. 20–26.

2. Ibid., p. 25.

3. The physiocrats' theories were not identical to modern economic theory. They believed that all wealth came from land, thus underestimating the productive potential of reproducible capital—something that is quite understandable before the Industrial Revolution. But their policy advice was strikingly similar to what a modern economist would have recommended, except, maybe, for their idea that all taxes should be substituted by a tax on land. For a discussion of the physiocrats' ideas, see Simon Schama, *Citizens* (New York: Vintage Books, 1990), pp. 81–88, and Durant and Durant, *Rousseau and Revolution,* (New York: Simon & Schuster, 1967), pp. 71–80, 858–65.

4. See Simon Schama, *Citizens*, pp. 83–85 and Durant and Durant, *Rousseau and Revolution*, pp. 858–59.

5. Ibid., pp. 85–86.

6. Ibid., p. 87.

7. See David S. Landes, *The Unbound Prometheus* (Cambridge: Cambridge University Press 1997), pp. 263–69.

8. As discussed later in the book, the welfare state can coexist with economic freedom. This is the case in Sweden and other Nordic countries. Yet, during the adjustment of these countries to industrialization, they had not yet created the welfare state and were examples of totally free economies with very small governments and no state-managed social security. For a good narrative of this process, see Franklin D. Scott, *Sweden: The Country's History* (Carbondale: Southern Illinois University Press, 1988).

CHAPTER 7

Divisiveness and Social Interest

What leads a society to become rigid or flexible? What did Britain, the United States, Sweden, and similar countries have that Germany, Russia, and the other countries that fell into destructiveness lacked? Why do some counties tend to retrogress to vertical shapes of social organization? Our previous analysis suggests that the answers to these questions are intimately related to the way different societies deal with the problem of harmonizing the chaotic diversity of their members with the need for a uniform social order. That is, the answer is related to the set of ideas that keep society functioning as a unified body and the way they can accommodate the social changes caused by a technological revolution.

In every society, the ideas underlying social order are complex and sometimes contradictory. This is inevitable because there is a tension between permanence and change, two basic elements of social life. In a previous chapter, we discussed social order as a capital good, a set of institutions that enable individuals to do things that they could not do in isolation—a public good from which every member of society can take a serving. We focused the discussion on the relationship between order and change—how social order builds on previous sets of order—and saw rigidity as a negative trait of a social system. Certainly, rigidity is a negative feature of a social system taken as a whole. Yet, to be functional, a social order needs some permanent elements, some aspects that would never change. It is precisely the set of permanent elements that gives identity to a society and, more importantly, what lends an essential predictability to its behavior. What is the use of a social order if it is not stable, if one cannot be sure that it will last? Growth and change need those permanent elements to flourish. We live inserted in time and stable connections between the past and the future are essential to calculate if it is worth investing today to get benefits in the future. This is true not just in economic terms but also in every other aspect of life. To build on an existing infrastructure—the secret for developing an advanced society—makes sense only if such infrastructure is to last.

Thus, society can work only when there is a minimum level of predictability that allows people to believe that they will be able to reap the benefits of their current actions. Institutions, the complex system of rules of behavior structuring societies, give this minimum level of predictability. To introduce predictability, institutions have to restrict the ways open for individual behavior. At the same time, they have to allow for individual freedoms to satisfy the people's craving for growth. This poses a contradiction in terms of the requirements for a social organization to succeed in the long term: change is the engine of social order but permanence is its mainstay. Resolving this contradiction is the key to creating a society out of a conglomerate of people.

It is in the solution that different societies find to this conflict between a predictable social order, as given by stable unifying ideas, and social change coming from individuals pushing for a redefinition of such ideas that we can find the key to the difference between societies that absorb rapid change in a healthy way, and those that either blow up or attain an unstable and destructive equilibrium.

History shows that there is one feature that distinguishes rigid societies from flexible ones: the relationship between economic and political power. Countries where these two powers are fused into a single composite dimension—so that the government controls the economy—are on the side of rigidity, while those where they are separate—so that economic matters are dealt with by the market—fall on the side of flexibility. I call the first kind of societies *one-dimensional*, because power has only one dimension in them. Both political and economic matters are settled in that single dimension, which is, politically. The Tsarist society, pre-Hitler Germany, pre-militarist Japan, and other societies that fell prey to violent revolutions and destructive regimes were like that, and they coped with the Industrial Revolution in ways that reinforced these traits. Societies where the economic and political powers are separate are *multidimensional* because they open opportunities for success and failure in each of these dimensions. The separation of political and economic powers creates an umbrella under which other dimensions of life—art, academic pursuits, the civil society—tend to flourish. The societies that adjusted harmoniously to the Industrial Revolution had this feature. They were multidimensional.

Yet, the intervention of the state in the economy is a symptom, not the cause of the problems of rigid societies. As we have seen several times in history, just liberalizing the economy is no guarantee that economic freedom will prevail. One country after another has liberalized its economy only to reimpose state intervention in the economy after a few years. Moreover, it is clear that the presence of capitalism does not make the difference. Pre-Nazi Germany, after all, was capitalistic in the sense that the majority of the enterprises were private but there was no economic freedom, and society was so rigid and one-dimensional that it collapsed under the pressures of industrialization. The same can be said about many other countries, including developed and developing ones.

At the core of the difference between the one-dimensional and multi-dimensional societies is the attitude that people take regarding the satisfaction of their need for stability and predictability in social relations—a need that, as we discussed earlier, is rational because a society cannot function without a minimum of predictability.

Societies can take one of two basic positions in their search for predictability. The first position is that of societies holding as their ultimate objective the achievement or preservation of a certain set of circumstances. These can be defined in many ways, most frequently in terms of a certain pattern of income distribution; or of a certain distribution of the relative power of the different sectors of society; or even of a certain way of organizing economic activities. People in these societies derive the sense of stability from the permanence of this state of affairs and consider that their governments are legitimate only to the extent to which they keep it in place. That is, for them, stability is defined in a primary, objective, material way. They tell individuals, *Your circumstances will not change.* To deliver on this promise, governments in these societies have to restrict the economic and political freedoms of their citizens, preventing them from straying into creating activities or relationships that could disrupt the existing balance. Thus, the government has to assume the control not just of political but also of economic matters—fusing in this way economic and political power into a single magnitude. Without such control, the government would not be able to keep in place the desired state of affairs, or further its attainment. This is the origin of the one-dimensional state. The feudal and mercantilist societies that exist in most of continental Europe were of this kind. The Communist and Nazi regimes that evolved from them are the extreme forms of this social organization. They justified their totalitarian control of society on the creation of the state of perfection. They told individuals, *Your circumstances will not change once we get to our paradise.* What they fixed was the set of circumstances that would prevail in that paradise.

The second position is that taken by societies wanting to have certainty regarding the rules of the game—which means certainty regarding individual rights. In these societies, everything can change as long as these rights are preserved. They tell individuals, *Your circumstances may change, but your rights will always be preserved.* People in these societies derive their security from the certainty that their integrity as individuals will always be protected. This is the mandate to their governments. Society develops multidimensions and flexibility. This was the route taken by the countries that adjusted harmoniously to the Industrial Revolution.

There is no nothing in between these two basic positions. By giving priority to maintain an achieved or dreamed material status, countries taking the first position are ready to sacrifice everything in the pursuance of their concrete objective. Individual rights take second priority when colliding with this objective. Giving priority to individual rights is also an exclusive proposition. If such a priority has been established there is no given status, social dream, or ideal that can have more importance than those rights. The first position focuses on keeping stable the results, while the second one focuses on keeping stable the processes; the first looks at the ends, the second at the means.

The choice of priorities gives shape to the mechanisms that society uses to keep social order in place. The maintenance of a certain state of affairs is associated with a vertical order—that which relies on hierarchies—and the maintenance of individual rights with a horizontal one—that which emerges among equals. We may visualize the vertical social order as a pyramid, the horizontal one as a web. The stability of the pyramid depends on the strength of its vertical structures—that is, on the coercive power of the central decision makers—while that of the web depends on the strength of the individual links tying one person to the next. That is, vertical societies depend on authoritarian structures, while horizontal ones on social cohesion.[1]

The priority given to individual rights—which restrict the power of the state over the individual—leads to self-government—which empowers individuals to defend and extend their liberties. In this way, the micro-liberties give birth to complete freedom and self-determination. The fully democratic societies of the twentieth century developed in this way—from the micro to the macro. While the opposite process also happens—the reinforcement of the microfreedoms by the macroinstitutional setting—experience also shows that democratic institutions are easily eroded without the support of the population values. The social cohesion that makes freedom and democracy possible is thus rooted in the individual.

The two systems have competed with each other for centuries, imbedded in the societies that chose each of them as the basis for their social order. Each has its own advantages in terms of their effectiveness in promoting the material welfare of the population. The vertical society is more focused; the horizontal one more flexible.

The unity of purpose provided by vertical, rigid structures of social organization gives them an advantage in terms of effectiveness during periods of steady technological changes. This was the case in the period of the Industrial Revolution when bigger of the same was better—as it was in the last quarter of the nineteenth century and in most of the twentieth. When technological change becomes turbulent and unpredictable, however, planning the structure of something so complex and so rapidly shifting as an entire economy becomes an impossibility. It is in those moments when the flexibility of horizontal societies shines in sharp contrast with the woes experienced by the vertical, rigid regimes.

In the long run, comprising periods of steady and turbulent technological progress, history has demonstrated that countries giving first priority to individual rights not only attained the objective of protecting those rights. They also achieved better results in terms of attaining better objective conditions of life than the societies in the other set of countries. This was natural because this kind of society is more amenable to change and progress for several reasons.

First, the social order of societies giving first priority to individual rights is quite resilient because it is based on something that can always be preserved. The social order of countries aiming at attaining or preserving a set of circumstances is fragile and prone to collapse into chaos because it is based on something that is naturally ephemeral.

Second, the rule of individual rights neatly reconciles the need for a social order with the possibility of change. Society does not see change as a threat, but as the normal manifestation of the freedom of the individual. In contrast, the population wanting to keep in place a state of affairs naturally develops a negative attitude to change. Anything that disturbs the social and political equilibrium is seen as immoral and illegitimate.

Third, societies basing their stability on individual rights tend to develop self-reliant individuals. For this reason, the overall adjustment of horizontal societies takes place day by day, through the infinite adjustments that individuals make in their daily activities. In contrast, societies based on the maintenance of a status quo tend to develop individuals who think that the government has to resolve their problems. Economic success comes to depend on political power because governments can grant subsidies and protection to some individuals and not to others or appoint as managers of the state enterprises only people of a certain party. Equally, the government has the power of vanquishing someone not only politically but also economically. This turns political conflicts into all-or-nothing affairs, in which the winners take all, politically and economically, and the losers lose everything. Within such an environment, political violence becomes rational for all parties, creating a fertile field for cold-blooded destructiveness to emerge. That is why one-dimensional, vertical societies, where the state controls the economy, are also prone to catastrophic revolutions.

Fourth, since multidimensional societies are free from these all-or-nothing incentives, they are also free from the propensity to violence that they elicit. That is, multidimensional societies are not just more conducive to change, but they are also less likely to fall into destructive infighting because losses in one dimension of life can be compensated with gains in another. This happens not just because people can move from politics to economics or the other way around, but also because they can move from national to local politics, or from any starting point to independent institutions, such as universities or civil society organizations. This cannot happen in vertical societies where all power, national and local, political and economic, has to be concentrated to ensure the unity of society. The multidimensionality of life also facilitates political compromise enormously, as politicians can give advantage to their opponents in one dimension in exchange for gaining an advantage in another. Compromise is easier when there are many issues at hand than when there is only one; also, it is easier when there are many layers of power than when there is only one, overwhelming central power.

All these features of the multidimensional societies make them much more amenable to change than those of the one-dimensional ones. They also make the social order of the former much more resilient to change than the latter. Since we know for sure that change is going to take place in the long run, we can be sure that the horizontal, multidimensional order is by far the best, not just because it is compatible with freedom, but also because it tends to be more successful in terms of material and humane progress.

If flexible societies have the advantage in the long run, why do so many societies choose vertical, rigid forms of organization?

In short, vertical order is the most common because it is the easiest to obtain. The vertical order subordinates the diversity of a conglomerate to the will of a central decision-maker. It uses coercion to create uniformity out of diversity. The horizontal order is much more difficult to obtain because it does not create uniformity. Rather, it harmonizes the strains of diversity to produce a collective will, leaving diversity in place. Reducing the dispersion of the results of diversity to an acceptable range requires a very strong basis of self-control on the part of the individuals—ultimately rooted in shared values of respect for the *individual* freedoms of everyone else. Verticality is the only way to create social order when such self-control does not exist.

Societies without self-control need tyrannies to do what they are unable to do when in freedom—to cooperate with each other in the minimum way that is essential for the operation of a society. For this reason, they like tyrannies and fall into chaos when they do not have them. Thus, the ultimate source of rigidity, corruption, and destructiveness is social divisiveness.

The Nazis prevailed in Germany because the German society was deeply fragmented by social and political conflicts that the democratic Weimar Republic was unable to resolve. As no political party or coalition among them was able to generate a clear majority during the 1920s, the president of the country governed by decree. Then, when the Great Depression hit the country, Germany turned, in just four years, from a country where the extremes represented less than 10 percent of the votes into one where half of the voters wanted to destroy democracy through either Nazism or Communism. The country could have gone either way. However, the Nazis were the ones that benefited the most from this polarization. Their share of total votes went up from 3 to 37 percent, while that of the Communists went from 11 to 14 percent.[2] Together, they represented 50 percent of the votes.

People in the other 50 percent of the voters were increasingly demoralized about the system, too. They were fragmented into five major parties and several splinter parties. The largest of them (the Social Democrats) carried only 20 percent of the votes in the last election before Hitler; the second (the Center) carried only 15 percent. These parties could not agree on a viable coalition. Between 1928 and the end of 1932, there were four elections for the Reichstag, two in 1932 alone, because no sustainable government could be formed. The only thing in which the Germans increasingly seemed to agree on was that democracy and freedom was not the solution to their problems. The legitimacy of the democratic system was reaching its end, killed by the fragmentation of special interests that had characterized German politics since the unification of the country.

The Nazis thrived in this environment, offering a national program, a vision of a new Germany where all sectors and social classes would be unified under ideas that were at the same time revolutionary and traditional. National Socialism was—as its name clearly indicated—a socialist doctrine and demanded a strong intervention of the government in the economy to resolve the social problems. Its socialism, however, was different from that of Marx. It rejected the notion of social warfare. The role of the state was not to take sides with the proletarians but to create a union among all sectors and classes under the objectives of the nation. The National Socialists did not oppose the private ownership of capital. Capitalists could exist, as long as they actively contributed to the fulfillment of the nation, as defined by the Nazi leaders. For them, capitalists and workers should not be fighting each other, but should unite under the guidance of the state. The National Socialists negated individual freedoms, not those *and* the private ownership of capital as the Marxists did.[3]

It was in this way that the Germans chose for themselves a regime that, while taking them to the past, as they wished, also imposed on them the order of slavery. Trying to protect from each other and from external competition, and trying to get ahead of their countrymen by using the power of the state, they laid out the foundations for the only social structure that can introduce order in a chaotic society: a tyranny.

While the Soviet Union was similar to Nazi Germany in the use of terror to give cohesion to society, there is a puzzling difference between the two of them in this respect. In both regimes the dictators drew a line splitting society into a majority and a minority and then gave cohesion to the majority by blaming the minority for all the problems of the country. Yet, in the case of the Nazis, they chose a group that could be defined in a permanent way as the attacked minority, so that the rest of the population could feel secure that terror would not be turned against them—at least, if they did not oppose the Nazi regime. The history of Nazi Germany clearly shows that Hitler was right that the Arian Germans would support the genocide. The Arian Germans accepted Nazism without a struggle and participated in the Holocaust quite willingly. There was no conflict among them regarding the Nazi policies. They became a unified country. The Communists, on the other hand, split society with a fuzzy line— bourgeois and proletarians—and kept on moving it through the years in such a way that, after a while, nobody could feel safe. And, still, the population supported their massacres. How could people cooperate in the genocide of themselves?

To understand the dynamics of Soviet destructiveness one has to look at its musical-chairs nature. The Party instructions made failure to denounce an enemy of the people proof of complicity. Since the Party also emphasized that the enemies were double-faced, so that an effort had to be made to discover them, the country as a whole became paranoiac in two ways—looking for enemies and fearing denunciations. If one failed to denounce someone who somebody else denounced, one was doomed. The Party warned against the passive members, who were trying to destroy the country by inaction, but also warned against the active wreckers, who would lead the country to destructive paths. Furthermore, the Party also warned against the careerists, who would denounce innocent people only to advance up the ladder of the Party. Within this system, the killers became the killed with predictable regularity. The Soviet citizens participated enthusiastically in this macabre game until they discovered that the missing chair was theirs.

As much as the Germans did, the killer Soviet citizens thought that they would be spared because they did not fit the description of the people that should be killed, the exploiters that Communists called *kulaks*. They all agreed that kulaks should be shot. The surprise came when they discovered that in one of the turns of the game they had been classified as kulaks. By that time, it was too late.

Social divisiveness was evident in what the Soviet citizens did and did not to defend themselves against the machinery of repression during the decades of terror. Looking at the first manifestation, it is clear that each of them thought that he or she could be spared if only he or she became ingratiated with the Communist executioners. For this purpose they, at best, remained silent. At worst, they denounced their friends, colleagues, families, and even participated in their killing. For them, this was easier and safer than trying to organize themselves against the terrible common threat they faced. They didn't care about what happened to their friends, as long as they could save their own skins, and they knew that their friends thought the same. Regarding the second manifestation, what they did not do, it is amazing that even highly placed military officers were unable to unite to defend themselves when Stalin was killing them one by one, with such regularity that it was predictable that all of them would die. They could not start a conspiracy against Stalin because they could not trust anybody, not even their own families. They knew that, as much as they themselves could sell their friends, their friends could sell them as well. Actually, they were *sure* that they would sell them. They knew in their own bones the divisiveness of Soviet society.

This was the crux of the matter. Marshall Tukhachevsky, one of the top Army officers killed by Stalin at the height of the Great Terror, passed this judgment on Soviet society. He told the magistrates that were condemning him to death in one of Stalin's fake trials:

To look on all this and remain silent is a crime. And for all these years we have looked on and remained silent. And for this both you and all of us deserve to be shot.[4]

One of the Arian Germans who were imprisoned by the Nazis, Martin Niemöller, a Protestant pastor, made a remark that was essentially similar to that of Marshall Tukhachevsky's in terms of the diagnosis of the reasons why terrorist governments are able to establish destructive regimes:

In Germany, the Nazis first came for the Communists, and I did not speak up because I was not a Communist. Then they came for the Jews, and I did not speak up because I was not a Jew. Then they came for the trade unionists, and I did not speak up because I was not a trade unionist. Then they came for the Catholics, and I did not speak up because I was Protestant. Then they came for me, and by that time, there was no one left to speak for me.[5]

That is, vertical regimes—and the destruction and corruption that come with them—are rooted in social divisiveness. Societies incapable of developing strong social bonds are liable to fall prey to them. Since divisive societies are the most common, vertical regimes are also the most common. Upgrading to a horizontal society requires a difficult feat: creating strong social bonds based on self-reliance and social interest. Not many societies—only the developed ones—have attained this feat.

Understanding the difference between the two kinds of society—the vertical and the horizontal—requires a shift in our perception of the conflicts that plagued the process. Influenced by the tragic history of ideological warfare, we frequently think of the politics of the Industrial Revolution as a long confrontation between the left and the right, which the right won with the demise of the Soviet Union. Yet, the difference between the modern, democratic state that triumphed at the end of the Industrial Revolution and the regimes that collapsed in the process lies in the shape of society, not in their ideological leanings in terms of what we call left and right in casual conversation. The difference was that one kind of society was horizontal while the other was vertical.

The classification of societies on left and right is confusing because the word *left* has two different meanings, both related to government intervention in society. First, there is the government intervention aimed at controlling the *economic* activity of a society, which fuses in one single dimension the political and economic power. This fusion is what gives a vertical shape to society. The extreme form of this intervention is that of prohibiting the private ownership of means of production. Yet, even milder forms tying together economic and political power—such as protecting local industry heavily or granting privileges to certain activities— also give a vertical shape to society because they make economic success a function of political access and connections. Second, there is the government intervention aimed at meeting the *social needs* of its citizens— providing, say, health, education, and unemployment security. This, the welfare state, is the mark of what we can call the democratic leftist societies. It does not necessarily lead to verticality unless it is accompanied with the merge of political and economic powers.

We can see the difference by comparing the Nordic with the Communist countries. Many people think of Communist regimes as the exacerbation of the features that constitute the left, in which the Nordic countries are included. The differences between the latter and the former, however, are not of degree but of substance. Certainly, the Nordic countries are on the left because their taxation is high, their governments are big and they provide a solid social safety net for their citizens. Yet, the central priority of these countries is firmly on the respect for the rights of the individual and their governments have always moved within the boundaries set by this priority. Their governments are big but not authoritarian. They have established their social security net because that is the will of the population, clearly expressed in free elections, and not because a despotic government has imposed it on them to force cooperation. The enormous difference is that, while Communist societies are vertical, the Nordic societies are horizontal. Thus, the difference between vertical and horizontal societies is not the same as that between societies on the left and on the right.

The welfare state might increase short-term social rigidity, but, as long as the welfare society is cohesive, it can rearrange itself to reduce such rigidity by changing its institutional setting. For this reason, shifts from right to left and vice versa never represented cataclysmic changes in the social order of horizontal societies. Respect for individual rights remained supreme when, for example, Britain or Sweden moved to the left to establish welfare states in the twentieth century, or when Franklin Delano Roosevelt established the New Deal in the United States. When the population of these countries decided to move back in the direction of the right in the 1980s and 1990s they did so within the same well-ordered processes of change characteristic of horizontal societies.[6] Sweden and other Nordic countries have remained well to the left of Britain and the United States. Yet, they are fundamentally similar to those countries and fundamentally different from the former Soviet Union. They represent the leftist side of horizontal societies.

On the other side of the ledger, the vertical shape of social order includes societies on both left and right, too. Communist societies are on the left while the Nazi societies are widely conceived as being on the right because the Nazis allowed the private ownership of means of production. The vertical shape of societies also includes societies that we do not classify in terms of left and right, such as the autocratic feudal societies. It also includes many other contemporary societies, such as those organized under militaristic regimes supported by a small group of proprietors, so common in Latin America in the recent past, which are neither Communist nor Nazi. Today's Asian religious tyrannies also fall into this category. It is irrelevant in all these cases whether the state justifies its claim to power based on socialistic, rightist, or religious grounds. Their dominant feature is the assertion of the power of the state over the freedom of the individuals. The confrontation that ended with the demise of the Soviet Union was between this kind of society and the horizontal ones, not between societies on the left or right.

Table 7.1 summarizes the features of the two kinds of society that emerge from the choice of what people want to keep predictable in their lives. Following the logical sequence of the origins of social order, the table first describes the features of the founding citizens and then those of the societies they create. Once a society has been created, the opposite causality starts to work, reinforcing in the population the individual features that the original creators reflected in the social order.

Table 7.1
Creative and Destructive Societies

Individual	Creative	Destructive
Attitude in pursuing self-interest	Self-reliant	Dependent on the state
Motivation	Self-interest and social interest	Self-interest exclusively
Values	Individualistic	Collectivistic
Links to others	Cohesive	Divisive
Society		
Social field	Strong	Weak
Shape	Horizontal	Vertical
Dimensions	Multidimensional	One-dimensional
Definition of stability	Keep individual rights in place	Maintain the status quo or attain a utopia
Role of the state	Keeper of individual rights	Coercive to keep the status quo in place or attain the utopia
Economy	Free	Controlled by the state
Social stance to change	Flexible	Rigid
Reaction to change	Adjustment	Chaos and Revolution
New regime	Harmonic with changes	Destructive

This summary marks the end of this part of the book. Our conclusions are simple. Vertical, rigid structures emerge in societies lacking social cohesion. They are the only mechanisms that such societies have to avoid chaos and establish a social order. Horizontal, flexible regimes are viable only in countries with strong social cohesion. The problem of attaining a smooth adjustment to the cataclysmic changes produced by a technological revolution is that of developing strong social cohesion—which is the same as developing social interest in the population. The key to success is the equilibrium between the two motivations of social behavior: individual interest and social interest.

Now we can turn to apply the lessons learned from the analysis of the past to meet the challenges that the new technological revolution is posing. This is what I do in the second part of the book.

NOTES

1. The distinction between the vertical and horizontal shapes of society and government goes as far back as the ideas of two British philosophers, Thomas Hobbes (1588–1679) and John Locke (1632–1704). Hobbes argued that social order

could be attained only if people subjected themselves to the absolute supremacy
of the state, which would protect them against their own brutish instincts. Locke,
in contrast, maintained that sovereignty did not reside in the state but with the
people, and that civil and natural law bounded the supremacy of the state.

2. See Samuel W. Mitcham Jr., *Why Hitler?* (Westport, Conn.: Praeger, 1996),
pp. 125, 136, 163.

3. For a discussion of the differences between conventional (Marxist) socialism
and National Socialism in the early twentieth century, see Zeev Sternhell, *The
Founding Myths of Israel* (Princeton, N.J.: Princeton University Press, 1998),
pp. 3–11.

4. Marshal Tukhachevsky, quoted in Robert C. Tucker, *Stalin in Power*, (New
York and London: W. W. Norton and Company, 1990), p. 440.

5. Quoted by Steven Paskuly, *Death Dealer, The Memoirs of the SS Kommandant
at Auschwithz*, ed. Rudolph Höss (New York: Prometheus Books, 1992), p. 110.

6. In the late 1940s and early 1950s a wave of nationalizations swept the developed world, affecting utilities mainly and, in some countries, industrial enterprises deemed as strategic. In Britain, health care was also nationalized. While this
trend tended to fuse the economic and political dimensions of life, it did so in a
limited portion of society. Private ownership of the means of production and the
general separation of economic and political activities remained in place—except
in those limited areas. In the 1980s, Margaret Thatcher initiated a reversal of this
fusion in Britain, unleashing a process that overtook most of the developed world.
The majority of government-owned utilities and industrial enterprises were pri-
vatized during the remaining two decades of the century.

PART II

The Road Ahead

CHAPTER 8

The Challenge

The main issues of the current transformation are very similar to those of the Industrial Revolution. A technological revolution is eroding the existing social order in all its dimensions. The reshuffling of production in accordance with the new competitive advantages is threatening privileges and established positions around the world, causing a deterioration of the income distribution at the national and international levels as well as an increasing instability in the world's financial markets. The increasing connectivity is also eroding the cultural basis of the social order in many countries, particularly in those that rely on strong vertical modes of organization. This has prompted the emergence of a strong resistance to the most visible of the consequences of connectivity: globalization. Radicalism is reemerging after having disappeared for at least twenty years in most developing countries and for almost a century in the developed ones. The tensions of the transformation have already exploded in the terrorist attacks against modernization carried out by members of some of the most rigid societies in the world. In the decades to come, these tensions will affect even the most flexible of our societies and we all will face the same choices of the Industrial Revolution: absorbing, harmonically, the changes induced by the new technologies on the one hand, or rejecting them and fall into stagnation or destructiveness on the other. The shape of the institutions that will arise from the transformation will be determined by this decision.

We do not know the specific shape that these institutions will take but we know the general principle on which they should be based. We understand quite clearly how tyrannical institutions are created using one single variable, self-interest, manifested either in terms of searching for economic well being or the will to power. Countries where citizens pursued their self-interest unrestrictedly, burdening the state with the task of providing the social cohesion needed to get the benefits of a unified society fell into stagnation and destructiveness. To understand how liberal institutions are created, however, we need another variable, the social glue that keeps society united in spite of the centrifugal forces of self-interest. This glue is social interest —the desire of the individuals for doing things right, in a way that they not only fulfill their own self-interest but also have a positive impact on society. It was only in those societies where social interest was strong that democracy and capitalism combined to create the modern industrial society. Societies where social interest was weak broke down during the transformation and fell under vertical tyrannical regimes and either stagnation or destructiveness.

This finding forces a change in the perspective of our ultimate quest— what to do in the difficult years of transition toward the connectivity world—from looking for the design of a system that would be consistent with the new relations created by connectivity to looking for the preconditions for such a system to emerge and work. This is the subject of this last part of the book. I start in this chapter with a brief restatement of the nature of the economic transformation we are living through.

Connectivity is causing a migration of labor to higher-value-added activities in all countries in accordance with each society's stock of knowledge and capacity to translate knowledge into productivity. This implies that activities generating value added too low for the levels of income of developed countries should be transferred to the developing ones, thus liberating resources in those countries to move up in the value-added ladder. This is what started to happen in the United States in the 1980s and 1990s and the result was that the country adjusted smoothly to the first stage of the revolution, releasing an astonishing amount of creativity. This stage is still in the future for most other countries, including both developed and developing ones. Further stages are still in the future even for the United States. The transformation is still beginning.

The process demands raising the skills of the population all over the world. In the developing countries, these should be upgraded to take over the activities displaced from the developed societies, and more. In the developed countries, the challenge is to upgrade the abilities of the unskilled that would lose their jobs to globalization, so that they could justify economically the wage advantage that they have over their counterparts in the developing countries. That is, for both developed and developing countries the problem is one of raising the skills of a considerable portion of their population. The faster this process takes place, the faster connectivity and the globalization of inputs of production would bring about a rapid increase in income in both the developed and developing countries.

The best policies to attain this rapid transformation are the liberal ones. The transformation should be left to run its course, day by day. Trying to stop it would only mean that it would gather steam to explode in destructive ways later on. Thus, rather than protecting the threatened activities, government policies should aim at accelerating the economic liberalization that started in force in the 1990s. They should also aim at investing heavily in education and other dimensions of human capital, taking advantage of the great possibilities that connectivity opens to carry education to all the population in the world.

Still, as we discussed in the previous part, resistance to change is gathering force and is likely to gain supporters as the transformation becomes more turbulent. The idea that defensive strategies—such as increasing protection against foreign competition or carrying out demographic policies to eliminate internal competition for jobs—are the best option may appeal to increasing sections of the population.

I discuss these ideas in the next chapter, showing that connectivity has turned them unviable even in terms of protecting the people their proponents want to protect.

CHAPTER 9

The False Solutions

Rebuilding social cohesion in the new kinds of relationships that are emerging with connectivity is the most important task at hand. Social cohesion, however, is not a policy variable. That is, governments cannot issue policies that would automatically produce or increase social cohesion. On the contrary, government actions are ultimately determined by the choices of their constituencies, which reveal the extent of social cohesion. Socially cohesive societies elect governments that put in place policies consistent with flexibility. Symmetrically, if a society chooses to oppose changes, a vertical government will be in power and its mandate to resist change will determine its policies. As it happened during the Industrial Revolution, trying to superimpose a horizontal mode of organization on an essentially vertical society is likely to fail. Sooner or later, the horizontal institutions would be bypassed and a vertical authority would be imposed. Increasing social cohesion is a problem of values that can be resolved only by concerted actions of leaders working on all dimensions of social life, emphasizing both self-reliance and social interest as the basis for social progress. This is not an easy task, particularly in these times when the popular idea is that the pursuance of self-interest exclusively is the key to success.

Still, government policies may play a crucial role in attaining a harmonious adjustment to the new technological revolution. In most societies, change and resistance to it will struggle against each other for a long time, and the general direction of policies will be uncertain. It is for these cases that discussing what governments can do is relevant because government leaders may exert a strong influence in the route that the country will take. Depending on the policies they choose, they can foster the triumph of the vertical or the horizontal trends in society.

I start the discussion of this subject in this chapter by looking at what government should not do, focusing on four ideas that are increasingly proposed in both developed and developing countries as the solutions to the problems posed by connectivity and globalization: increasing trade protection, increasing protection to existing jobs, demographic policies, and turning help for developing countries into a system of grants exclusively. The argument is that these policies, rather than helping find the solution to the problem, would aggravate it, because while enforcing undesirable vertical structures, they would fail in producing the results their supporters expected from them.

Protection has always prevented societies from getting the benefits of trade and has charged consumers with the costs of keeping in place inefficient activities. Through this mechanism, some sectors have benefited from the costs imposed on the rest of society. In this section I argue that while protection can still derail progress, connectivity has drastically reduced its power to increase the income of the sectors it is supposed to benefit in the developed countries.

To see how the power of protection to increase the incomes of the unskilled has declined in these countries we can think of a company working in the United States producing goods that require both sophisticated and simple components. The company produces the former locally and the latter in a low-wage country. The government, trying to please the trade unions, is willing to protect the domestic unskilled workers of such company. It offers the trade unions a choice of three potential strategies. One is to raise import tariffs on the inputs; the other is to raise tariffs on the final product; and the third is to raise tariffs on both. What would you advise the unions to accept, if their objective is to increase demand for the domestic unskilled workers and maximize their wages?

Advising the first option—tariffs on inputs—would create an incentive for the company to move the production of the sophisticated parts of the product to another developed country where inputs are not taxed. This would give the company an advantage over the local competitors, which would have to pay higher prices for the inputs while selling the final product in both the domestic and international markets at the same price as the company producing abroad. All companies in the same business would do the same. The activity would disappear and the workers would be fired. Advising the trade unions to accept the second option—raising import duties on the finished goods exclusively—would only increase the profitability of producing the unsophisticated components abroad. Advising the third option to the trade unions—to ask for increased import tariffs on both inputs and the finished products—would leave the situation unchanged for the unskilled workers. It would be as profitable to produce the unsophisticated part of the product abroad as when no protection existed. There would be a difference, however. The higher price of the finished good resulting from protection would reduce its demand in the domestic market, lowering the demand for the services of the workers producing it. Some additional local workers would be fired. Thus, you would reject all three government proposals.

There is another possibility that you may mention. That is forbidding the importation of all unsophisticated inputs and the finished products that contain them. This sounds better. It is a flawed solution, however, because unsophisticated parts are used in all products, so that the prohibition would have to be extended to all the goods sold in the economy and not even the United States can give itself the luxury of trying to produce everything it needs. Also, paying higher prices for those inputs would put all the American exporters of sophisticated products out of competition in the international markets. That is, to protect some groups of low-value-added producers the country would lose its competitiveness in the high-value-added markets.

Another variation that might come to your mind would be to forbid the importation of only the unsophisticated inputs. What would the producers of sophisticated goods do in such circumstances? They would do two things. First, they would establish or keep in operation plants abroad producing unsophisticated components to keep their international sales intact. To prevent this outcome, you may think of prohibiting investment in productive facilities in foreign countries. These companies, however, can make strategic alliances with companies' abroad and provide the funds to capitalize them from the United States. To prevent this, the government could prohibit the movements of capital for this purpose. Yet, as anyone knows, it is extremely difficult to control capital movements in the age of connectivity.

The second course of action would be to invest in labor saving technologies in the plants they kept in the United States to sell domestically. After all, the unsophisticated parts of production are the ones that can be automated more easily. They have not been automated today because the wages of the unskilled labor in developing countries do not justify doing so. If these wages increased because companies are forced to produce these goods in developed countries, automating would become an option. To prevent companies from regaining competitiveness by investing in laborsaving technologies, governments would have to ban laborsaving investment and research, directly or through labor legislation making it impossible to fire people. To enforce these measures, the government would have to intervene in yet other activities. And so on.

Following this logic, the United States would become a replica of some of the most backward countries in the world. The income of the country would go down, including that of the trade unions you are advising. An enormous portion of the resources that the United States now uses to produce high-value-added products would have to be redirected to produce low-value-added ones. Thinking along these lines shows that, in fact, the lack of protection helps to increase the overall level of wages in the United States because the imports of low-value-added components liberate the local labor force to produce high-value-added goods and services.

That is, you would have to tell the trade unions that, contrary to what the proponents of protection think or say, increasing protection would not result in either higher wages or higher employment in our increasingly connected world, where a substantial portion of international trade is in inputs for production. I arbitrarily placed the example in the United States but it is valid for any developed country.

The trade unions could point out that the situation is different for companies specializing in unsophisticated final products, which, of course, use only unsophisticated inputs. There, protection might still work. One example of these products is average textiles (high-quality textiles for expensive garments are a high-value-added activity where high-wage countries like Italy are quite competitive.) The activity is highly protected in the United States through a system of high import tariffs mixed with some duty-free quotas carefully calculated so that they do not spoil the market for the domestic producers. The trade unions can point out that the wages of the textile workers in the United States are still higher than those of their counterparts in the developing countries. You can then answer that, despite this protection, the real wages of the unskilled are going down in the United States because the American economy is not willing to pay more for low-value-added products.

Furthermore, a growing portion of the textiles and garments consumed in the country are produced abroad and the large American textile companies own and operate facilities abroad. That is, their shareholders have access to the worldwide labor market and they are using it to sell in the United States and other markets. The more protected the American market becomes, the more they will depend on producing outside the United States to compete in the world markets. They are free to move. It is only their American workers who are trapped within low-value-added activities inside the protected domestic labor markets. As expressed by an eminent trade theoretician, Ronald W. Jones:

Globalization and the increased degree of international mobility of inputs and factors have tended to create divisions within a nation between agents that are trapped by national boundaries and agents that are capable of relocating their activities abroad. Not all agents have equal abilities to take advantage of foreign opportunities. To protect the interests of those agents and firms that feel trapped within a country's borders, national governments will be tempted by measures that add friction to international mobility. For example, in the Asian financial crisis of the late 1990s, some governments and economists became enamored with the idea of taxing short-term capital movements. Part of the problem, of course, is that increased mobility of inputs tends to make supply elasticities higher. A disturbance to economies that alters their relative positions could more readily serve to encourage firms and even industries to shift the locale of their operations from one economy to another . . . Globalization and the increased mobility of productive inputs and factors pose serious challenges to the effectiveness of policies pursued by national governments in an attempt to aid special groups that are trapped by national boundaries.[1]

Yet another possibility is to create international arrangements that would extend internationally the power of governments to enforce taxation and redistribute income across sectors in society. Developed countries could associate to protect themselves against the imports of low-value-added goods from the developing countries, forcing all their residents to buy the low-value-added goods produced within their boundaries. As also noted by Ronald W. Jones:

Greater international mobility of factors for some agents and resulting increases in supply elasticities and location possibilities serve to make intercountry comparisons of public policies more relevant. This might lead to stiff international competition in the portfolio of taxes, regulations and benefits offered to private agents. Instead, the forces of globalization may herald a more concerted attempt to harmonize the offerings and takings of public sectors in an attempt to limit the attractions of international mobility.[2]

Following this approach, developed countries could associate with each other within a regime with two features: a customs union that would prevent the introduction of low-wage unsophisticated goods from developing countries and a uniform set of taxes and subsidies. This would allow them to impose in one stroke two restrictions to factor mobility. Local companies would not be interested in investing abroad because most of the purchasing power for finished goods in the world is concentrated in developed countries and consumers in those countries would be forced to pay the higher costs of unsophisticated goods and unsophisticated inputs of sophisticated goods.

Arranging such an association would be quite difficult, however, because all developed countries would have to accept that they would pay for the costs of the least efficient of them in each sector of the economy. American companies, for example, would have to cope with the costs of the most inefficient of the Japanese companies. Moreover, the developed

countries as a whole would experience a reduction in their standard of
life, as they would have to allocate a large portion of their resources to
produce the low-value-added goods and services that today are produced
in low-wage countries. The developed countries would experience retrogression, as resources that could, say, be used to produce highly sophisticated health equipment would then have to be used to produce fabrics
and clothes. With time, as we already discussed, companies would invest
in laborsaving technologies that would reduce the costs of producing the
unsophisticated portions of their products, which, in turn, would reduce
the demand for unskilled workers and, with it, their wages. If their wages
cannot move down, unemployment would increase. With time, trade
unions in all developed countries would have to understand that importing low-value-added goods from low-wage countries would lead to
higher wages in their own countries by liberating resources to produce
high-value-added goods.

That is, protection would not smooth out the transformation in the developed countries, even if all of them apply it in a coordinated way. One
clear example of the impotence[6] of protection and even subsidies to forestall the decline of employment in an activity that is being discarded by
technological progress is that of agriculture in the Great Plains in the
United States. In the 1930s, it took a farmer twenty hours to produce 100
bushels of wheat. By 1975, it took him only five hours, and today it takes
even less. Accordingly, agricultural employment in the region has been
falling steadily since the 1930s. Small farms are also disappearing in the
region, crowded out by bigger farms with the higher capital investments
that make the increases in productivity possible. The region is losing
population fast. The government tried to counteract these trends by
pumping subsidies and protecting the farmers against foreign competition
with measures that effectively banned imports of agricultural products.
Over the last 40 years, the inhabitants of the region became the benefici-
aries of the highest subsidies in the country, getting over $385 per capita
in 1998. Still, employment keeps on falling and property keeps on becoming more concentrated. The case also illustrates the perversity of subsidies
aimed at keeping in place activities or methods of production that are
already obsolete. They are worsening the distribution of income. About
80 percent of the subsidies go to 20 percent of the farmers, those with the
largest landholdings, so that the government program is protecting the
rich. Worse still, even if productivity has increased dramatically, agriculture in this region still produces losses. The subsidies now represent about
half of the incomes of these rich farmers.[3] The poor in other regions of the
country pay part of their taxes to subsidize them. The situation of other
declining activities, like textiles, is similar. Employment and real wages
keep on falling in spite of the government's heavy protection. That is,
protection can take away income from the unprotected activities and

transfer them to the protected ones, but it cannot increase the total income of the population.

Protection is more effective in developing countries than in developed ones for three main reasons. First, these countries do not have the ability to develop their own technologies. They have to import knowledge and machinery. Thus, if they live under a protective regime, they are left out from the economy of knowledge and their inefficient enterprises can survive without fearing that domestic competitors would pose a technological threat to their market positions. Second, with few exceptions, their entrepreneurs lack the abilities necessary to operate productive facilities in foreign countries. Thus, there is no danger that they would take their investments to other places to compete in the global markets. Third, protection is more pervasive to begin with so that producers and consumers have little room to go around it.

Still, keeping the power of protection in place to maintain the incomes of the privileged is also declining in developing countries. As we already discussed, protected activities depend on the exports of commodities to get the foreign exchange needed to pay for their imported inputs. In this way, the rate of growth of commodities' exports imposes a limit on the growth of the protected activities—which tend to include the entire industrial sector. The long-term decline in the prices of commodities is constraining even more the potential growth of the industrial sectors. Borrowing abroad to remove the foreign exchange constraint on the growth of industry—the solution that many developing countries tried during the 1970s, 1980s and 1990s—proved worse than the infirmity. After a short boom, these countries fell into terribly devastating financial crises.

It seems as if the developing countries are trapped. Increased protection would not cure their ailments. Yet, one of the arguments used by the proponents of increasing it is that the liberalization of the 1990s did not produce growth but, instead, stagnation. They point to the low rates of growth of these economies to support their argument.

The liberalization of the 1990s, however, was quite limited, so that it cannot be argued that liberal policies have failed in the developing countries. In fact, the problem is the reverse of what the supporters of protection are diagnosing. This is evident when the degree of economic freedom of developing countries is compared with that of the developed ones.

To make this comparison we can use the Index of Economic Freedom published by the Heritage Foundation and the *Wall Street Journal*.[4] The index goes from 1 to 5 in a reversed scale, so that the higher the index the more repressed the economy. The overall index for the developed countries in 2002 was 2.0, while it was 3.3, or 62 percent higher, for the developing ones. Regarding international trade freedom, the point of contention of globalization, the index was 1.9 for the developed countries and 3.8 for the developing ones, which means that protection is about twice as high in the latter. The average developing country is still quite far from being open to competition from abroad.

It is understandable that much is still to be done. Reforming an economy is not a task of a few years. The backwardness of the developing countries is still more visible if the Index of Competitiveness of the World Economic Forum is used in the comparison. This index includes dimensions such as institutional development and the sophistication of the entrepreneurs and the labor force, which are lagging even more in the developing countries. The problem is that it seems the momentum for change has faded and, worse still, that the political pendulum is starting to go the other way. The idea that protection and government intervention in the economy is the road to progress is still popular in the developing economies and is becoming more so, even if the evidence is that economic development is positively correlated with liberal economic policies.

There is another set of instruments that governments can use to protect the incomes of workers in weak or declining activities: regulations forbidding or increasing the costs of layoffs. These instruments, however, backfire. Aiming at preserving employment by making it difficult to fire people, they actually increase the cost of hiring new labor and therefore lower the rate of creation of new employment. The net result is less employment. Its victims are predominantly the young.

In fact, evidence shows that higher job security levels are associated with lower employment rates, both in country-specific studies and in regional cross-country analyses. The magnitude of the relationship is very high. James Heckman and Carmen Pagés, the authors of one of the most comprehensive analyses of this subject, covering 36 Latin American and developed countries, found that an increase in dismissal costs equivalent to one month of pay is associated with a 1.8 percentage point decline in employment rates. Since in Latin America the average severance payment is 3.04 months—or 25 percent of the annual wages—the estimated loss in employment is about 5.5 percent of the working population. Several studies on advanced Organization for Economic Cooperation and Development countries show similar effects.[5] Heckman and Pagés summarize their results with the following words:

Our evidence suggests that job security provisions are an extremely inefficient and inequality-increasing mechanism for providing income security for workers. They are inefficient because they reduce the demand for labor; they are inequality-increasing because some workers benefit while many others are hurt. Their impact on inequality is multifaceted: Job security increases inequality because it reduces the employment prospects for young, female and unskilled workers. It also increases inequality because it segregates the labor markets between workers with secure jobs and workers with very few prospects of becoming employed. Finally, job security provisions increase inequality if, as predicted by some theoretical studies and most of the available empirical evidence, they increase the size of the informal sector.[6]

The damaging impact of labor restrictions can be appreciated in continental Europe. From 1980 to 1997, employment creation in most European countries is just about, or is lagging behind, the growth of their working-age population.[7]

The official report issued by the Organization for Economic Cooperation and Development (the organization of the richest countries in the world) on the problems of unemployment afflicting its member countries found a close relationship between these problems and the restrictions to fire workers: the countries that create new jobs faster are those where such restrictions are lower. For this reason, the report recommended dismantling the mechanisms that today increase the cost of firing people in the rich countries.[8]

That is, all the mechanisms that governments mount to make it harder to fire workers actually backfire in terms of the ultimate objective of increasing overall employment. This is true also of another mechanism aimed at defending jobs: demographic policies.

Just as it happened during the Industrial Revolution, we are witnessing large migrations in our times. The direction of such migrations, however, is opposite to that of the old ones. In the nineteenth and early twentieth centuries, people migrated from the most to the less civilized parts of the world, while today the migrations go the other way. Countries with large communities of legal and illegal immigrants include the United States, Britain, the Nordic countries, Germany, France, and Japan. The migrants of the past looked for a primitive place where they could build a new world for themselves; those of the present look for an already existing social and economic infrastructure where they can insert their lives. They are looking for a more advanced social order.

The introduction of large groups of people with foreign cultures poses several problems to the host societies. One is that, while looking for a social order, immigrations pose an obvious challenge to the host societies' institutions, threatening the integrity of such order. The values, the traditions, and the self-image embedded in those institutions are diluted by the customs of the immigrating population. This also happened with the migrations of the nineteenth century. The circumstances, however, are different today. In the old migrations, the dissolution of the host society was seen as positive—even by some of the natives—because it meant the triumph of modernization. The immigrants, building on the strength of superior commercial and technological abilities, and sometimes on the strength of a colonial army, soon escalated to the higher echelons of their adopted society and launched it into a path of modernization. Thus, the cost of the dissolution of the traditional mores of the host society was at least partly compensated by its integration into a better-organized world. It was also inevitable. The host societies were too weak to prevent it.

The threat of dissolution to the host society in the current times goes in the opposite direction. The migrants to the developed countries have lower education and abilities than the average member of the host society. The migrants of today bring along the threat of dissolution without a substitute for the existing social order. The natives can easily see their presence as harbingers of the end of the traditions and values on which their society was built, and of the retrogression of their countries, or of large pockets inside them, into underdevelopment. Thus, the host societies see the immigrants as carriers of decay.

This problem is more acute in Europe and Japan than in the United States because societies in the former have been traditionally closed. They developed their commonalties on the basis of birth and generations of living together. Their perception of social linkages is inextricably mixed with nationality. The United States, by contrast, has always been a melting pot.

Another effect of the large migrations is the real or perceived impact that they have on the incomes of the unskilled in the developed countries. Willing to work for lower wages and increasing the supply of labor in their host societies, they tend to reduce the salaries of their competitors in the labor markets, which are the unskilled natives. Thus, unskilled foreigners have become the tangible symbol of the deterioration of the salaries or the increase in the unemployment of the uneducated natives that have been taking place in the last several decades, even if—as it is most frequently the case—the latter would not take the jobs that the immigrants take.

Furthermore, as the foreigners tend to be at the lower end of the educational ladder, they are in danger of becoming underclassed in their host societies. The segregation is already visible in the new planned communities, which tend to exclude immigrants and other minorities, while the old urban centers are becoming ghettos for the latter, and where the quality of education and social services is lower and the crime rate is higher. The creation of an underclass would contradict the basic principles of the host societies' social contract.

The three effects together—the threat of decay, the perceived threat to jobs, and the growing danger of engendering an underclass—may combine to elicit a xenophobic response from the natives, which can easily degenerate into violence of the neo-nazi kind. While it seems difficult to believe that this would lead to pogroms in the developed host societies, violence would increase the turmoil of the transformation and would give credibility to those proposing a return to a more comfortable past. Recent polls show that in the European Union, 14 percent of the population admit that they are intolerant toward minorities and a further 25 percent say that they are ambivalent.[9] The popularity of politicians promising to stop immigrations and restrictions to the rights of the immigrants already living in the developed countries has increased exponentially, as the 2002 presidential elections in France clearly showed.

This problem cannot be ignored. The poverty and lack of opportunities that prevail in developing countries pushes people to migrate to societies with a more productive social order; the demographic trends in the developed countries pull these people by offering them job opportunities once they arrive. In fact, most developed societies will increasingly depend on immigration to keep their economies working. The birth rate of the most advanced countries is now well below the rate of replacement, so that their populations will become older in the next 30 years and, in some cases, it will fall in absolute numbers. For example, if the current demographic trends do not change, people over 65 in Germany would become half of the country's population by 2030 while the total population would shrink from 82 to 73 million. As this happens, the working population would decline by 25 percent, from 40 to 30 million. A similar process would take place in Japan, Italy, France, Spain, Portugal, the Netherlands, Sweden, and even the United States.[10]

What contemporary proponents of demographic policies fear is that the decline in the working age population in the developed countries will force these countries to receive even more immigrants to keep their productive machinery going. To deal with this problem, one of them, Patrick Buchanan, recommends three policies to developed countries. First, they should aim at isolating their countries from the developing ones by tightening their immigration policies. Second, they should offer incentives for the locals to increase their rate of reproduction. Third, they should protect the activities where the nationals work against foreign competition.

Buchanan's recommendations are reactive and do not address the real problems of the transformation. As we have already discussed, protection cannot resolve the problems posed by a technological revolution, particularly in developed countries, because there the innovations that are disrupting the economy come not from the outside but from the inside. Restrictive immigration policies cannot resolve these problems, either. In fact, Buchanan's recommendations regarding trade and immigration are inconsistent with each other. The best policy that developed countries could adopt to stop massive immigrations is, precisely, trade liberalization, which would go a long way in spurring the creation of a more productive social order in the countries now exporting people. This would reduce the push toward emigration more effectively than any increase in the border patrols.

Moreover, while blaming the foreigners for the dissolution of contemporary developed societies he proceeds to identify the trends that have led to such dissolution; Buchanan mentions European socialism, the ideals of the sixties' generation in the United States, the New England liberals, the refusal of white young people to procreate, the Marxist Frankfurt School . . . all of them creations or actions of the people he wants to reproduce faster, the original western inhabitants of the United States. The names he mentions as the leaders of the erosion of values are all western as well. In one of the paragraphs of his introduction he writes,

A sense that America, too, is pulling apart along the seams of ethnicity and race is spreading. Moreover, America is just undergone a cultural revolution, with a new elite now occupying the commanding heights. Through its capture of the institutions that shape and transmit ideas, opinions, beliefs, and values—TV, the arts, entertainment, education—this elite is creating a new people. Not only ethnically and racially, but culturally and morally, we are no longer one people or "one nation under God."[11]

The people he is talking about are not foreigners or recently immigrated people. The new immigrants are not members of the elite and have no capacity to become a part of it because they lack the required education to integrate themselves even in the average rank and file of American society. This is precisely the problem we are discussing: that they do not have this ability. What Buchanan is really saying is that if the original natives keep on behaving as they are doing, and if they forget about the values that made their society great, the unassimilated foreigners will take over and will change the nature of American society. If the latter are not well educated and have not absorbed the American values, the change would be for the worse. Take the foreigners away from this reasoning and you still have a society in decay. It is clear that demographic policies cannot resolve a problem of values.

Thus, Buchanan's recommendations do not address the problems he set out to resolve. This, however, is not the only flaw in Buchanan's reasoning. There are other ones.

To begin with, even if we believe that a demographic policy like the one Buchanan is proposing would really resolve the problem, such a policy would have an effect only in the long term, in about 30 or 40 years. By that time, the effects of the current demographic trends he is worrying about would have already taken place. For example, Germany's economically active population would have declined from 40 to 30 million. No feasible demographic rate of growth of the Aryan Germans could possibly prevent this fall because many of the new Aryans born out of the government incentives would still be children and could not procreate. In the meantime, Germany could keep its economy going only by importing foreigners.

But even if we forget that, it is clear that Buchanan's demographic policy would be quite difficult to put in practice without destroying, in the process, the liberal values he avowedly wants to protect. It would be impossible to create incentives for the right kind of people to reproduce faster without establishing a policy of straightforward racism. If this were not done, the policy would backfire. The immigrants are already reproducing faster than the originally local population in all developed countries. If the incentives were extended to them, they would reproduce much faster than the right people would, both because their natural birth trend is higher and because they would tend to react more effectively to the incentives—they are poorer and need the extra income badly. The alternative, establish a racist incentives policy, would be a first step toward a new Nazism.

While not the same, the current situation reminds us of the problem that the elites faced in Europe during the nineteenth century. At the time, the elites saw the influence of the poor, uneducated masses increasing quickly in their societies. They feared that in time they would destroy social order with their ignorant attitudes and lack of culture. It took a decisive action of society as a whole to forestall that possibility by raising the poor and ignorant to educational levels that would ensure an orderly management of society.

Doing this, trying to integrate the immigrants, is not a straightforward task, either. It is in fact more difficult than the task that the now developed countries faced in the nineteenth and early twentieth centuries because, in addition to poverty and lack of education, many of the immigrants come from truly alien cultures, with different customs and different features. The environment of the 1950s, of which Buchanan is quite nostalgic, was certainly more comfortable. But returning to those years seems to be impossible. The world is becoming one and the demographic trends are a concrete reality, whether we like it or not. It would be better to try to make the best out of the new interrelated world, integrating the immigrants and as many of the people living in developing countries into the advantages of connectivity.

Regarding *future* immigrations, each country can make its own sovereign decision. Yet, as Buchanan himself points out, without immigration the population of Europe and Japan would decline sharply; the population would become old; pension funds would have serious problems in meeting their obligations; locals would be forced to provide the low salaried services now provided by the immigrants; and the economy would decline. It is unlikely that countries would opt for this road.

In summary, the problems that Buchanan and many others have posed in reference to immigration are real and cannot be ignored. Their solutions, however, cannot be found in isolationism. The host societies have a vested interest in liberalizing trade to reduce the incentives to migrate;

in raising the economic productivity of the immigrants to the levels of the natives; and in integrating them into the mainstream values that give structure to their social lives, thus ensuring that the main character of their societies would survive. As any other society in the world, they have to fill the gaps in their connectivity networks. While improving their productive skills is a complicated problem, integrating the immigrants within the system of social bonds that gives cohesion to their societies is even more so. For these societies to work as a unified entity, the immigrants must cease to feel as immigrants, and become full members of the mainstream of society. Thus, a redefinition of social bonds is also needed in those countries where such bonds have been based, for many centuries, on racial identity and a shared past.

All of the false solutions that we have discussed in this chapter are surrounded by mythical auras of righteousness. None, however, commands a bigger aura than the idea that rich countries should give money away to the poor ones. The arguments presented to support this idea range from the naïve—that granting money would cure poverty in those countries—to the malicious—that the rich countries are rich because the poor countries are poor and should therefore compensate them for the damage they have inflicted upon them. In fact, if given under these premises, donations work precisely in the direction of deterring progress by stifling the development of self-reliance.

There is no doubt that donations may play a positive role if wisely granted, particularly in the poorest of the developing countries. Yet, as we have seen before, the main reason why poor countries are poor is not lack of resources but the self-imposed scourge of official interventionism aimed at protecting politically powerful groups in the domestic economies and the lack of attention to social objectives such as the education of the population. The developed countries are not to blame for the damage that developing countries inflict on themselves by adopting regressive policies.

The inefficacy of grants to spur economic growth is exemplified by the case of Africa, which has received enormous amounts of granted money in the last 30 years. Yet, rather than growing, most of the sub-Saharan African countries have become poorer as the money flowed in. The true solution is not there but in something that the grandiloquent calls to pour even more money on the developing countries do not mention: liberalize the trade of the developed countries with the developing ones, treating them like equals. As I discuss in a subsequent chapter, developed countries tend to pursue liberal trade policies in most products, the exception being the low-value-added ones that could suffer in the competition with developing countries. If the developed countries really want to help the developing ones, the best action they could take would be to liberalize these markets under arrangements that would also liberalize the markets of the developing countries.

In fact, going ahead with trade liberalization is the only course of action that presents a probability of success in creating a superior social order out of the tensions of the Connectivity Revolution. Economically, it is the only course that could generate growth and employment as the new technologies spur new activities around the world. With time, this process would even reverse the trend of commodity prices to fall, as demand for them would increase faster with the overall economic growth. The other road—protectionism and its associated restrictions on domestic economic freedom—is a blind alley leading to decay and destructiveness. In one sentence, we should aim at getting the benefits of the natural processes that are changing our world, not at stopping them in a vain attempt to eliminate the disruptions of change.

NOTES

1. See Ronald W. Jones, *Globalization and the Theory of Input Trade* (Cambridge, Mass.: MIT Press, 2000), pp. 155–57.

2. Ibid., pp. 155–57.

3. See "The Future of Farming in the Great American Desert," *The Economist*, 13 December 2001.

4. The index is available on the Internet at www.heritage.org.

5. Data from James Heckman and Carmen Pagés, The Cost of Job Security Regulation: Evidence from Latin American Markets, Working Paper #430, Research Department (Washington, D.C.: Inter-American Development Bank, 2000). This paper also provides a good review of the result of other studies on severance payments, which tend to confirm the negative impact these have on employment generation.

6. Ibid.

7. Pietro Garibaldi and Paolo Mauro, Deconstructing Job Creation IMF Working paper, WP/99/109, International Monetary Fund (Washington, D.C.: International Monetary Fund, 1999), pp. 3–5.

8. *The OECD Jobs Study: Implementing the Strategy* (Paris: OECD, 1996), p. 15.

9. See "How Restive Are European Muslims?" *The Economist*, 18 October 2001.

10. See Peter Drucker, "The Next Society: A Survey of the Near Future," *The Economist*, 1 November 2001.

11. Patrick Buchanan, *The Death of the West: How Dying Populations and Immigrant Invasions Are Threatening Our Country and Civilization* (New York: Thomas Dune Books, 2002), pp. 4–5.

CHAPTER 10

Politics and the New International Order

The problem of generating support for liberal policies is conceptually similar in developed and developing countries. In essence, the problem is that at any given moment, there are more people profiting from the old system than from the new one. To resolve it, it is necessary to reverse those proportions. Looking at the experience of the now developed countries during the Industrial Revolution may be useful in identifying the sectors and groups that naturally tend to support liberal policies.

The experience of the Industrial Revolution is not clear-cut, however. The allies and rivals of liberal policies were different in each of the now developed countries, so that, for example, in some of them the capitalists were supportive of liberal policies and protectionist in others. In some countries farmers were protectionist while in others they were liberals. The situation was more complex at the individual level. For example, as a rule workers were protectionists regarding the activities where they worked and liberal regarding the goods they bought. One instance of this behavior was evident more recently, in the 1980s in the United States. At that time, several observers noted that, while the United Auto Workers pushed for protection against imported competition, the parking lots of the factories where they worked were full of Japanese cars. Thus, the politics of protection and liberalization can get extremely complex. Is it possible to create sustainable coalitions to support free trade within this complexity? This is the subject of this chapter.

Examining who was for and who was against protection and liberal economic policies during the Industrial Revolution, Ronald Rogowski has shown that factors of production—labor, land, and capital—were not consistent in their preferences across countries. The same group was protectionist in some countries and supportive of liberal policies in others.[1] Rogowski explains these differences by looking at the relative scarcity of factors of production in each of the countries. Factors tended to be protectionist when they were relatively scarce in one country while they tended to be free traders when they were relatively abundant. In this fashion, British labor and capital were free traders because they were relatively abundant, while landowners were protectionist because land was scarce. In the United States land was abundant and therefore free trader while capital and labor were scarce and for this reason they were protectionist. In Germany labor was free trader because it was abundant while capital and land were protectionist because they were scarce.

Why should scarce factors favor protection while abundant ones favor free trade? The answer is that the relatively scarce factors collect a premium on their scarcity. For example, workers can earn higher salaries in a country where they are scarcer than in a country where they are abundant. When a country opens to international trade, the scarce factors become less scarce and their income is reduced naturally. For example, goods requiring much capital to be produced would be expensive in a country where this factor is scarce and cheap in another where it is not. If trade were open between the two countries, the price of the goods would fall in the first one, reducing the rents of capital prevailing there. The owners of capital would be unhappy, while the workers and the owners of land would be happy, because they would have to pay less for the goods in question.

Thus, it was logical that, being scarce in the United States, workers would be protectionists in that country, while, being abundant in Britain, they would be free traders there. Since the situation of capital was the same, it was logical that capital and workers allied to push for protection in the United States and to push for free trade in Britain. In Germany, however, capital and labor were not allied. There, labor (abundant) was left alone in its support for free trade while capital and land (scarce) allied with each other to promote protection.

While Rogowski's analysis produced results that closely mirrored reality during the nineteenth century, some important anomalies arose in his model of the twentieth century. We can mention three of the anomalies. First, during the Great Depression of the 1930s, all sectors in all countries turned protectionist, regardless of their relative abundance. Second, current landowners are protectionist all over the world, also regardless of the relative abundance of land in different countries. Third, the same can be said regarding textiles. These examples show that relative abundance is not the only determinant of the position that sectors take regarding international trade: sectors with declining relative or absolute earnings also tend to demand protection, regardless of their relative abundance or scarcity. This reverses Rogowski's logic. Rather than demanding protection because they are scarce, these sectors demand protection to become scarce in a world where competition in their field is springing up everywhere. This is what all sectors in all countries did during the Great Depression, when all of them were declining; it is the same that all sectors did in the developing countries during the twentieth century; and it is what all agricultural and textile sectors in the world are doing today.

Also differently from Rogowski's framework, currently we find no country fully committed to free trade as Britain, Denmark, and other countries were in the nineteenth century. Still, trade among developed countries tends to be free except for the declining products, such as agriculture and textiles. This may be taken, in Rogowski's terms, as a manifestation that capital and workers in high-value-added production have become abundant in all of these countries and they have allied with each other to adopt free trade, while workers and capitalists in declining activities have allied with each other and with landowners to promote protection. The result, however, has not been a confrontation of attitudes to free trade like the ones that took place in the nineteenth century. Rather, the result was a political arrangement that produced a split trade policy in which the growing sectors have supported free trade—or something close to it—for their own products while supporting protection for the declining ones.

To understand how this has happened, it is interesting to note that not all declining industries received protection in the developed countries during the last 20 or 30 years. Many of these, even if initially protected, were allowed to decline because the costs of protection were transferred to many other, more sophisticated products and reduced their competitiveness. During this period, protection concentrated on activities that do not produce important inputs for the sophisticated industries and those that do not tax the more sophisticated consumers excessively. The population of the developed countries can easily afford more expensive food and textiles and the high-value-added industries are not affected by higher prices for food. Therefore, it is cheap for politicians promoting policies in other subjects to buy the support of those promoting the protection of agriculture and textiles by agreeing to protect those activities. It should be added to this that farmers tend to be quite vociferous and uncompromising in those countries, particularly in Europe. Thus, politicians seeking their support for other matters are forced to accept their demands for protection.

This became the natural coalition in developed countries. It is not a single coalition against free trade but a series of coalitions on other subjects of policy that support protection to agriculture, textiles, and similar low-value-added activities just to get the votes needed for decisions regarding those other subjects. Since these are the products where developing countries can compete, the world has become asymmetrical. Trade is freer among developed countries than between them and the developing ones.

Ominously, on March 6, 2002, the United States imposed punitive tariffs on imported steel, going as high as 30 percent, adducing that steel imports were damaging the American steel sector. The problem is that steel has become a commodity that can be produced even in unsophisticated countries. Its production had already declined substantially in the United States when the government issued its protective measure. The problem only got worse since the drastic downsizing of the 1980s, when the problem became critical for the first time. *The Economist* reported that in 2000 the average cost of production of steel in the United States exceeded US$300 per ton for integrated producers and US$275 for mini-mills. Europe, Japan, and China had substantially lower costs. South America's was just over US$175.[2]

The tariffs imposed in 2002 were supposedly temporary, established for not more than three years. Their life could be much shorter if the United States is defeated in the World Trade Organization (WTO) and the United States yields to the decision of this institution. The important point, however, is that steel is a major input for many other products, and raising its cost artificially will have a severe negative impact on the competitiveness of those products. American cars, engines, and engineering products in general would face competition in both the domestic and the international markets from firms paying much less for steel. They would have what in economics jargon is called "negative protection."

In the long run, companies producing these goods would be forced to adopt strategies to avoid bankruptcy, which could include reducing the steel content of their products, substituting it with plastic or aluminum alloys; producing their goods outside the United States and importing them for local sales; or abandon the production of those goods that contain much steel. In fact, a large number of the engines included in cars produced in the United States are manufactured in Mexico and other places. As we discussed in the previous chapter, actions like this would defeat the purpose of the measure. More dangerously, if the steel lobby is able to keep the measure in place, the users of steel may also demand protection, at least to the point of offsetting the impact of higher steel costs.

This is unlikely to happen with steel. Most likely, the protective measures will be temporary. The United States already adjusted them by opening loopholes through which some competition from abroad can enter the country without discrimination. But the measure shows a trend that, if continued, could trigger a chain reaction of protective measures that in the end would cripple the American economy and endanger international trade. Processes like the one that swept the world in the last quarter of the nineteenth century or like that which destroyed international trade in the 1930s would take place, with dire consequences for the world economy. A world depression could not be ruled out and, with it, the unleashing of unpredictable social conflicts.

While the certain retaliation of the trade partners would have these undesirable effects, the worst effect of this measure would be the triggering of a race for state protection to ensure the economic success of specific sectors. With time, this would create the environment for political conflicts between sectors, further eroding the social cohesion and self-reliance that have been the basis of the American success. The problems of modern times are too complex to increase their complexity in this artificial way.

In developing societies, protection and other obstacles to the mobility of factors is not the result of the disinterest of the most powerful coalitions, as it seems to be the case in the developed countries. On the contrary, they are manifestations of the political clout of the most powerful political sectors. Governments of these societies are forced to dispense favors to many different groups to be able to govern. They tend to do it through protection and regulations because these apportion income to politically powerful groups without requiring government cash expenditures. With time, such arrangements result in the maze of privileges to different sectors characteristic of underdeveloped societies. The complexity of those systems is such that it is difficult to determine what sectors are more privileged than others, because the advantages obtained by some sectors are compensated by the advantages granted to other sectors. However, in net terms, it is clear that there is an alliance between landowners, capitalists, and industrial workers to artificially increase the rents of land, capital, and primitive industrial skills.

The political scenario of developing countries is rooted in the divisiveness of their societies. As a result of their fragmentation, they have become prey to the rule of small elites, which have managed these countries for centuries. The composition of these elites has changed over time. In the nineteenth century, they included landowners, the military, and politicians that served them. They were successful in stifling the industrialization of their countries. In the twentieth century, they supported industrialization but they co-opted the emerging economic and social groups in a way that resembled Germany in the late nineteenth century. These elites repressed the labor movements. The resulting confrontation between capitalists and landowners on the one side, and workers on the other, led to the triumph of the extreme left in many countries, like Cuba, Vietnam, Kampuchea, and China. In most of them, however, the conflict was resolved with the incorporation of the industrial workers to the commanding elites through the protection that labor regulations established for them. This consolidated a coalition that has dominated the developing countries for decades on end. When seen from the perspective of political economy, it is easy to understand why developing countries pursue policies that are irrational from the point of view of society as a whole: they are profitable for the coalitions that hold political power.

Generally speaking, these coalitions developed two models of restrictive economic regimes. One is what we call the Latin American model, which we also call the model of private ownership and high economic instability; the other is the model for the rest of the developing world, which we call the model of government ownership of enterprises in industry, services and low levels of instability. The two models are mixed— many governments in Latin America owned substantial portions of the productive capacity and some countries outside Latin America have experienced serious economic instability. However, the differences in degree allow for a conceptual distinction.

In the Latin American model, the main partners of the elite coalition are the agrarian, industrial, and financial capitalists. They support protection for obvious reasons. Protection granted to agricultural products does not result in conflicts with the industrialists because, typically, industrialists do not use domestic agricultural products as inputs. The agrarian capitalists sell their commodities in raw forms in the international markets while industrialists tend to import duty free semifinished goods that they turn into protected final goods. Protection to agricultural products affects the costs of production of industrialists only through an indirect channel: it increases the price of food, thus reducing the real wage of workers. For this reason, industrialists have to pay higher wages than in a free trade economy to pay a given real wage. On the other hand, protection of industrial products does increase the cost of production of agricultural commodities in countries where farmers are forced to buy protected machinery, equipment, and chemicals from the domestic industry. But bearing with these effects is the price that landowners and industrialists pay for the mutual support in their struggle to get more protection.

The main partners also support inflation and devaluations because these mechanisms afford them profits in several dimensions. First, they keep the real wages low. Second, since all the members of these groups keep their savings in foreign currency, they gain in acquisitive power in the domestic market when the currency is devalued. Third, in the case of the financial capitalists, the policy of inflation and devaluations works as a protective barrier as effectively as import tariffs do for farmers and industrialists. Highly unstable financial environments keep away competition from foreign banks, allowing them to charge the large intermediation spreads characteristic of the developing countries. The main partners tolerate regulations affording protection to the industrial workers because such protection buys the support of the industrial trade unions for the overall economic model.

The share of the industrial workers in the deal is poor. Their salaries are still very low and they are kept so by the devaluations. Yet, they are higher than those of the rest of the workers and they have their jobs assured. Since they know that such privileges depend on the maintenance of protection for the enterprises where they work, they and their trade unions have become strong defenders of protection and restrictions to the mobility of factors of production.

This alliance proved overwhelming for almost a century. Its excesses, however, debilitated it in the 1980s and 1990s through the processes that led to the liberalization of their economies, already discussed in previous chapters. While weakened, however, the old alliance is still strong and protection, even if lower than at the mid-century, has remained high in the developing countries, hindering their capacity to grow and adjust. The failure of the mixed system that has emerged from the incomplete reforms is playing back into the hands of the old alliance, which is pointing out the lack of growth of the decade after the reforms and demanding to go back to higher rates of protection.

In the model of extensive government ownership of productive enterprises that is more common outside Latin America, the senior partners include capitalists and bureaucrats managing the state-owned enterprises. As in Latin America, workers in the industrial- and government-owned service enterprises are junior partners. In those countries, inflation and instability tend to be lower than in Latin America, not because they have more fiscal and monetary discipline but because they repress the financial markets more effectively. At the same time, protection and regulations restricting the mobility of factors tend to be more asphyxiating. In India, for example, the bureaucrats became so powerful that even as late as the mid-1980s government permits were needed for every production run of every product. If, for example, a company wanted to produce light bulbs, it had to specify, when requesting the permit, the design and the number of units to be produced. If, in the midst of the production run management decided to change the color of the bulbs, it had to request permission to do it. In many countries, government-owned companies become more powerful than the government itself because they control more cash and were not subject to the procedures of government auditing agencies.

In general, the hybrid regimes that emerged from the liberalization of the 1990s are failing to spur the growth that the liberal politicians had promised and this is strengthening the political position of the old elites. They point to the more stable times when they controlled everything in the economy and blame the new politicians for the low growth of the last decade. Of course, they would not be able to reproduce the calm conditions of the linear times of 20 or 30 years ago. But they can derail the process of reforms and with this, close the opportunities that connectivity and globalization is opening for them.

In summary, the identity of the members of the elites that control developing countries and the details of the mechanisms they use to promote their interests may diverge, but the effects are the same: poverty, ignorance, and backwardness.

The facts of the political economy of adjustment seem disheartening. We have identified two major problems that should be resolved.

- First, developed countries would have to challenge politically their most inefficient sectors to dismantle the schemes that today protect them against foreign competition mostly in activities lagging in value added per worker.
- Second, developing countries would have to overcome the coalition that has dominated them for the best part of two centuries to liberalize their trade regimes, to eliminate their own asphyxiating regulations, and impose fiscal, monetary, and financial discipline.

In both cases, relatively small groups that command significant power in their own local states are deterring a process that would benefit many countries. The political symbiosis in each of the sets of countries makes it very difficult to weaken and overcome these coalitions.

This is precisely the problem that worried Alexander Hamilton and James Madison when designing the shape of the government of the United States. They tried to resolve it through the creation of the federal government. They rightly guessed that a federal government would be freer than local governments to deal with local interest groups. We do not have that choice in our times. A federal government imposing the common good on countries is unfeasible. Political integration is out of the question. But some kind of international political institution could help.

What kind of international institutional setting should prevail to facilitate the transformation and maximize the benefits of connectivity at the global level?

Multilateral official financial institutions, such as the International Monetary Fund and the World Bank, have struggled for decades to help carrying out the required reforms. However, their leverage, while substantial, is not enough to break the power of the controlling elites in the developing countries and is nonexistent in the case of the developed ones.

We need stronger mechanisms to break resistance to change. This can be achieved in the developing countries by creating a credible prospect of growth associated with liberal policies. This can only be provided by access to the developed markets. All voters in developing countries—except for those living in radicalized countries—understand the potential for growth associated with integrating their economies with those of the most advanced countries in the world. It is to integrate themselves within those more developed societies that so many of them migrate or try to migrate to them. Getting such integration can easily become a common purpose that would give unity to their societies, starting the process of social, political, and economic development that has been denied to them by their own fragmentation.

Thus, the liberalization of developing countries and with it, the possibility of eliminating poverty worldwide, passes through the liberalization of the developed ones. The solution hinges on finding a way to facilitate the liberalization of developed countries. The problem is what to do to help the workers that would be displaced by the liberal trade regime in those countries. In the long term, these countries have effective educational systems that would easily upgrade the potential of these workers to increase the value added they could produce. In the short term, there is no other solution but the judicious use of social security.

Theoretically, in economies where the workers that would be displaced by technological change are in a minority, the gains in efficiency that the economy would obtain with the transformation would be enough to remunerate the innovators and still leave something to compensate the losers through social security benefits. This would oil the process. Workers who would not sink in poverty as a result of the introduction of modern methods of production would tend to oppose modernization with less virulence than people who would have no alternative source of income if they were fired. The United States used a mechanism like this, the Trade Promotion Act, to smooth out the introduction of the North American Free Trade Agreement (NAFTA) in the 1990s. The law, still in force, provides income and training to the people displaced by the new patterns of trade.

The solution, however, is not that simple. Social security also results in stiffening rigidities, mainly because funding social security requires heavy taxation that adds to the cost of production for local enterprises, reducing their competitiveness relative to those of countries where such taxation does not exist or is lower. It was for this reason that Bismarck introduced protection for the German enterprises at the same time that it imposed the social security system on them. Thus, in Europe, the notion that the government would protect the consumption of unemployed workers became linked to the understanding that the government would also prevent the failure of the big enterprises that provide a good portion of the employment.

Such understanding produced a system of regulation that suffocates the creation of new firms and new activities in Europe. This trapped the region within traditional industrial activities with a declining value added per potentially employed worker. While in the United States the economy has already evolved away from low-value-added jobs in many industries, this has not happened as yet in Europe. Industrial jobs in the United States have already come down to about 17 percent of the labor force but in Europe industrial employment still accounts for around 35 percent. Many of the activities performed by these workers can be carried out more cheaply in countries with lower wages and lower social security benefits. To reduce their costs of production, continental European companies are investing abroad but their economies are not generating the jobs needed to replace those that they are exporting. As in Japan, resources generated by the efficient enterprises are taken away from production and invest-ment to keep an inefficient system in place. The more rigid the salaries and regulations, the more unemployed there are, the higher the payroll taxes needed, the higher the costs of producing in Europe, and the stronger the trend of European companies to invest abroad to reduce their costs.

There are other problems with the social security approach. In the initial years of the transformation, the higher efficiency of the new methods of production would leave preciously scarce resources available for the com-pensation of unemployed workers and failing enterprises. It takes a con-siderable time for the new methods to render their benefits and, as we have seen throughout this book, economies undergoing radical transfor-mations are prone to recessions and even depressions. These circum-stances have come around when the European countries have little room for maneuver to increase the benefits of their social security systems.

The average government subsidies and transfers in the 12 largest econ-omies in Europe increased from 10.8 percent of GDP to 26.8 percent from 1960 to 1995 and remain to this day around that figure. With such levels of transfers, total government expenditures increased from 28 to over 43 percent of GDP in the same period.[3] Given these figures, it is not realistic to believe that the social security transfers could be increased from their already high levels. On the contrary, they will probably have to be reduced because heavy taxation is one of the reasons why European countries cannot create new economic activities and enterprises. Short of dictatorial measures, there is nothing that European governments can do to stop the investments that European companies are carrying out in East Europe and other regions with lower wages except lowering the costs of hiring work-ers in their own countries. The only instrument that they have to do this is reducing the payroll taxes and taxation in general. This, however, means that social security benefits should be reduced precisely when they would be most needed if new growth were not spurred inside their local econ-omies to replace the jobs transferred to the lower-wage countries. The result is a vicious circle.

Yet, for all its shortcomings, a judiciously designed social security sys-tem may be the only solution that countries have to assuage the pain of the transformation. Social security reform should concentrate on both reducing the overall level of benefits—27 percent of GDP is too high a burden to carry in the increasingly competitive world markets—while targeting them on the poorest sectors of the population. Even half the current amount would facilitate the integration of these sectors to the new world of connectivity if the benefits were targeted. Of course, this would require a shift in the mechanisms used to fund the social security systems, from payroll contributions to general taxation, because those funding the system would not receive its direct benefits. They would go to the poor. The more affluent could be shifted to private pension systems. This, of course, implies a sacrifice of the latter. The sacrifices that they would have to make if the process is not facilitated, however, would be much worse.

This solution is not available for the developing countries. They are too poor to carry out significant transfers from one part of the population to another. The only solution available for these countries is to accelerate their growth, which means accelerating their integration in the world economy.

What would be better? Work in the integration of the world all at once or by trade blocks? The first is the aim of the WTO. The second is what could be done by extending the European Union and NAFTA.

The emergence of these two processes has elicited a heated controversy in some quarters. Integrating the world in all dimensions of economic activity would be the best in a theoretical world. A single economic space maximizes the opportunities for an efficient use for all factors of production and reduces transaction cost in all places, in such a way that the potential for growth of any locality would increase when inserted within a larger economy. It is obvious that, for example, New York gains from being part of a single economic space with the rest of the United States. So does any small city or county in the Midwest or on the Pacific shore. The same logic applies to Paris, Marseilles, or any other place in France and now in the European Union. It would apply equally if all places in the world became parts of a single economy. In fact, the integration of localities into larger economic spaces was one of the engines for the tremendous economic development that accompanied the Industrial Revolution. Thus, attaining this total integration at the global level would be the best that we can attain. Moreover, it would be the best not just for the future connected economy but also for the transformation process because larger economic spaces would maximize the dimensions of adjustment. The mobile factors of production—labor and capital—would flow to the places and activities where they could be best used. The costs of adjustment would be lower around the globe.

Taking the approach of the regional trade blocks is obviously inferior to the creation of one single global trade space. Regional blocks keep protection in place against those not included in the block and the gains of trade are not fully realized. Moreover, there is no guarantee that the trade blocks would eventually merge into a single world market. Such blocks have a crucial advantage, however: they are easier to create, by several orders of magnitude, than a world trade order. In practice, a combination of regional blocks with a longer-term effort to liberalize trade worldwide seems to be the best, just because a rapid global liberalization is not feasible. In the imperfect world we live, forming increasingly large trade blocks can be the best way of attaining the worldwide liberalization. This is what has been happening in fact.

Trade blocks have another crucial advantage. Because they are negotiated among smaller numbers of participants, they are more amenable to full economic integration than global treaties that just liberalize trade. The two regional efforts—the EU and NAFTA—have gone a long way in the creation of integrated economic spaces, where not only trade rules but also other economic regulations are homologated. Countries become partners rather than just potential traders. For this reason, they have proven to be quite effective vehicles of modernization—or, said in another way, effective vehicles to export the social order of the most developed partners. Mexico is benefiting enormously from its participation in NAFTA, well beyond the gains it obtained from the trade liberalization. Modernity is spreading fast across the country, factors of production are becoming more mobile, the enforcement of the rule of law has improved drastically, and even political processes are becoming more transparent and democratic.

The same happened in Spain and Portugal when they entered the European Union. Their societies became more horizontal and multidimensional. This benefited not only those societies but also their more advanced partners, which in addition to a larger market, got more secure neighbors. Trade blocks could play a key role in the creation of a new, more harmonious world order. Trade blocks could also become a vehicle for worldwide liberalization if they negotiate in the WTO with a single voice.

Today's trade blocks are opening the door for a rapid liberalization of the world's economy. They, however, have a crippling defect in setting in motion modernization processes in the developing countries: they are not automatically open to new entrants. The entry of each potential partner depends on arbitrary decisions of the members of the blocks and the terms and conditions are negotiated from zero. This works against the logic of networks and gravely retards the process of globalization, hindering the adjustment to the new connected world. It is different from the membership rules of the WTO, which is open to all entrants willing to comply with the rules binding the existing members. This kind of arrangement, if adopted by trading blocks, would greatly accelerate the dissemination of free trade and would create strong incentives for modernization in developing countries if the conditions of access forced the adoption of liberal policies, modern commercial legislation, and transparent procedures in the domestic markets. The certainty that meeting these requirements would automatically give them access to a trade block would give a strong reason for countries to dismantle the damaging regulations that today restrict the mobility of resources, to enforce the rule of law, and become more democratic.

To use trade blocks as vehicles of modernization it is essential that the rules be fixed and binding on all members equally, so that it would be clear to every potential member what it needs to do to enter the block. There would be nothing to negotiate, just like entering the WTO. Even transition periods should be fixed. The only valid reason to reject an application would be that the applicant does not meet the conditions for access. Member countries violating one of the fundamental covenants would be automatically suspended or expelled. In this way, trading blocks could create the foundations for the new international order that must be created to replace the one that now is crumbling. There would be mechanisms to export the most valuable of commodities, an efficient social order from the developed to the developing countries.

This is not a new idea. This was the way the Hanseatic League was organized in the early centuries of the last millennium with great success. Today, the European Union is applying it in a limited way to absorb within its structure some of the formerly Communist countries in East Europe, also with great success. The Union has provided assurances to the countries included in the compact that they would be accepted as members of the Union as soon as they comply with strict and well-defined conditions of social order. These countries have decided that becoming members of the Union is a high priority for them, and are making extremely fast progress in meeting the Union's conditions.

If it is true that trading blocks can become vehicles to expand efficient social order into the developing countries, the problem is how to create in rich and developing countries the twin coalitions that would make it possible to expand them. The problem is much easier to resolve in the developing countries than in the developed ones. Growth has been so slow in most of the former that the possibility of getting access to larger markets is an attractive political message. It can give a powerful common purpose to the developing societies, strong enough to break the remnants of the old protectionist coalition. The examples of Spain, Portugal, Mexico, and now the formerly Communist countries, are encouraging enough to be set as paradigms. If the general voters understand what they could gain, they will provide the national consensus required to dismantle the inefficient schemes now in place.

In contrast, eliminating protection to agricultural and textile products is not among the issues that can unify the developed societies under a common purpose. Most people in the United States are not even aware that the problem exists. The minorities that would be affected by liberalization, however, are quite vocal and easily turn violent. Thus, it is not easy to find strong support for the elimination of the protectionist policies.

Voters in developed countries should weigh the problems that could come from the dismantling of protection for low-value-added activities against the much worse ones that would come about if liberal economic and political regimes fail to spur growth n the developing countries for lack of access to larger markets. If this happens, the developing world would sink in the stagnation or the destructiveness that are the by-products of illiberal regimes.

Some developing countries have already chosen a destructive path. Not much can be done about them and it would be naïve to believe that their choice could have been affected by opening the markets of the developed countries to their agricultural and industrial exports. But the important point is preventing others from becoming sympathizers of these or new focuses of violence and terrorism. Altogether, this is a case in which solidarity coincides with self-interest.

Mobilizing support in the rich counties for an integration of their economies with those of the developing ones may prove to be very difficult. The indifference that people in the developed countries show for the trade regime of low-value-added activities is not confined to this matter. It seems to be extending to all communal issues, betraying a weakening of the social bonds that helped these countries to adjust harmoniously to industrialization. In fact, it seems that connectivity itself is eroding the social bonds that gave cohesion to the modern industrial state.

This problem is the subject of the next chapter.

NOTES

1. Roland Rogowski, *Commerce and Coalitions: How Trade Affects Domestic Political Arrangements* (Princeton, N.J.: Princeton University Press, 1989).

2. "Smeltdown," *The Economist*, 18 October 2001.

3. See Vito Tanzi, Globalization and the Future of Social Protection IMF Working Paper WP/00/12, International Monetary Fund, (Washington D.C.: International Monetary Fund, 2000) pp. 8–9.

CHAPTER 11

The Problem of Social Cohesion

Social bonds are very weak in the developing countries. In fact, that is why these societies are underdeveloped and have resorted to vertical structures to keep social order in place. While many societies have made remarkable progress in recent times with the introduction of effective democratic institutions, social cohesion remains weak and democracy fragile. The old divisiveness that caused their underdevelopment and led to their vertical shapes of social organization is returning as the rapid improvements that people expected in the quality of their lives as a result of political and economic liberalization are not materializing. Rather, in many of these countries, liberalization has not reverted the process of decay that had started in the more vertical times for all the reasons we discussed in part one. Many people in those countries, forgetting that the old regimes had become nonviable, are longing today for the simplistic one-dimensional organization, idealizing the stability of vertical structures. Theirs is the typical problem created by the rapid dissolution of the old order and the slow buildup of the new one. The success or failure of the Connectivity Revolution to create a more horizontal world will crucially depend on the nature and smoothness of this transition. What should emerge is as a superior form of social organization, based on strong social bonds and more horizontal structures—not a return to the vertical order of the past.

The problem of the transition, however, is not exclusive to the developing countries. As expressed by Richard Sennet in words I quoted in a previous chapter, social cohesion seems to be weakening in the developed countries as well. As this happens, the developed societies are acquiring some of the traits of the underdeveloped ones.

I discuss this worrying problem in this chapter, starting with an examination of the relationship between social bonds and underdevelopment.

The lack of strong social bonds is evident in each and every one of the dimensions of social life of developing countries. In these societies there is a widespread cynicism about politicians and political institutions; traditionally, the emphasis in social relations has been on the differences between different groups rather than on their commonalities; factions have dominated the political environment, and communal life has not existed.

The social fragmentation of underdeveloped societies is not limited to the economic cleavage that separates rich from poor. It exists inside the rich and the poor groups as well. It is for this reason that these countries have shown a remarkable inability to create stable political regimes. For centuries, they showed a tendency to stage continuous revolutions and coups, each of which led by people who heralded the dawn of a new era for their countries only to be overthrown, sooner or later, by another group making the same claim.

This weakness, which was common to all developing countries, from Latin America to Africa to Asia, made room for the conquest of the latter two by small contingents from the industrial countries, which were able to dominate the countries by playing one domestic group against the other. In the late eighteenth century, for example, a small group of commercial clerks led by Robert Clive conquered an enormous territory in India by creating and dissolving alliances with local princes until they dominated all of them, establishing the foundations for the British Empire in India. Later, other employees of the British East India Company completed the task by using essentially the same strategy. Africa and most of Asia fell into foreign domination in this way during the nineteenth century. This weakness of the locals, more than the technological superiority of the westerners, was the reason why the latter could conquer and retain for centuries countries with many more inhabitants than the imperial center. This did not happen in Latin America because the United States proclaimed the Monroe Doctrine early in the nineteenth century. However, the newly independent Latin countries established records of both lengthy dictatorships and frequency of coups. Up to the mid-1980s, for example, Bolivia had had more governments than years of independence.

The inability to create a sustainable political regime and the existence of this rigid line splitting society are evidences of a lack of social cohesion between rich and poor, rich and rich and poor and poor. Society as a whole, and groups inside society, cannot organize themselves to attain a common purpose for a prolonged time. People in these countries define themselves in terms of what makes them different from other members of the same society rather than in terms of their commonalities, something that is both a cause and a consequence for the lack of communal life. With all these problems, the different groups are in a perpetual conflict that forestalls any possibility of development for all of them.

The poor themselves achieve much less than what they could because they cannot organize themselves to improve their condition. Some of the most impressive examples of what a poor community can do to improve its conditions and start on the road to progress are given by instances in which non-poor people have taken the time to organize them for the attainment of one common purpose. This is a repetition of the success that civic groups had during the Industrial Revolution in the elimination of poverty in the countries that adjusted harmoniously to industrialization. In most of the current cases, however, the organizers are not local nationals but foreigners, people from developed countries. Most often than not, they are volunteers that travel far and suffer the conditions of poverty to help their faraway brethrens. These foreigners do not have any comparative advantage to do this work in terms of formal education or wealth over the higher classes of the country they travel to help. Yet, the latter are seldom seen in those activities. There is no real interest in the upper classes of developing societies in resolving the problem of poverty; no sense of communality with the poor; no sense of urgency to resolve their problem and no understanding that poverty is bad for the rich segment because it traps countries in underdevelopment.

The lack of social cohesion is also visible in a phenomenon that is common to all developing countries: the stark difference between the bad quality of public facilities—such as roads, parks, sewerage systems, and the like—and the high, or at least adequate, quality of the private homes of the upper and middle classes. From India to Latin America, from Africa to the Middle East, it is common to travel through terribly deteriorated and sometimes dangerous roads to enter luxurious houses that seem to have been transported directly from the developed world. In many countries, while private schools are excellent, public schools are a disaster. The same happens regarding health facilities and even public security. In Brazil, for example, the amount that the affluent spends in private security is at least 30 percent more than the total budget of public police. Private guards outnumber the police three to one.[1] The situation is likely to be similar in many other developing countries that do not carry statistics about the subject.

The coexistence of private affluence and public decay in the developing countries has been frequently attributed to the difference in efficiency existing between the private and the public sector, and it has been one of the arguments for privatization of public facilities. Such difference is a reality and some of these problems have been resolved when privatizations have been properly carried out. But the problem is deeper than this. There is a generalized lack of concern for the fate of the overall society. People do not care if the road is rotten as long as their home is comfortable and secure. They do not care if the children of other people are badly educated or not educated at all as long as theirs are well-educated, and they do not care about the quality of the public health services as long as theirs is good. As long as this problem is not resolved, the "developing countries," which is the politically correct term for them, will be not more than "underdeveloped societies," which is the accurate term for many of them.

Hernando de Soto, the famous Peruvian social scientist I already quoted, has repeatedly pointed out that poverty is largely a problem caused by the lack of access of the poor to the social capital imbedded in the institutions of the more affluent part of society. Just getting such access would do much to reduce poverty. The case of the migrations from the developing to developed countries confirms this perception. People who are dirt poor in the former tend to increase their standard of living dramatically when they migrate to the latter. Even if many—if not most—of these people remain poor under the measure of poverty of the developed countries, they get out of poverty by the measure of the developing ones.

Social bonds are much stronger in developed societies—in fact, this is why they are developed. Yet, the last few decades have shown manifestations of what appears to be a weakening of such bonds in these societies too. The roots of those trends are complex. Not all of them can be attributed to the Connectivity Revolution; many are the result of the natural evolution of the industrial society. Yet, connectivity reinforces all of them and, when taken together, they seem to evidence the erosion of social bonds that is characteristic of a deep technological transformation. Such erosion is visible in the abandonment of communal life; the crisis of political institutions and the increasing power of political factions.

Robert D. Putnam, a Harvard professor of sociology, raises these concerns, focused on the United States, in a book called *Bowling Alone: The Collapse and Revival of American Community*. He shows how communal life has declined in the United States in the recent past—including participation in political, civic, religious, philanthropic, and informal social events. A small sample of his findings suffices to show the decline in communal life and the progressive isolation of the individual.[2] In the United States:

- participation in civic organizations halved from 1969 to 1997.
- active involvement in community organizations fell by 45 percent between 1985 and 1994.

- the number of people who took any leadership role in any civic organization went down by more than 50 percent in the same period.
- regarding clubs, if the current trend were projected into the future, they would disappear within the next 20 years.
- the same trend is appreciable in professional associations. For example, the membership of the American Institute of Architects, while increasing substantially in absolute terms, declined as a percent of the number of architects, from 51 in 1963 to 37 in 1997; that of nurses from 18 to 9 between 1977 and 1998; and so on.
- people are participating less in church activities and these activities involve less communal tasks than 40 years ago.
- people entertain and visit other people less frequently.
- friendships in the work place and the neighborhood are declining, too.
- the people who have contributed to some charity in the last month declined from almost 50 percent in 1980 to slightly over 30 percent in 1995 while the percent of national income going to philanthropic organizations has declined by 30 percent. United Way giving has come down from its peak at 15 percent of family income in 1930 to about 5 percent in 1997.

All of these symptoms betray an increasing isolation of the individual, which, as we have seen in a previous chapter, Richard Sennet attributes to the fleeting nature of the relationships that the new world of connectivity is bringing about in the workplace, the neighborhood, and in general.

The effects of the increasing isolation of the individuals are not limited to interaction with friends and acquaintances. It also has direct implications for families. For example, the membership of the parent-teacher associations went down from 47 percent of the parents with kids 18 and under in the late 1950s to less than 20 percent in the mid-1990s. This is happening precisely when education is becoming more important.

Problems of declining participation in civic and communal activities have been observed in Europe, too. Anthony Giddens, a British professor, points this out in a recent book.[3] Quoting a study carried out by Peter Hall in the United Kingdom,[4] he observes that the membership of organizations devoted to voluntary work have remained unchanged in that country since the 1950s. He also notes, however, that this is the aggregate result of an increase in the participation of the more affluent parts of the population and a decline in the participation of the poorer communities.

The problem that Giddens is pointing to is increasing the social divide within the poorer citizens and between them and the richer ones. Society is becoming more fragmented as "the sweep of economic and social changes" is marginalizing a good portion of the population.

Giddens also points to two of the aspects of the dissolution of social order in the communities in Europe—the chaotic environment created by petty crime in the cities and the migration toward secluded areas it is eliciting:

One of the most significant innovations in criminology in recent years has been the discovery that the decay of day-to-day civility relates directly to criminality. For a long while attention was focused on almost exclusively upon serious crime—robbery, assault or violence. More minor crimes and forms of public disorder, however, tend to have a cumulative effect. In European and American cities, when asked to describe their problems, residents of troubled neighborhoods mention abandoned cars, graffiti, prostitution, youth gangs and similar phenomena.

People act on their anxieties about these issues: they leave the areas in question if they can, or they buy heavy locks for their doors and bars for their windows, and abandon public facilities. Disorderly behavior unchecked signals to citizens that the area is unsafe. . . . As they withdraw physically, they also withdraw from roles of mutual support with fellow citizens, thereby relinquishing the social controls that formerly helped to maintain civility within the community.[5]

This trend has reached its extreme in the creation of protected communities separated from the rest of society. In the United States, 47 million people, equivalent to a sixth of the population, live in 230,000 of these planned communities, paying US$35 billion in fees to cover their communities' needs for protection, maintenance of common areas, education and in many cases, health. All these communities share a feature in common: they try to be as self-sufficient as possible.[6] This is a legitimate response to a worrying problem, the decline of the general quality of life in the cities, in itself a manifestation of the weakening social interest in developed societies. However, it also betrays the surrender to geographical fragmentation as a solution to the growing cleavages of American society. In turn, this mechanism will tend to deepen the gaps that are emerging between different groups in the country. However justified, the fly to seclusion tends to nurture the idea that one can live comfortably in the midst of a society that is dissolving in crime and low levels of education.[7] This used to happen only in developing countries. In fact, developed societies are becoming similar to the developing ones in this crucial respect. The strength of existing institutions is such that, even if this fundamental engine of social cohesion is weakening, the damaging results are not yet visible. The economy keeps on expanding, the institutions keep on working, and everything seems fine. But society is weakening at the core.

Another sign of fragmentation is given by the increase in radicalism that we discussed in part one. The radicals are very small minorities that carry little weight in democratic elections. Yet, they have acquired great importance in the recent past because they are playing in a political vacuum caused by the increasing cynicism over both government and party politics that has been taking place the last several decades in the most developed societies. The decline of the prestige of political institutions is apparent all over the world. Politicians, who used to be heroes in the first half of the twentieth century, are progressively seen as corrupt individuals bent on pursuing their careers without paying any attention to the needs of their countries. When asked, "How much of the time do you trust the government in Washington to do the right thing?" the percent of Americans answering "most of the time" dropped from 76 in 1964 to 25 in 1994.[8] The cynicism is becoming evident in the changes in the participation in political activities. Within 20 years, from 1973–1974 to 1993–1994, the percent of the population that worked for a political party decreased by 42 percent; that which participated in any of 12 different political activities, by 25 percent; those who wrote to a congressman or senator, by 23; those who held or ran for a political office, by 16 percent.[9]

Mistrust in politicians is old and even traditional in democratic countries. In fact, the institutional setting of democracies aims at minimizing the deleterious effect that untrustworthy politicians may have in the life of society. Scandals and personalized attacks have been common before. In none of these cases, however, people lost confidence in the democratic process, even if the personalized attacks were much worse than anything that has been observed in modern times. What is new and dangerous in our times is the transference of mistrust from the individual politicians to the institutions. Subtly but surely, the legitimacy of democratic institutions is declining all over the world.

One of the symptoms of the decline of the legitimacy of the institutional setting of democracy is the emergence of a host of single-issue organizations that claim to be more legitimate than elected officials. Amazingly, this claim has been taken as face value in the political scenarios of all countries. As this happens, the focus of politics is shifting from political parties, organizations concerned with the overall situation of the country, to organizations concerned only with narrow issues. This is a vehicle for social fragmentation, of which radicals can take swift advantage. In fact, they are already taking advantage of this phenomenon to create their own single-issue organizations, acquiring a good stage to give the impression that their ideas are more popular than they are.

Any of these organizations now claims to be more legitimate than the elected representatives of the people and feels entitled to disturb and even prevent the meetings of world leaders "in the name of the people." They claim to be a part of "the civil society," wrapping themselves in the mantle of organizations of civic work. They reinforce each other in their claims, so that now this new kind of civil society has become the ultimate judge of the governments' actions.

The idea that these groups are more legitimate politically than elected representatives gained intellectual currency as many sociologists noted that civil society organizations, while common in democracies, did not exist in tyrannical regimes. In a classical non sequitur, this observation led to the conclusion that they are the basis of democracy and the natural auditors of governments. Some authors have called them the "social capital," meaning that they embody the society's capacity to organize itself in a democratic way. Through this claim, these organizations appropriate for themselves what is the true capital of a society, the entire institutional setting, which includes the Supreme Court, the Legislative Branch, the laws, the organization of businesses, and so on.

Certainly, civil society organizations played a crucial role in the development of democracy and economic freedom. Yet, we must distinguish between two kinds of civil society organizations. One category comprises civic institutions of the kind that helped to build the social cohesion required for the harmonious adjustment to the Industrial Revolution. They were, and still are, apolitical. They want to advance a certain objective and their members associate to work together in attaining it through their own efforts. In this way, people organize themselves to help hospitals, or to tend the needy, or to preserve nature. The Swedish institutions that helped resolve the social problems of their country during the nineteenth century are prime examples of this kind of organization. The Salvation Army, the Red Cross, the British Friendly Societies, and the Boy Scouts are also among thousands of these positive groups.

These, however, are not the ones that have emerged in the last few decades to dominate the current political scenario and claim legitimacy as the foundations of democracy. They do not organize the personal participation of citizens in the solution of society's problems. Instead, they aim at influencing the government into taking action in favor of single-issue interests. They are essentially political but they campaign outside the established democratic institutions and have a vested interest in subverting them, so that they can attain their objectives without having to win elections. Typically, their constituents do not know each other. Their participation is limited to reading the mail, promotional material sent by these organizations, and writing checks for them if they like their stated objectives. They participate by proxy, granting funds and legitimacy to the managers of these organizations.

Delegating political participation to people who have not been elected and have power but no responsibility may generate severe problems. The enormous amounts of money that these institutions mobilize give their managers astonishing political power, which they can use within the loosely defined frameworks in which they operate. They become kingmakers because they can support or destroy politicians. The temptation to use this power for personal benefit is strong. This temptation also exists for politicians. They, however, have not just power but also responsibility.

The dominance of single-issue organizations that require no more than a check from their members is another symptom of the withdrawal from communal life and social interest that we discussed in previous paragraphs. Surrendering personal contact is extremely dangerous for the political process. As expressed by Putnam:

A politics without face-to-face socializing and organizing might take the form of a Perot-style electronic town hall, a kind of plebiscitary democracy. Many opinions would be heard, but only as a muddle of disembodied voices, neither engaging with one another nor offering much guidance to decision makers . . . Citizenship is not a spectator sport . . .
Without such face-to-face interaction, without immediate feedback, without being forced to examine our opinions under the light of other citizens' scrutiny, we find it easier to hawk quick fixes and to demonize anyone who disagrees. Anonymity is fundamental anathema to deliberation.[10]

Naturally, when most people stop participating in political activities, those are increasingly left in the hands of extremists. This is happening in the United States. According to data provided by the Roper Social and Political Trends Survey, while participation in politics has declined throughout, it has declined much more in people describing themselves as middle-of-the-road, so that the political activity at the grass roots level is increasingly under the control of the polarized extremes. This is not to say that the American society is becoming polarized. On the contrary, the proportion of Americans describing themselves as middle-of-the-road is increasing. They, however, are not participating, and are leaving the field to those who do not think like them.[11] Noting that in a 1998 primary election in his home state of Missouri the voter turnout was lower than 15 percent, Richard Gephardt, a leading Democrat in the United States, expresses the same concern:

Partly as a reaction to the partisan dogfighting that they see on their nightly news, Americans everywhere have been turning away from politics, not bothering to vote, not bothering to hope. The result, of course, is a vicious circle, because, as fewer people vote, the influence of those at the extremes—who do vote—becomes ever greater.[12]

These developments have not resulted in a radicalization of the American society mainly because they take a long time to have an effect. Even if declining, the middle-of-the-road people still constitute a massive majority. People belonging to the most radical of these organizations—like those that disrupt the meetings of world leaders with violent demonstrations against globalization—cannot win an election, at least in this moment. The impact they have on government actions is similar to that of mobs attacking palaces in the nineteenth century: they were not the majority and were not representative. Yet, they were able to set siege on governments and change the perception of reality for the majority of the people.

When thinking that civil society organizations of this kind are the basis of democracy we should remember that the German Weimar Republic that preceded the accession of Hitler was full of them and that the number and membership of these organizations increased exponentially as the breakdown of democracy was nearing. Not one of the enthusiasts of the civil society could call for more social capital. These organizations included associations of former soldiers, youngsters, workers, professionals, entrepreneurs, housewives, cranks, criminals, racial fanatics, children, teenagers, common citizens, and local fellows. These people shared a worldview and gave themselves rules of conduct. They organized all kinds of civic activities. They elected their leaders and then obeyed them blindly. They even wore uniforms to look alike and press their point on the rest of the population. Different from the façade organizations that Communists were so fond of creating elsewhere, the German Communist and Nazi organizations were authentic. They manifested the existence of a strong social capital in the sense that is given today to this term. Yet, the main purpose of most of them was to destroy democracy—either from the left or from the right.[13] They eventually succeeded. They created a rigid and inhuman social capital. This was only logical. The political system that is consistent with this vision of democracy is fascism. It takes only some time for all sectors in society to realize that the best way to influence government is to organize themselves in pressure groups, which then become what the fascists called the live forces of the nation. This would turn the clock back to the rigid feudal forms of organization, destroying democracy in the process.

Another extreme example of a dangerous group with a knack to organize itself for a common purpose is the Mafia. As in the case of the German Communist, Nazi, nationalist and militarist organizations, mafias tend to arise within weak political structures. They fill the vacuum left by such weakness. Their proliferation, rather than being the sign of a strong basis for democracy, is a clear sign of its decay.

Even if not legitimate, factions are changing the nature of politics from the management of the broad interests of a nation into actions and reactions regarding the single issues that they raise. Taken to its extreme, the substitution of single-issue for all-encompassing politics would throw society into disorder. It would defeat the socially unifying forces in society, fragmenting it into the disarray of conflicting individual interests. This is the perfect setting for a violent confrontation of differing views on how to manage the new society that is emerging from connectivity.

Overall, though radicalism is growing in developed societies, the problem in these societies is not one of destructive attitudes in their population but one of progressive indifference for the fate of society. Paradoxically, even if justified on the cynicism about politics and politicians that is so fashionable nowadays, this indifference betrays a worrying complacency with things as they are. Cynicism is the retreat of people who do not want to participate because they are too busy with their own personal concerns.

Putnam attributes the decline in social interest to four main factors. First, he thinks that the pressures of time and money in an increasingly complex society, particularly in two-career families, account for about 10 percent of the phenomenon. Second, he thinks that suburbanization, commuting, and sprawl account for another 10 percent. Third, electronic entertainment, particularly television, accounts for 25 percent. Fourth, he also finds a very worrying fact: those trends are mainly driven by generational differences. People of older generations tend to keep their social participation at the old levels. The decline is mostly the result of the drastically lower social interest shown by the younger generations. The traditions of participation are being lost as the old retire or die. As the younger mature, those traditions are in danger of disappearing altogether. Putnam thinks that this generational change accounts for a full 50 percent of the phenomenon in our times.[14] If we interpret this last factor not as a cause in itself but as a vehicle for the change in attitudes, the percentage of each of the other factors would be doubled, so that electronic entertainment, a part of connectivity, would account for 50 percent of the decline in social participation.[15]

Yet, the reasons behind the disengagement of the new generations may be deeper. They may be related to a mistaken sense of security that the world outside our most immediate surroundings will work automatically, so that we can have the benefits of a modern and humane society without us having to participate in its maintenance and renovation. Gradually, people become used to this isolationist attitude and to its consequences.

Complacency could also be a symptom of a more worrying trend: the substitution of principles by circumstances—in this case the rates of unemployment and economic growth—as the main aspect of life that people think should not be allowed to change. In fact, all the problems I reviewed in the previous sections suggest that people are happy as long as they can carry on with their own personal activities and objectives, which in the aggregate, are related with being employed and earning higher incomes each year, high enough to allow for a separation from society as a whole into the secluded neighborhoods we already discussed. This looks like what has been traditional in the developing countries.

Commenting on the similar disruption of social bonds that accompanied the radical transformation that industrialization prompted in the American society starting in the 1870s, Robert D. Putnam wrote:

But even as these problems were erupting, Americans were beginning to fix them. Within a few decades around the turn of the century, a quickening sense of crisis, coupled with inspired grassroots and national leadership, produced an extraordinary burst of social inventiveness and political reform. In fact, most of the major community institutions in American life today were invented or refurbished in that most fecund period of civic innovation in American history.[16]

The quickening sense of crisis that prompted the renewal of the institutional life of the United States 100 years ago still does not seem to be there in the current transformation. Pushing the government to resolve all the issues of the transformation while focusing all private initiatives on making money will not do it. On the contrary, it would reinforce the fragmentation of modern society.

A system like this can work as long as the inertial quality of the existing institutions assures the functioning of society. There is a moment, however, when, for lack of broad participation, the quality of institutions begins to fade and social order deteriorates—either in the sense of increasing disorder or in the sense of the emergence of a social order that is not humane, free, or democratic. When this happens, the legitimacy of the liberal regime that today flourishes in advanced societies would also decline. As expressed by Sennet,

I do know that a regime which provides human beings no deep reason to care about one other cannot long preserve its legitimacy.[17]

John Stuart Mill, a famous British economist of the nineteenth century who spent his life explaining the advantages of economic freedom, expressed with the following words the danger faced when people forget the value of social interest:

[When this happens] ... the intelligence and sentiments of the whole people are given up to the material interests, and, when these are provided for, to the amusement and ornamentation of private life. But to say this is to say, if the whole testimony of history is worth a thing, that the era of national decline has arrived ...[18]

Retrogressing to forms of social organization characteristic of underdevelopment is precisely this, national decline. The consequences of such a decline go well beyond the national boundaries of the developed countries. If the social bonds of the most advanced societies fail, the probabilities of attaining a smooth transition to a better world would be quite small for the entire world.

NOTES

1. See "Bullet-proof in Aphaville," *The Economist*, 16 August 2001.
2. All the data quoted in the next several bullets are from Robert D. Putnam,

Bowling Alone: The Collapse and Revival of American Community (New York: Simon & Schuster, 2000), pp. 48–133.

3. See, for example, Anthony Giddens, *The Third Way: The Renewal of Social Democracy*, (Cambridge, U.K.: Polity Press, 1998), pp. 51–52.

4. Peter Hall, "Social Capital in Britain," mimeo, Center for European Studies, (Cambridge: Harvard University Press, 1997).

5. Anthony Giddens, *The Third Way: The Renewal of Social Democracy*, pp. 81–87.

6. See "The Growth of Private Communities, America's New Utopias," *The Economist*, 1 September 2001.

7. For a discussion of the impact of connectivity on the urban environment, see Joel Kotkin, *The New Geography: How the Digital Revolution Is Reshaping the American Landscape* (New York: Random House, 2000).

8. University of Washington, Graduate School of Public Affairs, Trust in Government Project (Seattle: University of Washington, Graduate School of Public Affairs, 1998).

9. The data is from the Roper Social and Political Trends Survey, 1973–1994, quoted by Robert D. Putnam, *Bowling Alone*, p. 45.

10. Ibid., pp. 341–342.

11. Ibid., p. 342.

12. Richard Gephardt, *An Even Better Place: America in the 21st Century* (New York: Public Affairs, 1999), p. 18.

13. For information about these groups see, for example, Peter Fritzsche, *Germans into Nazis* (Cambridge: Harvard University Press, 1998), pp. 122–136 and Anton Kaes, Martin Jay, and Edward Dimendber, eds., *The Weimar Republic Sourcebook* (Berkeley: University of California Press, 1994).

14. Ibid., p. 283.

15. Putnam's results show quite clearly that the older generations have kept their rate of social participation at levels similar to those of the midyears of the century. The decline has come about mainly because new generations with low inclination to participate have entered the population. There must be some reasons, however, for this decline in the participation rate of the new generations. Putnam's analysis seems to suggest that the pressure of time and money, suburbanization and electronic entertainment have had a less marked impact in terms of reducing social participation on the older rather than in the new generations. Robert D. Putnam, *Bowling Alone*.

16. Ibid., p. 368.

17. Richard Sennet, *The Corrosion of Character: The Personal Consequences of Work in the New Capitalism* (New York and London: W.W. Norton & Company, 1998), p. 148.

18. John Stuart Mill, *Considerations on Representative Government* (Amherst, N.Y.: Prometheus Books, 1991), p. 59.

CHAPTER 12

Forever Flowing

We have reached the end of the book. We started it with two fundamental questions: What makes the difference between the societies that react positively to technological changes, creating a superior social order from them, and those that react negatively to them, generating in the process bloody revolutions and destructive regimes? What are the policies that governments and societies can adopt to ease the transition toward the more humane and efficient society that connectivity is offering, avoiding a repetition, at a higher level of technological power of destruction, of the tragic events of the twentieth century?

We found the answer to the first question in the first part of the book. The problem of attaining a smooth adjustment to the cataclysmic changes produced by a technological revolution is that of developing strong social cohesion—which is the same as developing social interest in the population. The key to success is the equilibrium between the two motivations of social behavior: individual interest and social interest.

As we discussed the second question in the second part of the book, we found that, as the countries that created the modern industrial state discovered centuries ago, the best strategy for a harmonious adjustment would be to expand our conception of our own society to include those who live in it but are not part of it. This is true for both the developing societies—which are by definition fragmented by racial and economic differences—and the developed ones—which are in danger of becoming so under the turbulences created by the rapid social transformations elicited by the Connectivity Revolution. Developing social interest and its associated social cohesion is a tall order. Yet, this seems to be the only solution to the problems posed by the momentous transformations we are facing. Countries failing to do that in the previous transformation—the Industrial Revolution—fell into stagnation, destructiveness, or both.

What can governments do to promote such integration? In this respect, we found that the old preindustrial institutional setting, which aimed at preserving the shape of society unchanged through time, guaranteeing a place in society to every one, introduces a fatal rigidity in society, delaying adjustment until the forces of change become overwhelming and the adjustment takes place catastrophically. Certainly, some vertical, highly interventionist societies—such as Nazi Germany—attained both economic growth and the elimination of poverty during the Industrial Revolution. Yet, they did that by repressing the freedoms and rights of the workers their regimes were supposedly defending. In the end, such regimes collapse under the weight of their own destructiveness. Moreover, the nature of the transformation now taking place—the worldwide integration of production processes—is eroding one of the fundamental instruments that governments have used to give shape to society: protection against domestic and international competition. Thus, the integration of society cannot be forced. It has to come from within its members. This is the most difficult dimension of the transformation that is waiting for us, particularly after the fall of the Soviet Union, which was interpreted all over the world as a proof that the best way to attain social progress is for individuals to mind only their own business. But this was what the countries that responded harmoniously to the challenges of the Industrial Revolution did. The welfare state was created only after these countries developed. The social problems of their transformation were resolved primarily by civil society organizations that combated alcoholism, poverty, and marginality—as well as by the instillment in all members of society of self-reliance and social interest. Democracy was created on the basis of active participation and can be maintained only on the same basis.

Developing countries have a tough agenda in front of them. Rather than making the same mistakes that left them out of the Industrial Revolution over the last two centuries, they should move in the direction of opening their economies and developing sustainable democratic institutions. While their poverty problems are a problem for the rest of the world, they must take responsibility for them and develop the social interest and self-reliance needed to resolve them. Economically, they should open to the benefits of connectivity and globalization, and socially, they must invest in educating their populations. Quite importantly, they must aim at extending the penetration of connectivity to their poorest citizens—something that would help these people to integrate into their own societies and the rest of the world. At the turn of the millennium, the countries with the lowest incomes represent a fifth of the world's population and produce one percent of the world's GDP. They, however, account for only

0.2 percent of its Internet subscribers.[1] The main efforts to change this reality must come from the poor countries themselves.

Yet, a new institutional setting is needed to channel the new relations that are springing up as a result of connectivity and globalization. Without it, the process can easily become chaotic, particularly in the developing countries, where it can actually become violent. Given the close interconnections of the modern world, the problems of the developing countries are increasingly problems of the developed ones. The network of modernity must be extended to the Third World, breaking the local schemes of vested interests that are profiting from the backwardness of those countries, and supporting those who are open to change. This cannot be done with wars of conquest. Rather, it can be done by creating strong incentives for these countries to enter the mainstream of progress, mainly by giving them access to the markets of developed countries within an institutional setting conducive to progress. This implies liberalizing trade on the low-value-added activities still operating in developed countries—a politically difficult task that carries with it serious social problems for those countries. Given the economic power of developed societies, however, the problem is solvable. These societies have the means to alleviate the pains of the transformation of their weakest members while giving them the tools needed to increase their productivity in the new knowledge-driven world that is emerging in the twenty-first century.

In theory, the best way to create an institutional setting amenable to the new world would be by promoting a worldwide economic integration. This process is already in progress in trade terms through the negotiations organized by the WTO. It, however, could take too long for what is needed. Moreover, the process is too narrow; trade integration is just part of the needed integration. Institutional development is also needed—performing what Giandomenico Majone calls deep integration.[2] This dimension of integration could be as useful as that of trade for the developing countries. The best mechanism to achieve it may be the regional integration treaties, such as the European Union and the NAFTA. To maximize their impact, however, such treaties should be open to all countries willing to comply with a defined set of requirements. This was the way the amazingly successful Hanseatic League grew and prospered in the early centuries of the past millennium, extending institutional development all over the north of Europe, reaching from London in England to Novgorod in Russia. As the case of the East European countries has shown quite clearly, the prospect of becoming a member of a successful club may be a strong incentive for less-developed countries to modernize their economies and societies. This can create the momentum to dispose of the vested interests that are holding those countries hostage to backwardness. The integration itself, once attained, creates a self-sustaining process of integration and growth. With time, this would lead to a more peaceful and safe world.

This transformation is likely to have no end. As Lucretius, a famous Greek philosopher, wrote more than two thousand years ago:

> No single thing abides, but all things flow.
> Figment to figment clings; the things thus grow
> until we know and name them. By degrees
> they melt, and are no more the things we know.[3]

Technological progress was very slow through most of history. It started to accelerate in the late eighteenth century and has kept on accelerating ever since. Thus, creating horizontal, flexible societies is likely to generate increasing benefits through time. For this, self-reliance and social interest are essential.

Thus, recovering and developing social interest to support the social cohesion that is the basis of flexible, horizontal societies is the great challenge posed by the Connectivity Revolution. Countries able to do it will go ahead to create a superior form of society; those failing to do it will go into increasing social conflict and either stagnation, destructiveness, or both.

This is the main message of this book. It is something we have to remember in the difficult, worldwide transformation that we all will confront in the incoming decades and beyond. Only in this way would we legate to our children the most glaring of all miracles: the miracle of a sustainable and humane social order.

NOTES

1. See Phillip S. Muller, "Harvesting the Digital Dividend," in *Summary Report, International Policy Dialogue on Network Readiness, Education and Human Capacity Development for Participating in the Global Networked Economy and Society* (Berlin: German Foundation for International Development, 2002), p. 35.

2. See Giandomenico Majone, *The Internationalization of Regulation: Implications for Developing Countries*, paper presented at the International Conference on Innovation and Change in Regulation and Competition, October 2003, Mandaluyoung City, Metro Manila, Philippines. Dr. Majone is a professor in the European University in Florence, Italy.

3. Quoted by Will Durant in *The Story of Philosophy* (New York: Pocket Books, Simon and Schuster 1953), p. 100.

Bibliography

Aganbeyan, Abel. *Inside Perestroika: The Future of the Soviet Economy*. New York: Harper and Row, 1990.

Allen, William Sheridan. *The Nazi Seizure of Power: The Experience of a Single German Town, 1922–1945*. New York: Franklin Watts, 1984.

"American Productivity, The New 'New Economy,' " *The Economist*. 11 September 2003.

Andrew, Cristopher and Oleg Gordievsky. *KGB: The Inside Story*. London: Hodder & Stoughton, 1990.

Ansbacher, Heinz, and Rowena Ansbacher, eds. *The Individual Psychology of Alfred Adler*. New York: Harper Torchbooks, 1964.

Arnot, Bob. *Controlling Soviet Labor: Experimental Change from Brezhnev to Gorbachev*. Amrock, N.Y.: M. E. Sharpe, 1988.

Aslund, Anders. *Gorbachev's Struggle for Economic Reform*. Ithaca, N.Y.: Cornell University Press, 1989.

Bairoch, Paul. "Europe's Gross National Product: 1800–1975." *The Journal of European Economic History* 5 (1976).

———. "International Industrialization Levels from 1750 to 1980." *The Journal of European Economic History* 11 (1982).

Bankier, David. *The Germans and the Final Solution: Public Opinion under Nazism*. Oxford: Blackwell, 1996.

Barraclough, Geoffrey. *The Origins of Modern Germany*. New York and London: W. W. Norton & Co., 1984.

Bellon, Bernard P. *Mercedes in Peace and War: German Automobile Workers, 1903–1945*. New York: Columbia University Press, 1990.

Bennet, William J. *The Death of Outrage*. New York: The Free Press, 1998.

Berkowitz, Bruce. *The New Face of War: How War Will Be Fought in the 21st Century*. New York: The Free Press, 2003.

Bhagwati, Jagdish. *A Stream of Windows: Unsettling Reflections on Trade, Immigration, and Democracy.* Cambridge: MIT Press, 2000.

———. *The Wind of the Hundred Days: How Washington Mismanaged Globalization.* Cambridge: MIT Press, 2000.

Billington, James H. *The Icon and the Axe: An Interpretative History of the Russian Culture.* New York: Vintage Books, 1970.

Birth of a New Nation: Profiles in Cyberspace. Baltimore, Md.: Algora Publishing, 1996.

Blackbourn, David, and Geoff Eley. *The Peculiarities of German History: Bourgeois Society and Politics in Nineteenth Century Germany.* New York and Oxford: Oxford University Press, 1984.

Bloom, Alan. *The Closing of the American Mind.* New York: Simon & Schuster, 1987.

Brookhiser, Richard. *Alexander Hamilton: American.* New York: The Free Press, 1999.

Brovkin, Vladimir N. *The Mensheviks after October: Socialist Opposition and the Rise of the Bolshevik Dictatorship.* Ithaca and London: Cornell University Press, 1987.

Bukharin, Nikolai, and Preobrazhensky. *The ABC of Communism.* Ann Arbor: University of Michigan Press, 1988.

Bullock, Allan. *Hitler: A Study in Tyranny.* New York: HarperPerennial, 1962.

———. *Hitler: A Study in Tyranny.* Abridged. New York: HarperPerennial, 1991.

———. *Hitler and Stalin: Parallel Lives.* New York: Alfred A. Knopf, 1992.

Burke, Edmund. *Reflections on the Revolution in France.* Indianapolis and Cambridge: Hackett Publishing Company, 1987.

Burnham, James. *The Machiavellians: Defenders of Freedom. A Defense of Political Truth against Wishful Thinking.* Washington, D.C.: Gateway Editions, 1943.

Calleo, David. *The German Problem Reconsidered: Germany and the World Order, 1870 to the Present.* Cambridge: Cambridge University Press, 1990.

Campbell, Joseph. *The Portable Jung.* New York: Penguin Books, 1981.

Cannadine, David. *The Decline and Fall of the British Aristocracy.* New Haven and London: Yale University Press, 1990.

Chartier, Roger. *The Cultural Origins of the French Revolution.* Durham and London: Duke University Press, 1991.

Clark, Ronald W. *Lenin: A Biography.* New York: Harper and Row, 1990.

Cohen, Stephen F. *Bukharin and the Bolshevik Revolution: A Political Biography, 1888–1938.* New York and Oxford: Oxford University Press, 1980.

Conquest, Robert. *The Great Terror: A Reassessment.* New York and Oxford: Oxford University Press, 1990.

———. *The Harvest of Sorrow: Soviet Collectivization and the Terror-Famine.* New York and Oxford: Oxford University Press, 1986.

Cooper, John, ed., and D. S. Hutchinson, assoc. ed. *Plato: Complete Works.* Indianapolis and Cambridge: Hackett Publishing Company, 1997.

Craig, Gordon A. *The Politics of the Prussian Army, 1640–1945.* New York and Oxford: Oxford University Press, 1964.

Davies, R. W. *The Soviet Collective Farm, 1929–1930.* London: Macmillan, 1980.

———. *The Soviet Economy in Turmoil, 1929–1930.* Cambridge and London: Harvard University Press, 1989.

———, ed. *From Tsarism to the New Economic Policy: Continuity and Change in the Economy of the USSR.* Ithaca: Cornell University Press, 1990.

de Madariaga, Isabel. *Russia in the Age of Catherine the Great.* New Haven and London: Yale University Press, 1981.

D'Encausse, Helene Carrere. *Lenin, Revolution and Power.* London and New York: Longman, 1982.

———. *Stalin: Order through Terror.* London and New York: London, 1981.

Desai, Padma. *The Soviet Economy: Problems and Prospects.* Oxford: Blackwell, 1990.

De Soto, Hernando. *The Mystery of Capital: Why Capitalism Triumphs in the West and Fails Everywhere Else.* New York: Basic Books, 2000.

———. *The Other Path.* New York: Harper & Row, 1989.

De Tocqueville, Alexis. *Democracy in America.* New York: Vintage Books, 1945.

Disraeli, Benjamin. *Sybil or The Two Nations.* New York and Oxford: Oxford University Press, 1981.

Djilas, Milovan. *The New Class: An Analysis of the Communist System.* New York: Harcourt Brace Jovanovich, 1983.

Doder, Dusko. *Shadows and Whispers: Power Politics inside the Kremlin from Brezhnev to Gorbachev.* New York: Penguin Books, 1988.

Dolot, Miron. *Execution by Hunger.* New York and London: W. W. Norton & Co., 1987.

Durant, Will. *The Story of Philosophy.* New York: Pocket Books, Simon and Schuster, 1953.

Durant, Will, and Ariel Durant. *Rousseau and Revolution.* New York: Simon and Schuster, 1967.

Easterly, William. *The Lost Decades: Developing Countries' Stagnation in Spite of Policy Reforms 1980–1998.* Washington D.C.: The World Bank, 2001.

Easterly, William, and Ross Levine. *It's Not Factor Accumulation: Stylized Facts and Growth Models.* Washington, D.C.: Preliminary Version, The World Bank, Policy Research Group, 2000.

Ellis, Joseph J. *American Sphinx: The Character of Thomas Jefferson.* New York: Random House, 1998.

———. *Founding Fathers: The Revolutionary Generation.* New York: Alfred A. Knopf, 2000.

Engels, Friedrich. *Anti-During.* Peking: Foreign Languages Press, 1976.

Esposito, John, ed. *The Oxford History of Islam.* Oxford: Oxford University Press, 1999.

Fairbanks, Michael, and Stace Lindsay. *Plowing the Sea: Nurturing the Hidden Sources of Growth in the Developing World.* Boston, Mass.: Harvard Business School Press, 1997.

Farland, Mark. *Khrushchev.* 2nd Scarborough ed., New York: Stein and Day, 1979.

Feldman, Gerald D. *Army, Industry and Labor in Germany, 1914–1918.* Providence and Oxford: Berg Publishers, 1992.

Friedman, Thomas. *The Lexus and the Olive Tree: Understanding Globalization.* New York: Farrar Straus & Giroux, 1999.

Fritzsche, Peter. *Germans into Nazis.* Cambridge and London: Harvard University Press, 1998.

Galbraith, John Kenneth. *The Great Crash, 1929.* Boston and New York: Houghton Mifflin Co., 1997.

Gatrell, Peter. *The Tsarist Economy 1850–1917.* London: Batsford, 1986.

Gephardt, Richard. *An Even Better Place: America in the 21st Century.* New York: Public Affairs, 1999.

Gibbon, Edward. *The Decline and Fall of the Roman Empire:* New York: Alfred A. Knopf, 1994.

Giddens, Anthony. *The Third Way: The Renewal of Social Democracy.* Cambridge, U.K.: Polity Press, 1998.

Ginzburg, Eugenia Semyonovna. *Journey into the Whirlwind.* New York: Harcourt Brace Jovanovich, 1967.

Goldhagen, Daniel Jonah. *Hitler's Willing Executioners: Ordinary Germans and the Holocaust.* New York: Vintage Books, 1997.

Gorbachev, Mikhail. *Perestroika: New Thinking for Our Country and the World.* New York: Harper and Row, 1988.

Gordon, Robert J. "Five Puzzless in the Behavior of Productivity, Investment, and Innovation," 10 September 2003, draft of chapter for *World Economic Forum, Global Competitiveness Report, 2003–2004.* Available in the author's Web site in Northwestern.edu.

Granick, David. *Chinese State Enterprises: A Regional Property Rights Analysis.* Chicago: University of Chicago Press, 1990.

Gregory, Paul R., and Robert C. Stuart. *Soviet Economic Structure and Performance.* 3rd ed., New York: Harper and Row, 1986.

Grey, Loren. *Alfred Adler, The Forgotten Prophet: A Vision for the 21st Century.* Westport, Conn.: Praeger, 1998.

Grossman, Vasily. *Forever Flowing.* New York: Harper and Row, 1970.

Hackett Fischer, David. *Albion's Seed: Four British Folkways in America.* New York and Oxford: Oxford University Press, 1991.

Haffner, Sebastian. *The Ailing Empire: Germany from Bismarck to Hitler.* New York: Fromm International Publishing Corporation, 1989.

———. *Failure of a Revolution: Germany 1918–1919.* Chicago: Banner Press, 1986.

Haggard, Stephan, and Robert R. Kaufman. *The Political Economy of Democratic Transitions.* Princeton, N.J.: Princeton University Press, 1995.

Hamilton, Alexander. *Selected Writings and Speeches of Alexander Hamilton.* Ed. Morton J. Frisch. Washington: American Enterprise Institute for Public Policy Research, 1985.

Hegel, G. W. F. *Introduction to the Philosophy of History.* Indianapolis and Cambridge: Hackett Publishing Co., 1988.

Heiber, Helmut. *The Weimar Republic.* Oxford, U.K.: Blackwell, 1993.

Hemsley, John. *The Lost Empire: Perceptions of Soviet Policy Shifts in the 1990s.* London: Brasseys, 1991.

Herrnstein, Richard J., and Charles Murray. *The Bell Curve: Intelligence and Class Structure in American Life.* New York: Free Press Paperbacks, 1994.

Hilberg, Raul. *The Destruction of the European Jews.* New York: Holmes and Meier, 1985.

———. *Perpetrators, Victims, Bystanders: The Jewish Catastrophe 1933–1945.* New York: HarperPerennial, 1992.

Himmelfarb, Gertrude. *The Demoralization of Society: From Victorian Virtues to Modern Values.* New York: Random House, 1996.

Hitler, Adolf. *Mein Kampf.* Boston: Houghton Mifflin Company, 1971.

Hobsbawm, Eric. *The Age of Empire, 1875–1914.* New York: Vintage Books, 1989.

Höss, Rudolph. *Death Dealer: The Memoirs of the SS Kommandant at Auschwitz.* New York: Prometheus Books, 1992.

Hough, Jerry, and Merle Fainsod. *How the Soviet Union Is Governed.* Cambridge and London: Harvard University Press, 1979.

Hunley, J. D. *The Life and Thought of Friedrich Engels: A Reinterpretation.* New Haven and London: Yale University Press, 1991.

Huntington, Samuel P. *The Clash of Civilizations and the Remaking of World Order.* New York: Simon & Schuster, 1996.

International Monetary Fund, The World Bank, Organization for Economic Co-operation and Development, European Bank for Reconstruction and Development. *A Study of the Soviet Economy.* 3 vols, 1991.

Jicai, Feng. *Voices from the Whirlwind: An Oral History of the Chinese Cultural Revolution.* New York: Pantheon Books, 1991.

Johnson, Paul. *The Birth of the Modern World Society, 1815–1830.* New York: HarperCollins, 1991.

———. *A History of the American People.* New York: HarperCollins, 1997.

———. *Modern Times: The World from the Twenties to the Nineties.* New York: HarperPerennial, 1992.

Jones, Ronald W. *Globalization and the Theory of Input Trade.* Cambridge: MIT Press, 2000.

Juergensmeyer, Mark. *Terror in the Mind of God: The Global Rise of Religious Violence.* Berkeley: University of California Press, 2000.

Jung, Carl. *The Portable Jung.* Ed. Joseph Campbell. New York: Penguin Books, 1971.

Kagarlitsky, Boris. *The Twilight of Globalization: Property, State and Capitalism.* London and Sterling, Va.: Pluto Press, 2000.

Kaiser, Robert G. *Why Gorbachev Happened: His Triumphs and Failures.* New York: Simon and Schuster, 1991.

Karnow, Stanley. *Mao and China: A Legacy of Turmoil.* New York: Penguin Books, 1990.

Kaufmann, Walter. *Basic Writings of Nietzsche.* New York: The Modern Library, 1968.

———. *Nietzsche: Philosopher, Psychologist, Antichrist.* Princeton, N.J.: Princeton University Press, 1978.

———. *The Portable Nietzsche.* New York: Penguin, 1976.

Keegan, John. *The First World War.* New York: Random House, 1998.

Kennedy, Paul. *The Rise and Fall of the Great Powers: Economic Change and Military Conflict from 1500 to 2000.* New York: Vintage Books, 1989.

Kenwood, A. G., and A. L. Longheed. *The Growth of the International Economy.* London: Routledge, 1999.

Kershaw, Ian. *The Hitler Myth, Image and Reality in the Third Reich.* New York and Oxford: Oxford University Press, 1987.

Keynes, John Maynard. *The Economic Consequences of Peace.* New York: Penguin Books, 1995.

Khrushchev, Nikita. *Khrushchev Remembers: The Glasnost Tapes.* Boston: Little, Brown and Company, 1990.

Kimball, Roger. *Tenured Radicals: How Politics Has Corrupted Our Higher Education.* Chicago: Ivan R. Dee, 1998.

Kindleberger, Charles P. *Manias, Panics and Crashes for 1700–1940.* New York: John Wiley & Sons, 1996.

Kolakowsky, Leszek. *Main Currents of Marxism: 1. The Founders.* New York and Oxford: Oxford University Press, 1988.

———. *Main Currents of Marxism: 2. The Golden Age.* New York and Oxford: Oxford University Press, 1988.

———. *Main Currents of Marxism: 3. The Breakdown.* New York and Oxford: Oxford University Press, 1988.

Kotkin, Joel. *The New Geography: How the Digital Revolution Is Reshaping the American Landscape.* New York: Random House, 2000.

Kotkin, Stephen. *Steeltown, USSR: Soviet Society in the Gorbachev Era.* Berkeley and Los Angeles: University of California Press, 1991.

Krugman, Paul. *The Return of Depression Economics.* New York and London: W. W. Norton & Co., 1999.

Kuromiya, Hiroaki. *Stalin's Industrial Revolution: Politics and Workers, 1928–1932.* Cambridge: Cambridge University Press, 1990.

Lacqueur, Walter. *Stalin: The Glasnost Revelations.* New York: Charles Scribner's Sons, 1990.

Landes, David. *The Unbound Prometheus: Technological Change and Industrial Development in Western Europe from 1750 to the Present.* Cambridge: Cambridge University Press, 1969.

———. *The Wealth and Poverty of Nations: Why Some Are So Rich and Some So Poor.* New York: W. W. Norton & Co., 1998.

Lefebvre, Georges. *The Coming of the French Revolution.* Princeton, N.J.: Princeton University Press, 1989.

Legget, George. *The Cheka: Lenin's Political Police.* New York and Oxford: Oxford University Press, 1981.

Lesourne, Jacques. *The Economics of Order and Disorder.* Oxford: Clarendon Press, 1992.

Lewin, Moshe. *The Gorbachev Phenomenon: A Historical Interpretation.* Berkeley and Los Angeles: University of California Press, 1988.

Liesner, Thelma. *Economic Statistics 1900–1983.* London: The Economist Publications Ltd, 1985.

Lincoln, W. Bruce. *The Great Reforms, Autocracy, Bureaucracy, and the Politics of Change in Imperial Russia.* Dekalb, Ill.: Northern Illinois University Press, 1990.

———. *In the Vanguard of Reform: Russia's Enlightened Bureaucrats, 1825–1861.* Dekalb, Ill.: Northern Illinois University Press, 1982.

———. *The Romanovs: Autocrats of All the Russias.* New York: Anchor Books, 1981.

Linden, Carl A. *Khruschev and the Soviet Leadership.* Baltimore: Johns Hopkins University Press, 1990.

Lourie, Richard. *Russia Speaks: From the Revolution to the Present.* New York: Harper and Collins, 1991.

Machiavelli, Niccolo. *The Prince.* London: Penguin Books, 1981.

Maddison, Angus. *Dynamic Forces in Capitalist Development: A Long-Run Comparative View.* New York and Oxford: Oxford University Press, 1991.

———. *Monitoring the World Economy, 1820–92.* Paris: Organization for Economic Co-operation and Development, Development Centre, 1995.

Majone, Giandomenico. *The Internationalization of Regulation: Implications for Developing Countries.* Paper presented at the International Conference on Innovation and Change in Regulation and Competition, October 2003, Mandaluyoung City, Metro Manila, Philippines.

Marx, Karl. *Capital, Volume I.* New York: Vintage Books Edition, 1977.

Marx, Karl, and Friedrich Engels. *The Communist Manifesto.* New York: Penguin Classics, 1967.

———. *The Marx-Engels Reader.* Ed. Robert C. Tucker, 2d ed. New York and London: W. W. Norton & Co., 1978.

Massie, Robert K. *Dreadnaught.* New York: Random House, 1992.

———. *Peter the Great: His Life and World.* New York: Ballantine Books, 1980.

Mathias, Peter. *The First Industrial Nation: An Economic History of Britain, 1700–1914.* London: Methuen & Co., 1969.

Mayer, Arno. *The Persistence of the Old Regime.* New York: Pantheon Books, 1981.

Mazower, Mark. *Dark Continent: Europe's Twentieth Century.* New York: Alfred A. Knopf, 1999

McCauley, Martin. *Khruschev and the Development of Soviet Agriculture, 1953–1964.* London: Macmillan, 1976.

———. *The Russian Revolution and the Soviet State 1917–1921: Selected Documents.* London: MacMillan Press in Association with the School of Slavonic and East European Studies, University of London, 1990.

McDonald, Forrest. *Alexander Hamilton: A Biography.* New York and London: W.W. Norton & Co., 1982.

Medvedev, Grigori. *The Truth about Chernobyl.* New York: Basic Books, 1991.

Medvedev, Roy. *Let History Judge: The Origins and Consequences of Stalinism.* New York: Columbia University Press, 1989.

Medvedev, Roy, and Giulietto Chiesa. *Times of Change: An Insider's View of Russia's Transformation.* New York: Pantheon Books, 1989.

Medvedev, Zhores. *The Legacy of Chernobyl.* New York and London: W. W. Norton & Co., 1990.

Meisner, Maurice. *Mao's China and After.* New York: The Free Press, 1986.

Mill, John Stuart. *Considerations on Representative Government.* Amherst, N.Y.: Prometheus Books, 1991.

———. *Principles of Political Economy.* New York and Oxford: Oxford University Press, 1994.

Mitcham, Samuel W. *Why Hitler? The Genesis of the Nazi Reich.* Westport, Conn.: Praeger, 1996.

Moore, Barrington, Jr. *Social Origins of Dictatorship and Democracy: Lord and Peasant in the Making of the Modern World.* Boston: Beacon Press, 1993.

Morgan, Kenneth, ed. *The Oxford History of Britain.* New York and Oxford: Oxford University Press, 1990.

Morris, James. *Heaven's Command: An Imperial Progress.* New York: Harcourt Brace Jovanovich, 1973.

———. *Pax Britannica: The Climax of an Empire.* New York: Harcourt, Brace and World, 1968.

Morrison, John. *Boris Yeltsin: from Bolshevik to Democrat.* New York: Dutton, 1991.

Mosca, Gaetano. *The Ruling Class.* New York: McGraw-Hill Book Company, 1939.

Mosse, George L. *The Crisis of German Ideology: Intellectual Origins of the Third Reich.* New York: Howard Hertig, 1964.

Muller, Phillip S. "Harvesting the Digital Dividend," in *Summary Report, International Policy Dialogue on Network Readiness, Education and Human Capacity Development for Participating in the Global Networked Economy and Society.* Berlin: German Foundation for International Development, 2002.

Nahailo, Bohdan, and Victor Swoboda. *Soviet Disunion: A History of the Nationalities Problem in the USSR.* New York: The Free Press, 1989.

Nietzsche, Friedrich. *The Portable Nietzsche.* Ed. Walter Kaufmann. New York: Penguin Books, 1976.

Nove, Alec. *An Economic History of the Soviet Union.* London: Penguin, 1989.

O'Meara, Patrick, Howard D. Mehlinger, Matthew Krain, and Roxana Ma Newman, eds. *Globalization and the Challenges of the New Century.* Bloomington and Indianapolis: Indiana University Press, 2000.

O'Rourke, Kevin H., and Jeffrey G. Williamson. *Globalization and History: The Evolution of a Nineteenth Century Atlantic Economy.* Cambridge: MIT Press, 2000.

Overy, R. J. *The Nazi Economic Recovery, 1932–1938.* Cambridge: Cambridge University Press, 1996.

Oxenstierna, Susanne. *From Labour Shortage to Unemployment? The Soviet Labour Market in the 1980s.* Stockholm: The University of Stockholm, 1990.

Parente, Stephen L., and Edward C. Prescott. *Barriers to Riches.* Walras-Pareto Lectures, Ecole des Hautes Etudes Commerciales, Université de Lausanne. Cambridge: MIT Press, 2000.

Paul, Allen. *Katyn: The Untold Story of Stalin's Polish Massacre.* New York: Charles Scribner's Sons, 1991.

Peukert, Detlev J. K. *The Weimar Republic.* New York: Hill and Wang, 1993, p. 282.

Pipes, Richard. *Property and Freedom.* New York: Vintage Books; Random House, 2000.

———. *Russia under the Old Regime.* New York: Charles Scribner's Sons, 1974.

———. *The Russian Revolution.* New York: Alfred A. Knopf, 1990.

Polanyi, Karl. *The Great Transformation: The Political and Economic Origins of Our Times.* Boston: Beacon Press, 2001.

Porter, Michael. *The Competitive Advantage of Nations.* New York: The Free Press, Macmillan, 1990.

Prigogine, Ilya. *From Being to Becoming: Time and Complexity in the Physical Sciences.* New York: W. H. Freeman and Company, 1980.

Prigogine, Ilya, and Isabelle Stengers. *Order out of Chaos: Man's New Dialogue with Nature.* New York: Bantam Books, 1984.

Putnam, Robert D. *Bowling Alone: The Collapse and Revival of American Community.* New York: Simon & Schuster, 2000.

Raeff, Marc. *Origins of the Russian Inteligentsia.* New York: Harcourt Brace Jovanovich, 1966.

Reed, John. *Ten Days That Shook the World.* London: Penguin Books, 1977.

Reichmann, Eva G. *Hostages of Civilization: A Study of the Causes of Anti-Semitism.* Boston: Beacon Press, 1951.

Robertson, Priscilla. *Revolutions of 1848: A Social History.* Princeton, N.J.: Princeton University Press, 1971.

Rodrik, Dani. *Has Globalization Gone Too Far?* Washington, D.C.: Institute for International Economics, 1997.

Rogowski, Roland. *Commerce and Coalitions: How Trade Affects Domestic Political Arrangements.* Princeton, N.J.: Princeton University Press, 1989.

Rosenbaum, Ron. *Explaining Hitler.* New York: Random House, 1998.

Roth, Cecil. *The Spanish Inquisition.* New York and London: W. W. Norton & Co., 1964.

Ruelle, David. *Chance and Chaos.* Princeton, N.J.: Princeton University Press, 1991.

Rupert, Mark. *Ideologies of Globalization: Contending Visions for a New World Order.* RIPE Series in Global Political Economy. London and New York: Routledge, 2000.

Salisbury, Harrison E. *Black Night, White Snow: Russia's Revolutions, 1905–1917.* New York: Da Capo, 1977.

Schama, Simon. *Citizens: A Chronicle of the French Revolution.* New York: Vintage Books, 1990.

Schmitt, Carl. *The Crisis of Parliamentary Democracy.* Cambridge: MIT Press, 2001.

———. *Political Romanticism.* Cambridge: MIT Press, 2001.

Schulze, Hagen. *The Course of German Nationalism: From Frederick the Great to Bismarck, 1763–1867.* Cambridge: Cambridge University Press, 1991.

Schumpeter, Joseph A. *Capitalism, Socialism and Democracy.* New York: Harper Torchbooks, 1975.

Scott, Franklin D. *Sweden: The Country's History.* Carbondale: Southern Illinois University Press, 1988.

Sennet, Richard. *The Corrosion of Character: The Personal Consequences of Work in the New Capitalism.* New York and London: W. W. Norton & Co., 1998.

Shirer, William. *The Rise and Fall of the Third Reich: A History of Nazi Germany.* New York: Fawcett Crest, 1983.

Shlapentokh, Vladimir. *Public and Private Life of the Soviet People: Changing Values in Post-Stalinist Russia.* New York and Oxford: Oxford University Press, 1989.

Singer, Peter. *Hegel.* New York and Oxford: Oxford University Press, 1983.

Smith, Adam. *Wealth of Nations.* New York: Prometheus Books, 1991.

Smith, Henrick. *The New Russians.* New York: Random House, 1990.

———. *The Russians.* New York: Ballantine Books, 1976.

Spengler, Oswald. *The Decline of the West.* Abridged, New York and Oxford: Oxford University Press, 1932.

Stiglitz, Joseph E. *Globalization and its Discontents.* New York and London: W.W. Norton & Co., 2002.

Thurow, Lester. *Head to Head: The Coming Economic Battle Among Japan, Europe and America.* New York: William Morrow and Company, 1992.

Tiersky, Ronald. *Ordinary Stalinism, Democratic Centralism and the Question of Communist Political Development.* Boston: George Allen and Unwin, 1985.

Toynbee, Arnold. *A Study of History.* 2 vols. Abridgement by D. C. Somervell, New York and Oxford: Oxford University Press, 1957.

Trotsky, Leon. *The History of the Russian Revolution.* New York: Pathfinder, 1980.

———. *The Revolution Betrayed: What Is the Soviet Union and Where Is It Going?* New York: Pathfinder, 1972.

Tsipko, Alexander S. *Is Stalinism Really Dead? The Future of Perestroika As a Moral Revolution.* San Francisco: Harper, 1990.

Tuchman, Barbara. *The Guns of August.* New York: Bantam Books, 1967.

———. *The Proud Tower: A Portrait of the World before the War, 1890–1914. New York:* Bantam Books, 1967.

Tucker, Robert C. *The Marx-Engels Reader.* New York and London: W. W. Norton & Co., 1978.

———. *Stalin As Revolutionary: A Study in History and Personality.* New York and London: W. W. Norton and Company, 1974.

———. *Stalin in Power: The Revolution from Above, 1928–1941.* New York and London: W. W. Norton & Co., 1990.

———, ed. *The Lenin Anthology.* New York and London: W. W. Norton & Co., 1975.

Turner, Henry Ashby Jr. *German Big Business and the Rise of Hitler.* New York and Oxford: Oxford University Press, 1985.

Vaksberg, Arkady. *Stalin's Prosecutor: The Life of Andrei Vyshinsky.* New York: Grove Weinfeld, 1990.

Van Ark, Bart, et al., *ICT and Productivity in Europe and the United States: Where Do the Differences Come From?* Paper for the SOM PhD Conference, 29 January 2003, De Niewe Academie, Groningen. Available at r,c.inklaar@eco.rug.nl.

Weber, Eugen. *The Hollow Years: France in the 1930s.* New York and London: W. W. Norton & Co., 1994.

White, Stephen. *Gorbachev in Power.* Cambridge: Cambridge University Press, 1990.

Wilson, Edmund *To the Finland Station: A Study on the Writing and Acting of History.* New York: Farrar, Straus and Giroux, 1972.

Windschuttle, Keith. *The Killing of History: How Literary Critics and Social Theorists Are Murdering Our Past.* San Francisco: Encounter Books, 1996.

Winiecki, Jan. *The Distorted World of Soviet-Type Economies.* Pittsburgh: University of Pittsburgh Press, 1988.

Womack, James P., Daniel T. Jones, and Daniel Roos. *The Machine That Changed the World. The Story of Lean Production.* New York: HarperPerennial, 1991.

Wood, Gordon S. *The Radicalism of the American Revolution.* New York: Random House, 1993.

Yeltsin, Boris. *Against the Grain: An Autobiography.* New York: Summit Books, 1990.

Zaslavskaya, Tatyana. *The Second Socialist Revolution: An Alternative Soviet Strategy.* Bloomington and Indianapolis: Indiana University Press, 1990.

Ziegler, Herbert. *Nazi Germany's New Aristocracy: The SS Leadership, 1925–1939.* Princeton, N.J.: Princeton University Press, 1989.

Index

Socialism, 64
Socialists, and the genocide of Stalin, 58
Social security approach, 159–61
Soviet Union: citizens killed, 61; collapse and rebuilding of, 33–34; and decentralized economic decision, 6; destructiveness, 122; economy of, 65; failed at connectivity, 32–33; growth of the economy, 74; people in poverty, 34; use of terror, 122; vs. Britain and the U.S., 125; why it collapsed, 32
Spain: entrance to European Union, 162; investing in Latin America, 31
Spengler, Oswald, 100
Stalin, industrialized Russia, 74
Steel, 154; British vs. German, 111
Sweden, left of Britain and the U.S., 125

Taliban, 89
Technological: changes, to host societies, 70; progress made possible, 103; revolution, presently, 131; revolution and fundamentalism, 84; revolution and problems of transformation, 99; revolution and social change and order, 115; revolution as the cause of economic problems, 77; revolution begins to be visible, 5, 22; revolution's erosion of social bonds, 81; revolution's impact on society, 79
Telecommunications: bring a new economy, 3; and the Connectivity Revolution, 12; and the transfer of money, 6

Terrorism, and fundamentalism, 85–101. *See also* Christianity; Islam
Textiles, 46–47
Third World, in the nineteenth century, 19
Toynbee, Arnold, as a fundamentalist, 85; theory of, 103
Toyota: began horizontal coordination, 6–8; productivity indicators, 8
Trade blocks, 161–63
Trade liberalization, to create social order, 149

United States: as foremost country, 18–19; had financial instability, 31; nature of its citizens, 59; savings and investments, 42
Utopias, 70

Values, destruction of old, 83
Venezuela, crises in the 1990s, 30, 36
Vertical structure: and Communist societies, 125; of decision making, 15; and fundamentalists, 85, 91; to horizontal form, 96; includes, 125; most common, 120; policies which enforce, 136; and social order, 118–20, 123; struggles to keep in place, 112; superimposing horizontal, 135; upgrading to a horizontal society, 124
Virtual corporation, 17

World Trade Center: and events of September 11, xii–xiii; member rules, 162–63
World War II: effect on per capita income, 42; as the end of the Industrial Revolution, 5

About the Author

MANUEL HINDS is a consultant to private and public institutions, including the World Bank, the Inter-American Bank of Development, and the International Monetary Fund. He has worked on three processes of dramatic social change. As Minister of Finance of El Salvador in the first post–civil war government (1994–99), he helped to transform the devastated country into one that garnered investment grade-one status. Prior to that he worked as a consultant for the World Bank on Lebanon, Jordan, and the Occupied Territories (Palestine) during the peace processes of 1993–94. As Division Chief of Trade, Finance, and Private-Sector Development for Europe, the Middle East and North Africa at the World Bank (1986–92), he worked with the transformation of Eastern Europe (particularly Poland and the former Yugoslavia and former Soviet Union) from Communism to free-market economies.